EXPLORER'S GUIDES

Salt Lake City, Park City, Provo & Utah's High Country Resorts

ORER'S GUIDES

SECOND EDITION

Salt Lake City, Park City, Provo & Utah's High Country Resorts

A Great Destination

Christine Balaz

The Countryman Press
Woodstock, Vermont

OPPOSITE: *Salt Lake City Mormon Temple* Jonathan Echlin

Salt Lake City, Park City, Provo & Utah's High Country Resorts
ISBN 978-1-58157-124-0

Interior photographs by the author unless otherwise specified
Book design by Joanna Bodenweber
Composition by Chelsea Cloeter
Maps by Mapping Specialists, Ltd., Madison, WI © The Countryman Press

Published by The Countryman Press, P.O. Box 748, Woodstock, VT 05091

Distributed by W. W. Norton & Company, Inc., 500 Fifth Avenue, New York, NY 10110

Printed in the United States of America

10 9 8 7 6 5 4 3 2 1

EXPLORER'S GUIDES' GREAT DESTINATIONS

Recommended by *National Geographic Traveler* and *Travel + Leisure* magazines

A crisp and critical approach, for travelers who want to live like locals.—*USA Today*

Great Destinations™ guidebooks are known for their comprehensive, critical coverage of regions of extraordinary cultural interest and natural beauty. Each title in this series is continuously updated with each printing to ensure accurate and timely information. All the books contain more than one hundred photographs and maps.

The authors in this series are professional travel writers who have lived for many years in the regions they describe. Honest and painstakingly critical, full of information only a local can provide, **Great Destinations™** guidebooks give you all the practical knowledge you need to enjoy the best of each region.

Salt Lake Region

Logan

UTAH

WYOMING

Evanston

Huntsville

Ogden

Great
Salt
Lake

Antelope
Island

Coalville

San Lake City
International Airport

Salt Lake
City

Park City

Kamas

Sandy

Big Cottonwood
Canyon
Little Cottonwood
Canyon

Midway

Heber City

Sundance
Resort

Orem

Provo

Utah
Lake

Springville

Strawberry
Reservoir

Spanish Fork

0   10 miles
0   10 kilometers

Contents

Introduction & Logistics

At the time of the penning of this book's first edition, Utah was a rapidly modernizing and exciting place to live. Today its pace of change is all that has stayed constant; infrastructural, cultural, and social improvements have all been noticeable and dynamic in just these last three years alone.

From the upscale and festive Main Street of Park City to the Mormon Tabernacle of Salt Lake City with its organ of 11,623 pipes, the climate and culture of this mountainous region range from pleasant to blustery, from raucous to reserved. One can find sanctuary in a mosque, squeeze into a local rock concert, or romp at a Utah Jazz NBA game. When it is 65 degrees in Salt Lake Valley, there might be fresh powder atop thick snowpack in the mountain resorts. In one day alone, you can literally take a bike ride in shorts and sunscreen, suit up for a midday ski, and finish with nine holes of golf. This is not an exaggeration or even a rarity.

As you explore this region, you will feel comfortable, yet intrigued. You will be amazed by the dramatic natural beauty and simultaneously challenged by the wealth of athletic pursuits and puzzled by religious juxtapositions. You will spot celebrities on the ski slopes of Park City and will enjoy the international cuisine and quaintness of old brick neighborhoods. Located at the base of some of the most impressive Rocky Mountain peaks, the greater Salt Lake region offers the perfect pairing of outdoor escapes and urban opportunities. Better still, this ideal combination is blended with convenience, accessibility, and affordability that you are unlikely to find anywhere else in the world.

From a distance, Salt Lake City, Provo, and Park City appear to be like many other western cities. Salt Lake City, with its modern skyscrapers, sits snugly against the foothills of

Salt Lake City and the Wasatch Front Jonathan Echlin

Salt Lake Library Main Branch   Jonathan Echlin

the craggy Wasatch Range. Perched high in the mountains, Park City's handsome Main Street is peppered with sagebrush scenery and attractive people. Provo is a cheerful university town with large, green lawns and clean boulevards. Contrary to their benign appearances, each of these cities has undergone a turbulent and formative history charged by the quest for religious freedom and clashing cultures.

Today the past is reflected by a unique and dynamic society. At once mysterious and familiar, Salt Lake Valley is a mixture of monuments to the fast-growing Mormon religion, as well as premier performance arts companies and entertainment venues. You will see the common box-store amenities of American civilization alongside uniquely stylized western boutiques. With just over 2 million residents, the Wasatch Front is home to Salt Lake International Airport and dozens of major corporate headquarters. A 30-minute drive to the east, Park City hosts the Sundance Film Festival, undeniably the most renowned independent film festival in the nation. Just 40 miles south of Salt Lake City, Provo is home to 35,000-student Brigham Young University and adjoining high-tech industries. Budding modernity and enduring history have coalesced into today's Wasatch Front.

Salt Lake Valley is part of the massive Great Basin, a landlocked depression with no outlet to any ocean. In ancient times, this basin intermittently filled with water. Lake Bonneville, whose high-water mark was struck some 15,000 years ago, would have covered most of Salt Lake City with more than 500 feet of water. Today, tiered ancient shorelines are still visible along the benches of Salt Lake City and Provo. With dozens of access points along the eastern edge of these cities, the extensive Bonneville Shoreline Trail System offers an unending web of trails that overlook the cityscapes below.

When not underwater, the Salt Lake and Utah valleys were home to non-European peo-

Fountain in front of the Salt Lake City Mormon Temple   Jonathan Echlin

ple as early as 12,000 years ago. These were the ancestors of the Shoshone, Ute, Paiute, Bannock, and Gosiute tribes. In the 1700s explorers, Catholic priests, and trappers all crossed through Utah, documenting its grand terrain and harvesting its abundant wildlife. Despite its plentiful land and wild beauty, Utah remained uninhabitable by most would-be settlers because of its harshly dry climate and isolation from populated seacoast cities.

On July 24, 1847, Mormon pioneer Brigham Young and 148 followers crossed into this open landscape after a grueling 1,300-mile journey from Illinois. Upon arrival, Young declared modern-day Salt Lake City "The Place" that marked the end of a flight from persecution and the beginning of a religious boom. Refugees from traditional American civilization, the Mormons brought dissident religious beliefs and misfit polygamist practices. Here they tucked themselves safely into a vast and formidably barren region.

Only the intrinsic organization and industriousness of the religion enabled them to overcome the oppressive aridness of the region; even before the federal bureaucracies, the

Mormons were able to find, tame, and distribute the scarce water resources and convert these lands into a productive growing region. Since that time, the area has undergone a rapid and expansive development.

With the water tapped and the foundations for civilization laid, other pioneers ventured to Utah to create lives for themselves. Miners perched high in the mountains of Park City, exploiting the region's silver and other precious mineral ore. Ranchers and soldiers began to trickle into the valley and live uneasily alongside their Mormon neighbors, building a life on the shoulders of the LDS civil infrastructure. The Mormons, who otherwise would have been happily settled among themselves, continued to endure attacks from these "gentiles" and even the U.S. government. Understandably weary of harassment in their holy land, members of the Church of Jesus Christ of Latter-day Saints grew increasingly hostile toward outsiders. Non-Mormon "heathens" often lived tucked away up in the canyons, literally afraid for their lives. One relic from these tumultuous days is Ruth's Diner, an establishment that was literally moved out of downtown and into a boxcar in Emigration Canyon, so as to no longer incur Mormon hostility. Today Ruth's Diner still serves famous "mile-high" biscuits with every meal.

Indeed, conflict yielded occasional violence between the two groups. The years 1857–58 brought the Utah War, a battle between Mormon settlers and the U.S. government for power in Utah. The Mormons had proposed an expansive sovereign nation called State of Deseret and had begun creating outposts, such as Moab, to establish rule over most of what today would be nearly all of the Southwest. President James Buchanan and the federal govern-

Signpost in downtown Salt Lake City |Jonathan Echlin

ment forcibly removed Brigham Young from gubernatorial office. Though this action was received gracefully in northern Utah, there was movement for upheaval in the south. Some men even bragged they had enough wives to stamp out the U.S. Army. In the first year of the war, a reactionary massacre was staged by the Mormons to avenge the violent death of their slain apostle Parley Pratt. The result was the death of 137 innocent pioneers passing through Utah, en route from Arkansas to California, at Mountain Meadows, just north of present-day St. George. Eventually, the reality of the overwhelming power of the United States subdued the flames of the Mormon resistance.

In 1896, the Transcontinental Railroad was completed just 56 miles west of Ogden at Promontory Point, commemorated today by the Golden Spike National Historic Site. The Utah Territory's newfound accessibility resulted in a population surge, and the United States began efforts to include Utah in the Union. A primary barrier stood in the way of this agreement: The polygamist practices of the Mormon religion could not be allowed into the Union. Conveniently, leaders of the Mormon Church had a divine revelation in 1890 that virtually eliminated polygamy from mainstream Latter-day Saints (LDS) religion practices. While it did not completely end plural marriages, it did enable Utah to be admitted into the United States in 1896. Although separatist Fundamental Latter-day Saints still practice illegal polygamy across the western United States and in British Columbia, the major branch of the Mormon religion has greatly normalized. Today Utah's diversifying residents coexist in a symbiotic relationship, with cultures blending and a variety of religions flourishing. Since Utah's inception as a state, Mormons and non-Mormons alike have prospered.

Currently, the Salt Lake region is blossoming as a cultural, economic, and educational center. Twice a year thousands of merchants from around the nation gather at the Salt Palace Convention Center for the famous Outdoor Retailer Show. The Sundance Film Festival has spurred the activity of filmmakers and film societies around the valley. The University of Utah, Westminster College, Brigham Young University, and Utah Valley University have a combined student total of 80,000. The Mormon religion is the fastest-growing religion in the world. Anyone can take a free guided tour through Temple Square in downtown Salt Lake City, marvel at the atypical architecture, and hear the history from a Mormon tour guide. As Mormonism has grown, so too has there been an influx of non-Mormons, diluting the LDS population within Salt Lake City proper to around 30 percent. What remains of yesteryear's Mormon dominance is a thought-provoking forum for the blending of cultures and dynamic self-reflection.

Utah's modern culture is purposeful and vibrant. Introspection is expressed through art, music, creative fashion, and even widespread tattooing. Although the Mormon/non-Mormon cohabitation is peaceful, this culture/counterculture phenomenon is a palpable platform for contemplation and action. It is clear that many of the residents—Jews, Mormons, Muslims, Christians, agnostics, atheists, outdoor enthusiasts, artists, students, vagrants, businesspeople, and immigrants—are deep in an identity search, visibly defining their conclusions through fashion and artistic expression.

This guidebook will be a roundup of pioneer history, religious freedom, world-class outdoor recreation, and cultural exploration. Such a young and spiritually self-aware community provides a visceral opportunity to investigate fine arts, faith, and modern architecture, while alternately exploring legendary mountain bike trails, paragliding, helicopter skiing, and rock climbing. Enjoy this impressive region as you see fit. Do not attempt to do everything; there is more than a lifetime of experiences to be had here.

Provo Temple overlooking Utah Lake Christine Balaz

GETTING THERE

By Car

As advertised, Salt Lake City truly is the "Crossroads of the West." In fact, it might be more accurate to describe the area as an Interstate nexus. Salt Lake City sits precisely at the junction of Interstates 15 and 80. Running north-south, I-15 originates in San Diego and connects Los Angeles and Las Vegas to Provo and Salt Lake City, before continuing up through Idaho, Montana, and into Alberta. Running east–west, I-80 begins in San Francisco, crosses Nevada and the Bonneville Salt Flats, Salt Lake City, Park City, and Wyoming before joining I-90 in Chicago and eventually terminating in Boston. Also in the vicinity of Salt Lake City are I-84, I-86, and I-70, all east–west pipelines. From the Northwest, I-84 brings travelers from Oregon, Washington, and the city of Boise into Utah and merges with I-15 just an hour north of Salt Lake City. Interstate 70 brings visitors from nearby Denver, Vail, and Aspen. When approaching the Wasatch region from I-70, a detour on US 191/6 will spare you a few hours of car time. A well-traveled, major highway, it sees regular maintenance and boasts high plateau scenery.

You should be aware that Utah renumbered its freeway exits in 2005. Do not expect exit numbers on old maps to be correct. Be alert and follow signage for place-names.

By Air

If arriving by airplane, you will land at **Salt Lake City International Airport (SLCIA)** (www.slcairport.com), a mere 15 minutes from downtown Salt Lake City. This airport currently presides as the largest hub in the Intermountain West, with three terminals, five concourses, and 80 gates. Efficient and accessible, it was ranked first in the nation for punctuality in 2005, and can be accessed directly from I-80. The airport services major commercial airlines including American, Continental, Delta, Frontier, JetBlue, SkyWest, Southwest, United, and U.S. Airways. Additionally, regional airlines offer trips to other cities in Utah including Provo, Moab, and St. George.

The modern SLCIA building was designed with user ease as the number-one priority. Although more than 20 million passengers tread its concourses annually, Salt Lake Airport retains the convenience of a small airport. This usability is greatly appreciated at the end of a long flight. Even the most weary red-eye traveler must only stumble with the flow of his fellow passengers; all signs point to the same egress. The many concourses lead to common terminals that funnel into the baggage-claim area and shared single-level street access. At the baggage claim, general information booths stand with multilingual help to assist with directions and distribute local brochures. Additionally, the airport has direct phone lines to major hotels, so that you may inquire about your shuttle or make a last-minute reservation. With only one strip of airport-street interface, car rentals, pickups, and shuttle services cannot be missed. Hail your taxi, hotel shuttle, or friend.

Once outside the airport, you have only to follow a series of large signs that lead away from the airport and toward I-80. The clear demarcation tells not only of impending roadways but also of the cities that can be reached by each path. Salt Lake City is a mere 10 minutes

Ski racks at Deer Valley Resort Jonathan Echlin

directly east on I-80, and Park City 20 minutes beyond. To reach Provo, take I-80 east toward Salt Lake City, quickly turning south onto I-215 southbound. This will intersect with southbound I-15 to eventually reach Provo. To access Alta, Brighton, Snowbird, or Solitude, travel east along I-80 through Salt Lake City. Once on the eastern side of the city, follow signs to the southbound eastern leg of the I-215 beltway, which will take you south toward the Cottonwood Canyons. Within five minutes, you will begin to see signage for "ski areas." A trail of these will escort you easily to the mountain of choice.

It should be noted that SLCIA is currently in the midst of a billion-dollar renovation that will improve baggage, parking, landscaping, and much more. The expansion arose from 15 years of deliberation and miraculously does not slow air travel or passenger pickup and drop-off. Rather, the only thing you will notice is the presence of construction cones indicating minor parking lot detours. Like the rest of Salt Lake City, the airport embraces its surrounding environment and has recently received national pollution prevention and clean air awards. Attempting to minimize impact to wild species, the airport built a 465-acre wetland in 1992 to compensate for lost wildlife habitat.

Hotel and Ski Shuttles

You can safely assume that most fine and major hotels in Salt Lake City include airport shuttle as part of their guest services. However, be sure to confirm with your hotel before arrival, as there is amazingly no public transportation between the airport and city. Most bed & breakfasts and modest lodging establishments do not include shuttle services due to lower guest volume. If you have come to Utah as a ski vacationer, a mountain shuttle service will be your preferred choice. Because so much of Utah's tourism is based on its phenomenal skiing, numerous ski-specific shuttles and limousines boast direct and speedy delivery to any of 11 ski areas within 60 miles of the airport. **All Resort Express** (1-877-658-3999; www.allresort.com), located at the airport, allows you to choose between shared ride or limousine service. Aptly named **Resort Transportation** (1-800-604-1525; www.utahski guide.com) offers private shuttle rides only. **Park City Transportation** (1-800-637-3803 or 435-649-5466; www.parkcitytransportation.com) runs private and shared shuttles to any Utah ski resort. **Xpress Shuttle** (1-800-397-0773; www.expressshuttleutah.com) provides private and shared transportation to the greater Salt Lake Area. **Yellow Express** (801-521-2100; www.yellowcabutah.com) is yet another private shuttle service for skiers during a busy ski season. Be sure to call ahead for all of these services.

Car Rentals

Alamo: www.alamo.com; Salt Lake City International Airport, 801-575-2211

Avis: www.avis.com; Salt Lake City International Airport, 801-575-2847; Downtown Salt Lake City, 255 South West Temple, 801-359-2177; Provo, 1200 Towne Centre Boulevard, Sears, 801-494-1529

Budget: www.budget.com; Salt Lake City International Airport, 801-575-2500; Downtown Salt Lake City, 750 South Main Street, 801-575-2500; Park City, 50 Shadow Ridge Hotel, 435-645-7555; Provo, 1475 North State Street, 801-377-9300

Dollar: www.dollar.com; Salt Lake City International Airport, 801-575-2580

Enterprise: www.enterprise.com; Salt Lake City International Airport, 801-537-7433; Downtown Salt Lake City, 843 South State Street, 801-534-1622; Park City, 6560 North Landmark Drive #300, 435-655-7277; Provo, 875 South 100 East, 801-377-7100

Hertz: www.hertz.com; Salt Lake City International Airport, 801-575-2683; Downtown Salt

Lake City, 730 South West Temple, 801-596-2670; Park City, 1895 Sidewinder Drive, Marriott Hotel, 435-655-0868; Provo, 656 South State Street, Orem, 801-434-4520
National: www.nationalcar.com; Salt Lake City International Airport, 801-575-2277
Rugged Rental: www.ruggedrental.com; Salt Lake City International Airport, 801-977-9111
Thrifty: www.thrifty.com; Salt Lake City International Airport, 801-265-6677; Downtown Salt Lake City, Radisson Hotel, 215 West South Temple, 801-355-7368

Airport Accommodations

In case of delayed, red-eye, or early-morning flights, a stay near the airport can alleviate a great deal of travel stress. Although the airport is very near Salt Lake City, none of these airport establishments are actually close enough to the city to call home for your entire trip. Following is a comprehensive list of airport lodging. During heavy travel times, these will often be booked to capacity.

Airport Comfort Inn: 200 North Admiral Byrd Road; 1-800-535-8742 or 801—746-5200; www.slccomfortinn.com

Airport Inn Hotel: 2333 West North Temple; 1-800-937-1688 or 801-539-0438; www.airportinnhotelslc.com

Baymont Inn & Suites–Airport: 2080 West North Temple; 1-877-229-6668 or 801-355-0088; www.baymontinns.com

Best Western Inn–Airport: 315 Admiral Byrd Road; 801-539-5005; www.bestwestern.com

Candlewood Suites Salt Lake City–Airport: 2170 West North Temple; 801-359-7500; www.candlewoodsuites.com

Comfort Suites–Airport: 171 North 2100 West; 801-715-8588; www.comfortsuites.com

Courtyard by Marriott–Airport: 4843 Douglas Corrigan Way; 801-532-4085; www.marriott.com

Days Inn–Airport: 1900 West North Temple; 801-539-8538 or 1-800-228-2800; www.daysinn.com

Fairfield Inn–Airport: 230 Admiral Byrd Road; 801-355-3331; www.sla-ffi.com

Hampton Inn–Airport: 307 Admiral Byrd Road; 801-530-0088; www.hamptoninnsalt lake.com

Hilton Salt Lake City–Airport: 5151 Wiley Post Way; 801-539-1515; www.hilton.com

La Quinta Inn–Airport: 4905 Wiley Post Way; 801-366-4444 or 1-800-531-5900; www.lq.com

Microtel Inn & Suites: 61 Tommy Thompson Road; 801-236-2800; www.microtel-inns .com

Motel 6–Airport: 1990 West North Temple; 801-364-1053; www.motel6.com

Quality Inn–Airport: 1659 West North Temple; 801-355-3047; www.qualityinn.com

Radisson Hotel–Airport: 2177 West North Temple; 801-364-5800; www.radisson.com

Residence Inn–Airport: 4883 Douglas Corrigan Way; 801-532-4101; www.marriott.com

Super 8–Airport: 223 North Jimmy Doolittle Road; 801-533-8878; www.super8.com

By Bus

Greyhound Bus Lines (300 South 600 West; 801-355-9579 or 1-800-231-2222; www.greyhound.com) offers affordable service to Salt Lake City from nearly anywhere in North America and has routes connecting Utah cities such as Moab, Provo, Ogden, St.

Salt Lake City's I-215 Beltway Christine Balaz

George, and Green River. Salt Lake City's station is located just a short cab ride or walk west of downtown. Once you are in Salt Lake City and Provo, **Utah Transit Authority** (or UTA: 801-377-7433; www.rideuta.com) will serve you as the cities' mass-transit service, with bus and rail service crisscrossing the downtown and university districts. Traveling with the UTA in their Free Ride Zone downtown can be a relaxing way to take in some of the sights at no cost. The **Park City Free Bus System** (435-615-5301) is the ideal means of transport within Park City, as well as between the ski areas and downtown. Once in Park City, you cannot miss the numerous buses and covered shelters. Savvy locals and tourists find this to be immensely easier than attempting to park downtown or find the day-skier lots at the major mountain resorts.

By Train
Amtrak (1-800-872-7245; www.amtrak.com) crosses Utah daily with stops in St. George, Provo, Salt Lake City, Ogden, and Green River. Direct routes from Los Angeles and San Diego, San Francisco, Denver, Portland, Seattle, and Vancouver cross some of the nation's desolately beautiful desert country, which can add a great deal of effortless sightseeing to your trip. Provo's station (300 West 600 South) is a dozen blocks southwest of Brigham Young University. Salt Lake City's station (340 South 600 West) shares a location with the Greyhound Bus station and so typically has ample cabs waiting to take you the few blocks toward downtown. Unfortunately, the Park City Greyhound stop was eliminated. If traveling to Park City, you will need to take a taxi or shuttle up the pass from Salt Lake City.

GETTING AROUND

In Utah you will need a car anywhere outside city centers. Public transportation improves annually, but is currently only fully developed in downtown areas. Because of Utah's expansiveness and relatively low population, public transportation to areas outside urban centers is rare, with popular outdoor destinations the exception.

Utah Transit Authority (UTA) operates canyon shuttle lines to Alta, Brighton, Snowbird, and Solitude that save you the hassle of snow tires and crowded parking. (Call 1-888-743-3882 or visit www.rideuta.com for route and schedule information.) Additionally, Utah's national parks run shuttle-bus lines to minimize congestion and provide more relaxed sightseeing.

Whether you decide to rent a car or not, you will probably need to familiarize yourself with the infamous Utah **"grid system."** Marrying Mormon faith and practicality, the grid system locates streets and addresses by position on a coordinate plane whose origin, "(0, 0)," is none other than the LDS Temple. Utah's early pioneers planned their cities before they were even built, so the great majority of Salt Lake City and Provo streets are still named according to this method. The actual "(0, 0)" of Salt Lake City occurs at Main Street and South Temple. Counting in any direction away from the temple, each street name has a value 100 greater than the last. Main Street is a north-south running road. The next parallel street to the east is called 100 East, followed by 200 East, 300 East and so on. The same logic follows for each cardinal direction. The next street to the south of South Temple is 100 South. So if you are trying to find the address "153 East 200 South" you know that this location is approximately 1.5 blocks east of Main Street on 200 South (Street), which is two blocks south of South Temple.

Downtown Salt Lake City sidewalk Jonathan Echlin

Further complicating the system, some streets also carry dual names: 100 East in Salt Lake City is more commonly called State Street, and Commonwealth Avenue is most often referred to as 2100 South. These streets will usually be signed with both names. Provo, modeled after Salt Lake City, also implements the grid system. Although the city map is not identical, it can be navigated similarly.

Many people find this system vexing at first, but most grow to appreciate it for its practicality. In fact, most locals encounter problems only when they stumble across a street without a numerical name. "Where is Highland Drive?" If you find this system nevertheless insurmountable, fret not. Park City, never an LDS town, has street names completely of its own choosing.

The Main Street Trolley in Park City Jonathan Echlin

Taxis

Ski vacationers and intoxicating evenings create most of the business for Utah's cab companies. Not surprisingly, Salt Lake City, Park City, and the ski resorts have the majority of taxi service. Provo's only cab companies are **Affordable Cab**, **Yellow Cab**, and **Taxi Van**, listed below. Although there are many taxi services in Salt Lake City, three companies, **City Cab**, **Ute Cab**, and **Yellow Cab** are the major companies. If you anticipate requiring a cab, jot down a few of these numbers so you can call for a ride. Because of Utah's spacious layout, hailing a taxi here can prove difficult.

Ace Cab Company: Park City, 435-649-8294

Advanced Transportation: Airport to Park City, Park City taxi, and Park City ski areas, 435-647-3999, 1-866-647-3999; www.advtransportation.com

Affordable Cab & Limousine Service: Provo taxi, 801-375-0000

City Cab Company: Salt Lake City taxi and ski areas, 801-363-5550

Daytrips Transportation: Airport to Park City, Park City taxi, 1-800 649-8294; www.daytrips.com

Freshtraks: Salt Lake City taxi and ski areas, 801-228-1330 or 1-888-840-1330

Murray Cab Company: Salt Lake City taxi, 801-328-5704
Park City Taxi: Airport to Park City, 435-658-2227 and 1-800-724 7767
Powder for the People: Airport to Park City, Park City taxi, and Park City ski areas, 435-649-6648 or 1-888-482-7547; www.powderforthepeople.com
Taxi Van: Provo taxi, 801-375-8833
Ute Cab: Airport to Salt Lake City, Salt Lake City taxi, 801-359-7788
Yellow Cab: Salt Lake City and ski areas, 801-521-2100; www.yellowcabutah.com

Public Transportation

Recent years have brought about a growth of the **Utah Transit Authority** (801-377-7433; www.rideuta.com), a system of aboveground trains and buses connecting the downtown districts of larger cities to the university and surrounding residential areas. A great feature of the UTA is the Free Ride Zone in downtown Salt Lake City, convenient for commuters and tourists alike. For more information, see www.rideuta.com. Another extremely popular aspect of the UTA is the canyon shuttle service, which takes skiers and snowboarders from the park-and-ride lot at the mouths of Big and Little Cottonwood Canyons to Alta, Brighton, Snowbird, and Solitude. This saves a good deal of gas and brake pads, as the base of the ski areas sit approximately 3,000 feet above the mouths of these long and steep canyons.

GENERAL INFORMATION

Weather

Utah's climate is wildly diverse. Though it is most often pleasant and sunny, it can turn severe with little or no warning. The desert sandstone and sagebrush of the South see summer highs in the triple digits with no shade. Yet, as soon as the sun dips below the horizon, the temperature of the bone-dry air drops dramatically. The mountain ecosystems range from lushly green canyons to alpine granite above the tree line. Fortunately, the dramatic elevation and terrain differences in the Salt Lake region make it possible for you to customize your weather. For cooler weather, head to the mountains; for sunny warmth, play in the valley. It would be a challenge to find a region anywhere in the world with better, more adaptable weather.

Annually, the Wasatch Mountains see more than 240 predominantly sunny days, yet miraculously manage to squeeze 500 epic inches—roughly *42 feet*—of the world's fluffiest snow out of the small number of clouds that do pass by. Every year champagne powder absolutely buries the mountains. Naturally, these peaks experience highly variable weather and are subject to temperature inversions. To ensure you dress properly for your adventure, check the weather for higher elevations. Recreation traditionally relegated to the summer months, such as golf and mountain biking, can actually be enjoyed nine months out of the year. Spring, summer, and fall blend to offer nearly endless summer. Drive higher in the mountains and you can play à la winter during the late fall, winter, and early spring.

Valley summer highs can intimidate a Yankee. Salt Lake City and Provo, each around 4,400 feet (1,340 m) above sea level, average around 90 degrees F (32 degrees C) during July, August, and September for daytime highs. Fortunately, these low-humidity days will not cook you, like a summer in Louisiana or even a humid 80-degree day in Massachusetts.

Skier jumping at Snowbird Resort Jonathan Echlin

Keep in mind that the air is dry and the mountains always offer an escape during these hot days. Park City, at 7,080 feet (2,150 m) above sea level, is usually 10 to 15 degrees cooler than the valleys below. If you prefer an even chillier getaway, choose one of the dozens of tree-shaded and stream-refrigerated Wasatch canyons, where even the most sizzling days might see a high of only 75 degrees. The summer nights in Utah cannot be beat and seem to be made for outdoor concerts and strolls.

The weather changes drastically with each passing season, but every month of the year shares a common element: ample clear days. The bright Utah sun shines through the winter months, warming the valleys to highs of 40 degrees F (5 degrees C). Snow often falls, but usually does not accumulate. Park City has average winter daytime highs around 25 degrees F (-4 degrees C) and maintains a charming winter snow covering.

Spring and fall are favorite seasons of Utahans. Usually temperate and pleasant, the air

High Little Cottonwood Canyon peaks in early summer Christine Balaz

temperature offers comfortable daytime temperatures and cozy evenings. During spring you can golf comfortably in the valley or enjoy the late-season snow dumps at the resorts. Fall extends summer and paints the hillside scrub oak saturated shades of yellow, orange, and red. Though the days grow shorter, you can still enjoy your favorite summer activities.

Many visitors to Utah are surprised by two things: the dryness of the air and the intensity of the sun. Guard yourself against parching and sunburn with fluids, sunscreen, and protective clothing. The importance of hydration does not disappear during the winter months, especially for skiers. Additionally, the consumption of (nonalcoholic) liquids helps you acclimatize to the altitude; do not forget that the valley sits at 4,400 feet (1,340 m) above sea level and the peaks of Alta soar to 11,000 feet (3,350 m).

Tours

Salt Lake City Tours (801-534-1001; www.saltlakecitytours.org) offers guided bus tours of Salt Lake City and the Great Salt Lake, as well as specialty tours through Temple Square and the world's largest open-pit mine, Kennecott Copper Mine. For a more adventuresome experience, take a bicycle ride with **Tailwind Bicycle Tours** (801-556-3290; www.tailwind tours.com) in Salt Lake City or Antelope Island State Park. If time allows, make an excursion to Monument Valley in southern Utah. When in downtown Salt Lake City, consider being towed around Temple Square in a horse-drawn cart with **Carriage for Hire** (801-363-8687; www.carriageforhire.net). The tours are convenient, festive, and informative, lasting about one hour and filling your brain with local history.

Local Taxes

Expect sales taxes in Utah to total somewhere around 6.5 percent. Local taxes vary; Salt Lake City's sales tax is 6.6 percent. Provo visitors and residents pay 6.25 percent of their purchase in taxes. Resort tax applies to ski areas, raising the tax in Alta to 8.1 percent and 7.35 percent in Park City. Meals and room tax apply at a rate of 5 and 3 percent, respectively. Liquor tax is included in the purchase price of booze and wine, and by law cannot be higher in resorts.

Liquor Laws

Utah liquor laws create much more anxiety than is necessary—especially in recent times, as some of the more stringent rules have disappeared or lessened as of 2009. Although slightly odd and described with strange jargon, they are worth discussing, but easily navigated. The rumors you have heard on this topic are most likely a combination of urban legend and truth. Beer is the most picked-on alcoholic beverage in Utah. Indeed, most beer here contains 3.2 percent alcohol by weight (abw), or 4.2 percent by volume. You can buy this beer in gas stations, grocery stores, and on draught in bars. "Real" beer does exist for legal purchase in Utah in liquor stores and bars. This beer, imported from other states and countries, is more heavily taxed. Thus it is more expensive in liquor stores, costing one to two dollars a bottle. Most bars and restaurants sell these "real" beers and charge a surprisingly ordinary price. Until the summer of 2009, the state government only allowed the sale of full-strength beer in bottles; but now, restaurants are allowed to serve full-strength draught beer—a welcome change for residents and visitors alike.

On reduced-alcohol beer: keep in mind that if you were to purchase an American lager outside Utah, its alcohol content would only be about 4.8 percent abw, and a "real" porter or stout would only contain around 3 or 4 percent abw. Therefore, many of these "Utah" beers available for purchase in a supermarket or convenience shop aren't even that much altered from their ordinary state. Needless to say, though, Belgian-style beers change quite a bit with lowered alcohol content. Surprisingly, the beer brewers of Utah have not been defeated; in fact, beer brewing has blossomed here. People theorize that the brewers in Utah craft such flavorful beer because their focus must remain only on quality, not on quantity of alcohol.

Another worry of visitors is the "private club." This source of great anxiety and mystery has just recently disappeared into history. Still, for curiosity's (and posterity's) sake, this term is worth discussing. "Private club" used to be Utah speak for "bar." In their existence, private clubs were neither private, nor exclusive. "Private club" was simply the legal term for an establishment that served primarily alcohol, and could serve drinks to customers regardless of whether they have ordered food. (In a restaurant with a liquor license, you must order food to be served alcohol.) To enter a "private club," one had to purchase membership to enter. Temporary memberships could be purchased at these bars for about five dollars, and many establishments with live acts would even waive any additional cover charge. These memberships admitted the purchaser and seven guests to the establishment for up to two weeks. Still, though, no person under the age of 21 is allowed in a Utah bar, even if the person is a young child accompanied by parents.

Oddly enough, wine and liquor have incurred very little additional regulation by Utah's otherwise harsh liquor laws. Available for purchase in the plentiful state liquor stores of Salt Lake City and Park City, they cost a fairly standard price, somewhat comparable with the national average. Be aware that liquor stores in Utah, as in many other states, close on Sundays, government holidays, and election days—and hours vary per store, so check online (www.alcbev.state.ut.us) for locations and hours in your vicinity.

Finally, the rumored concept of "dry city" in Utah actually does exist. In 1999 the Utah Supreme Court ruled that local cities had the authority to deny liquor licenses to establishments if the city's residents did not want alcohol served in their town. Though not many cities in Utah actually have passed the "dry law," you will occasionally notice beer missing from store coolers.

Each bottle sold in Utah (excepting those containing low-alcohol beer) has a small, pink sticker affixed to it as proof of purchase within Utah. Although a difficult law to enforce, the transport of any alcohol in Utah without a state liquor certificate is illegal.

Area Codes

Utah area codes are simple. The area code in and around Salt Lake City and Provo is 801. Area code 435 represents all other counties in the state, including Park City, Moab, and St. George. Utah is expected to soon have a new area code, 385, which will cover the same regions as the 801 area code, affecting Salt Lake, Davis, Morgan, Utah, and Weber counties, including Salt Lake City, Provo and Orem. This will take place in overlay fashion, i.e. existing 801 numbers will retain their area code, and new numbers created in the area will be assigned the 385 area code. Eventually 10-digit dialing will become mandatory.

Emergency Telephone Numbers

In case of emergency, dial 911. To report other situations, contact the Salt Lake City Police Department (320 East 200 South; 801-799-3768), the Park City Police Department (445 Marsac Avenue; 435-615-5500), or the Provo City Police Department (48 South 300 West; 801-852-6210).

Hospitals

Salt Lake City is a regional medical hub whose hospital roster includes **Alta View Hospital** (9660 South 1300 East, Sandy/Cottonwood Canyons; 801-501-2600), **Cottonwood Hospital** (5770 South 300 East, Murray; 801-314-5300), **IHC Instacare Sugarhouse** (2000 South 900 East, Sugarhouse; 801-464-7777), **LDS Hospital** (8th Avenue & C Street, Avenues; 801-408-1100), **Primary Children's Hospital** (5770 South 1500 West, Murray; 801-265-3000), **Saint Mark's Hospital** (1200 East 3900 South, Salt Lake City; 801-268-7111), **University Hospital** (50 North Medical Drive, University of Utah; 801-581-2121), and **US**

Trail running in Salt Lake's foothills Christine Balaz

Veterans Medical Center (500 Foothill Boulevard, Salt Lake City; 801-582-1565).

A small and very active town, Park City has a large number of hospitals and emergency clinics per capita, including **IHC Physicians Group Family Practice** (1612 West Ute Boulevard; 435-658-0179), **Park City Mountain Resort Urgent Care** (1493 Lowell Ave; 435-655-7970), **Snow Creek Emergency and Medical Center** (1600 Snow Creek Drive; 435-655-0055), **Summit Health Care** (1750 West Sun Peak Drive; 435-647-5740), and **University of Utah's Hospitals and Clinics–Summit Health Center** (1750 Sun Peak Drive; 435-647-0503).

Provo has research powerhouse Brigham Young University to thank for its state-of-the-art hospitals and specialty health-care facilities. **Central Utah Clinic** (1055 North 500 West #202; 801-429-8095), **Intermountain Health Care** (1034 North 500 West; 801-357-7448), and **Utah Valley Regional Medical Center** (1034 North 500 West; 801-357-7850) are the general hospitals I hope you will never have to see on your trip here.

Local Publications

The Wasatch Region prints many periodicals, each with its own specialty. The *Salt Lake Tribune* (www.sltrib.com) and *Deseret News* (www.deseretnews.com) both report the daily news, the latter being of the LDS persuasion. *Salt Lake Magazine* (www.saltlakemagazine.com), a

Hiking in Salt Lake's foothills Christine Balaz

high-end monthly magazine, has a comprehensive events listing and in-depth articles pertaining to the region's happenings and establishments. *Salt Lake City Weekly* (www.slweekly .com) and *In Utah This Week* (www.inthisweek.com), both free for the taking in coffee shops and newsstands, also include regional events calendars and local tidbits. *The Park Record* (www.parkrecord.com) prints daily news and upcoming activities pertaining to Park City. Utah County's *Daily Herald* (www.harktheherald.com) reports news for Provo and Orem.

Chambers of Commerce

The **Salt Lake Convention & Visitors Bureau** has three branches. One is located among the baggage claims in Terminals 1 and 2. Another (300 North State Street; 801-538-1030; www.visitsaltlake.com), adjacent to the southwest corner of the Capitol Building, high on Capitol Hill, also serves as Salt Lake City's **Utah Office of Tourism**. The third (90 South West Temple; 801-534-4900; www.visitsaltlake.com) is located inside the Salt Palace Convention Center, on the west end of downtown. **Salt Lake Chamber of Commerce** (175 East 400 South State Street; 801-364-3631; www.saltlakechamber.org) is another resource for free information on your trip.

Located within a mile of I-80, the **Park City Chamber of Commerce** (1826 Olympic Parkway; 435-658-9616; www.parkcityinfo.com) should be your first stop when traveling to Park City. Well-placed signs will lead you from the Kimball Junction/Park City exit directly to the Chamber. The Visitors Center shares an access road with the Utah Olympic Park and the highly visible Olympic Nordic ski jumps.

Located just south of Brigham Young University, **Utah Valley Convention and Visitors Bureau** (111 South University Avenue; 801-851-2100; www.utahvalley.org) has a convenient, central location, yet is removed from the bustle of campus. Before you embark on your trip, peruse the Web site. It offers many discounts and is an impressive collection of useful information such as maps, weather, and activity recommendations by season.

Handicapped Accessibility

Utah's abundance of recreation is not exclusively for the able-bodied. In fact, Utah has a hardcore community of handicapped athletes. The Wasatch region is home to many world-class organizations that exist solely to extend these experiences to Utah's handicapped residents and visitors. Park City is home to the **National Ability Center** (435-649-3991; www .nac1985.org). This offers more sports programs and events than most people will try in a lifetime, including bobsledding, water-skiing, cycling, snowboarding, and rugby. The **National Disabled Ski Team** is also based in Park City; its World Cup disabled athletes undergo rigorous training here. Although participation is restricted to these qualifying elite athletes, simply witnessing their fast-paced slalom sessions will inspire any onlooker. **Splore** (801-484-4128; www.splore.org) provides another exceptional resource for Utahans and visitors with disabilities. Located in Salt Lake City, this nonprofit organization is dedicated to making rafting, climbing, skiing, and many other activities accessible to those for whom the logistics of these activities would otherwise be a major obstacle. If you wish to access these services, plan ahead, as most of their trips require advanced booking.

Gay and Lesbian

Considering Salt Lake City's intermountain western location, there is a surprisingly prosperous gay community here. While an outright presence remains subdued, a thriving net-

Sugarhouse District   Jonathan Echlin

work of societies, clubs, and organizations connects gay and lesbian Salt Lake. Local gay publications advertise an array of activity groups, online communities, nightclubs, and even ranch retreats. Monthly *Q Salt Lake* (www.qsaltlake.com) and weekly *Pillar of the Gay, Lesbian, Bisexual and Transgender Community* are two free publications distributed in coffee shops and newsstands throughout Salt Lake City. These periodicals monitor relevant news, politics, and general happenings and have thorough club and activities listings. Several gay-friendly establishments provide community gathering places for visitors and residents alike.

For a night on the town, you might look up **Club Try-Angles** (251 West 900 South; 801-364-3203; www.clubtry-angles.com) for men and women (although usually mostly men), Jam (751 North 300 West; 801-891-1162; www.gaybarsaltlake.com), for men, **Mo Diggity's** (3424 South State Street; 801-832-9000;) for women, **and Paper Moon** (3737 South State Street; 801-713-0678) for women.

Child Care and Children's Gear Rental

If traveling with children, you may need a retreat on your vacation. Many hotels and ski resorts offer child care recommendations, and some even provide in-house sitting. **Guardian Angels** (Salt Lake City: 801-598-1229, Park City: 435-640-1229, or Provo: 801-310-2761; www.guardianangelbaby.com), one of Utah's only temporary child care services, has CPR-certified babysitters who travel to your hotel. Each sitter has multiple character reference letters on file. Guardian Angels also provides children's **gear rental**, such as strollers, cribs, and sleds, and even delivers groceries to indisposed parents.

Within Park City you have several choices. **Annie's Nannies of Park City** (435-615-1935) is an insured and licensed organization that offers infant care, general babysitting, and group play. **The Clubhouse** has three locations, one on Main Street (435-940-1607), one at Prospector Square (435-649-3168), and one at the Redstone Plaza of Kimball Junction (435-575-1607). Drop-in service is available with reservations. Arrangements for in-home service is can be made through the Main Street branch. **Baby's Away Equipment Rental** (435-645-8823 or 1-800-379-9030) provides equipment rentals for families traveling with young ones.

Particular to This Book

Abbreviations

MEALS SERVED	DAYS OF SERVICE	CREDIT CARDS
B—Breakfast	Sun.—Sunday	AE—American Express
L—Lunch	Mon.—Monday	DC—Diners Club
D—Dinner	Tues.—Tuesday	Disc—Discover
	Wed.—Wednesday	MC—MasterCard
	Thurs.—Thursday	V—Visa
	Fri.—Friday	
	Sat.—Saturday	

Relative Cost

Considering the quality of the Wasatch Front cuisine and accommodations, you can expect to be surprised by the low prices. Here is a general cost guide:

	Restaurants	Accommodations
Inexpensive	up to $15	up to $100
Moderate	$15 to $25	$100 to $175
Expensive	$25 to $35	$175 to $250
Very Expensive	more than $35	more than $250

I

SALT LAKE CITY

Salt Lake City, capital of Utah, is at once an outdoor mecca, a cultural hub, and a religious stronghold. It is flanked by the Wasatch Mountains immediately to the east, the Oquirrh Range to the west, and the Great Salt Lake to its northwest. Each of these geological features, especially the Wasatch, with its manifold canyons and 11,000-foot peaks, provides four-season recreational opportunities. With its international airport, multiple universities, and cultural societies, Salt Lake City is an intermountain gathering place for creative minds. As the holy land of the Church of Jesus Christ of Latter-day Saints, Salt Lake Valley is saturated in Latter-day Saints (LDS) pioneer history; as one of the major urban centers of the Rocky Mountains, it is a fascinating amalgamation of finance, adrenaline junkies, and culture.

Utah has the largest median household size in the country. In fact, Utah is arguably the most family-oriented state in the country. This goes hand in hand with the stereotype that all of Utah is Mormon. This is not true, of course, yet without Mormonism, modern Utah would not be what it is today. Contrary to urban legend, the Latter-day Saints are far from being Utah's only facet. The most striking part of your experience here will be awe of the Wasatch Mountains jutting dramatically out of the valley. You will be surprised by consistently beautiful weather and impressed by the Salt Lake Library's architecture and the Mormon Temple. The most tangible Mormon impact is the population's pervasive politeness and the region's low crime rates. In fact, locals cherish the exaggerated Mormon stereotype for the reason that it keeps Salt Lake City largely undiscovered. There is no other city with such superb weather, immediate proximity to world-class recreation, and abundant cultural opportunities that is so untapped and accessible.

It is true that Utah's politics are fundamentally conservative, and that the liquor laws are unusual. Regarding liquor, gone are the days of "private clubs" and lowered alcohol draught beer. Furthermore, Utah bars are all smoke-free by law, and your early morning ski adventures and evening symphony trips will leave you so exhausted that a trip to the bar might seem completely out of the question.

Utah is evolving rapidly, and locals sense changes with every passing year. With an annual growth rate of 29.6 percent, the state's population is growing at a rate more than double that of the nation (13.2 percent), and is the fifth-fastest growing state in the United States Salt Lake City is winning national recognition for its urban regrowth and public transportation improvements. Historic neighborhoods, once dilapidated, are now bourgeois; old railroad switching stations are weekly converting to artist rows filled with studios and creativity. With a now minority LDS population, the majority of Salt Lake is comprised of Catholics, Jews, atheists, Latinos, punk rockers, and outdoors people. The Mormon/

Historic downtown Salt Lake City Jonathan Echlin

non-Mormon dynamic has created a powerful platform on which self-identity is paramount. The faith and presence of the Latter-day Saints seems to bring out stronger-than-
usual interest in other religions and lifestyles. If you are Baptist or a punk rocker in Salt
Lake City, you will likely be very involved in your congregation or music scene. Salt Lake
City's residents are highly pragmatic, but in a broad spectrum of flavors.

Undoubtedly, Salt Lake City is breaching the cusp of rediscovery. A critical mass has
been reached whereby the outside world is recognizing the assets of the area and the silli-
ness of the anti-Mormon sentiment. In 2002, Salt Lake City revealed itself to the world
when it hosted the Winter Olympics. Though the party is since over, these remaining
world-class facilities are open for athlete training and public recreation at extremely low
cost. Five dollars will rent you a pair of speed skates and buy admission to the ice oval in
Kearns. The Sundance Film Festival, now the world's premier independent film festival,
takes place each year in Park City and Salt Lake City. Its presence in Salt Lake City is tangible year-round, with aspiring filmmakers residing here and the Salt Lake Film Society
offering several free public screenings and forums weekly. In 2003, the modern Salt Lake
City Public Library opened with national awards in architectural innovation. Currently the
Salt Lake International Airport, already a major hub for commercial airlines, is undergoing
a billion-dollar expansion effort.

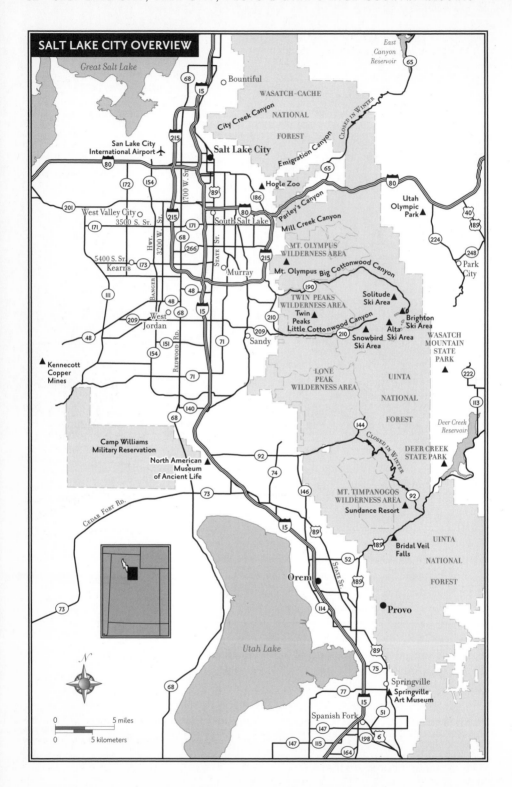

SALT LAKE CITY OVERVIEW

Great Salt Lake

East Canyon Reservoir

65

68
15

Bountiful

WASATCH-CACHE

City Creek Canyon

NATIONAL

FOREST

CLOSED IN WINTER

215

San Lake City International Airport ✈

Salt Lake City

Emigration Canyon

80

172   154

80

89

186

Hogle Zoo

65

Utah Olympic Park ▲

40
189

201

West Valley City
3500 S. St.

215

South Salt Lake

Parley's Canyon

Mill Creek Canyon

224

248

171

215

MT. OLYMPUS
WILDERNESS AREA

Big Cottonwood Canyon

Park City

5400 S. St.
Kearns

68
266

190

Solitude
Ski Area ▲

Murray

Mt. Olympus ▲

113

48

TWIN PEAKS
WILDERNESS AREA

Brighton
Ski Area ▲

111

48

Twin
Peaks ▲

WASATCH
MOUNTAIN
STATE
PARK

209

West
Jordan

68   15

Little Cottonwood Canyon

Alta
Ski Area ▲

48

209

151

210

Snowbird
Ski Area ▲

222

▲ Kennecott
Copper
Mines

154

71

Sandy

LONE
PEAK
WILDERNESS AREA

UINTA

113

71

NATIONAL

140

FOREST

Deer Creek
Reservoir

68

144

CLOSED IN WINTER

Camp Williams
Military Reservation

92

DEER CREEK
STATE PARK ▲

North American
Museum
of Ancient Life

74

146

MT. TIMPANOGOS
WILDERNESS AREA

92

73

CEDAR FORT RD.

Sundance Resort

UINTA

15

89

189

Bridal Veil ▲
Falls

NATIONAL

52

Orem ●

89

FOREST

73

114

Provo ●

N

Utah Lake

89

75

68

Springville

Springville
Art Museum ▲

0   5 miles

77

15

51

0   5 kilometers

Spanish Fork

147   115

147

198   6

164

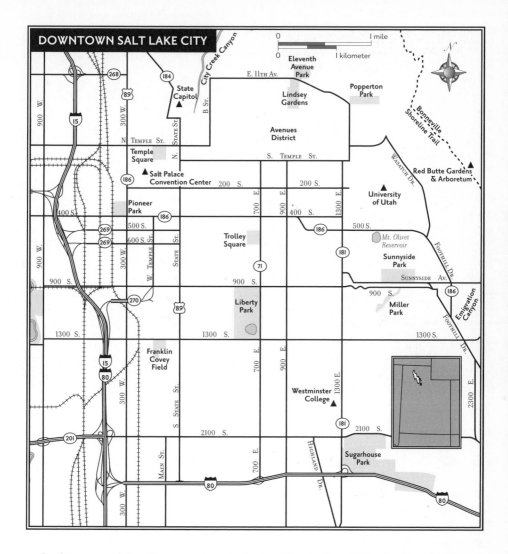

Looking around the city you may see students cycling to class, Orthodox Jews strolling with their families, artists, immigrants, spandex-clad fitness enthusiasts, Mormon missionaries, musicians, and tourists. Each is here to sample and enjoy all of the offerings of the area, from the cuisine to the ski resorts in the canyons, to the menagerie of artists giving free outdoor concerts all summer at the Gallivan Center downtown.

With this thriving influx of culture, Salt Lake City now enjoys all of the cosmopolitan benefits of a major metropolitan area. Because Salt Lake is still largely undiscovered, its entertainment prices do not reflect the quality of the presentation. Quality of living is not compromised by crowding. Salt Lake City's restaurants now habitually receive national acclaim, and its venues consistently attract headlining artists like the Rolling Stones and Shania Twain. Utah's license plates boast "The Best Snow on Earth." Indeed, roughly 500 inches of snow fall on the Wasatch every year, and it is up to 50 percent lighter than snow almost anywhere else.

The city lights Jonathan Echlin

Salt Lake City residents live a in a bubble; they enjoy a lower cost of living and less crowding than other urban dwellers and the shortest distance to premium outdoor areas (and the longest seasons to enjoy them), yet still reap all the benefits of living in a large city. Truly spoiled, Salt Lake City residents are within a 2.5-hour flight of 50 percent of U.S. cities.

Salt Lake City has a heightened sense of existence. The history of the Mormon/non-Mormon interactions here, once marked by violence, now enriches the city and the identities of its residents. Cultural fairs and religious festivals of all varieties take place throughout every year. The mountains enhance the quality of life. They are what sculpt the bodies here and what attract skiers from around the world. They keep you cool in the summer and they squeeze feet of snow out of the clouds passing by in the winter. Their spring runoff is what first allowed the Mormon pioneers to settle here, and their canyons are where the non-Mormons first erected their own mining cities.

When you walk around the city, you will notice how its significant history and mountainous geography manifest in everything that happens here. The peaceful streets, safe because of the strong LDS values, are almost all 132 feet wide, as called for in the Book of Mormon. The Wasatch peaks are never out of your sight, and rarely far from your mind. You cannot drive anywhere without seeing the Alta snowflake bumper sticker, or go many weeks in the fall without hearing about a major ski film premiering somewhere in the valley.

Salt Lake City's downtown streets are dwarfed by modern glass high-rises. The University of Utah's Huntsman Cancer Institute drives medical research and standards worldwide.

The I-215 beltway was recently added to the interstate system, making the whole city no farther than 45 minutes from any ski area in the Wasatch. The commingling of cultures and mountainous surroundings is what has created Salt Lake City and what will carry it into the future. The constant drive of its residents to define themselves does not allow the city to linger in the past or remain isolated in the craggy Wasatch. It continually strides forward, birthplace of new businesses, and new home to the adventurous.

LOCAL HISTORY

For as long as 12,000 years the Salt Lake Valley has been home to many different societies of indigenous people. These were ancestors and people of the Shoshone, Ute, Paiute, Bannock, Navajo, and Gosiute tribes, whose names appear as the names of mountains, roads, and towns across the region. Because of the wide annual temperature range and dry climate of this region, most of these tribes subsisted as bands of nomadic peoples, migrating seasonally. There is evidence, however, of some basic horticulture that produced maize, beans, and squash.

In some instances, farming begot a stationary lifestyle that allowed for craft specialization and the emergence of artistic expression. Artifacts evidence the historical presence of sophisticated tool making and fine basket weaving. Some of these pieces can be seen on display in the Museum of Ancient Life at Thanksgiving Point or in the Museum of Fine Arts at the University of Utah.

The first Europeans to encounter these peoples were the missionary-explorers Dominguez and Escalante, who had set out to establish a northern route between missions in Santa Fe, New Mexico and Monterey, California. After a tortuous and winding trek up the length of western Colorado and northeastern Utah, their party was paralyzed by inclement weather. Defeated, they turned back to Santa Fe, but not without making positive records of Utah's landscape and peoples. The only Europeans who forged success in Utah around this time were trappers, who, like the indigenous tribes, lived by means of hunting and gathering. When European fashion grew weary of pelts and furs and switched to silk, the trapping profession became null. The fur trappers also receded from the region.

Salt Lake Valley remained "uncivilized" until 1847, when pioneer and Mormon leader Brigham Young arrived in the valley after an unforgiving westerly pilgrimage. Young brought with him 148 people, including only three women and two children, all fleeing persecution and seeking their promised land. They crossed into the Salt Lake Valley via Emigration Canyon, where today many road cyclists take an afternoon spin. Sighting the Great Salt Lake, Young declared, "This is the place!" Today a monument to this "discovery" stands on the Wasatch Benches, on the east side of town. Contrary to rumor, Young did not mistake the lake for the Pacific Ocean. Rather, he had deliberately sought this region specifically because its inhospitable climate left it almost untouched by western government.

The year 1848 brought more hard times, including a swarm of crickets that descended on Salt Lake Valley, devouring the Mormons' fledgling crops. As if to confirm the place of the settlers in Salt Lake Valley, a flock of tens of thousands of California gulls followed, and within a few days had eaten the menacing crickets. Grateful to this heaven-sent bird, the Utahans made the California gull their state bird.

Things eventually went well for the Mormons, the only group of European Americans organized and industrious enough to collect, store, and allocate the desperately scarce Utah water. Because of the harshly dry climate and the unfavorable reputation of the Mormons, they were left entirely to themselves to cultivate their own religion and population. The Mormons enjoyed their intimate, well-planned community cemented by shared faith. City plans were drawn within weeks of arrival, all as dictated in the Book of Mormon. Ground was immediately broken for the Temple.

In 1849 Utahans proposed an independent Mormon state, Deseret, which would have covered most of the Southwest. The U.S. government refused to accept this proposition and created the provisional Territory of Utah in 1850. (Utah would not be granted statehood until the Mormon Church agreed to rid polygamy from its practices.) In spite of this, the Mormons moved forward with their plan. They founded towns, such as St. George and Moab, to establish control over Deseret. In 1857 President James Buchanan dispatched troops to the area to replace Governor Brigham Young with a leader of his own choice, Alfred Cumming. Naturally much of the Mormon community reacted negatively, although rarely was the dissidence violent. Mail service to the territory was cut off without warning and 2,500 troops were sent in. Perceiving this as religious persecution, the Mormons reacted in a hostile manner. Both sides' edginess gave way to battle. From 1857 to 1858, the government and territory fought against each other in the Utah War. An unfortunate tangent to this war was the 1857 Mountain Meadows Massacre, during which California-bound settlers were slain by vengeful Mormon hands.

In 1862 President Abraham Lincoln, unsettled by the growing population of the Utah Mormons, grew afraid that the Mormons might take secessionist interest in the Civil War in the hopes that they might be granted their state of Deseret by the Confederacy. To quell

Mormon rebellion and prevent alliance with the South, Lincoln sent Colonel Patrick Connor and his California-Nevada Volunteers to maintain some sort of governmental awareness of the political climate in Utah. They established Fort Douglas, which remains on the University of Utah campus today.

Suspicions gave way to cautious trust, and the troops relaxed. They began to explore the hills in search of the then American dream—mining. They foraged upward and eastward through Big Cottonwood Canyon, and then down into Park City where they discovered a major vein of silver. They also found precious metals in Parleys, Big Cottonwood, and Little Cottonwood Canyons. Immediately, the mining industry went off. Once word spread of the bounty of precious metals, it was not long before Utah began to attract prospectors from around the country. From the 1860s to the 1920s, hundreds of mines were established in the surrounding area, and tons of copper, gold, lead, and silver were picked from the hills. In the 1860s Alta and Park City became established towns in an otherwise Mormon state. At one point, Alta had as many as six breweries and 26 bars. Today, Hellgate is the name of the point in Little Cottonwood Canyon where two limestone cliffs create a cataract in the canyon just below Alta. Named in the heyday of Alta's mining days, Hellgate makes clear the Mormon perception of the miners' activities.

In 1869 the Transcontinental Railroad was completed. Utah would change instantly. First, hordes of rail workers were suddenly laid off and idle in Utah. Second, Utah was con-

Sprague Library | Jonathan Echlin

nected to the rest of the United States by state-of-the-art travel means. At once would-be miners poured into Park City and the Cottonwood Canyons. Ranchers came, too, as well as the economic entourage that follows wealth. Many lived right in Salt Lake City, despite the poor welcome they received from their neighbors. The influx of miners and other settlers created enough commerce for other businesses to become firmly established. Increasingly, the original Mormon plan for Salt Lake City dissolved. With a diversifying economy and population, a new business district and a ghetto developed within the city. An established red-light district even formed near the business quarter.

In 1880 Rowland Hall–St. Mark's School, an Episcopal school, was opened to educate the children of area miners and ranchers. A dozen or so cigar factories were enjoying healthy business. In 1871 the first Catholic Church was opened, and 1899 marked the groundbreaking for the Cathedral of the Madeleine, an ornate Catholic cathedral in the Avenues district.

Salt Lake City and County Building, Washington Square Jonathan Echlin

Utah State Capitol Building on Capitol Hill Jonathan Echlin

Jews began arriving in Salt Lake City as early as 1849, and by 1857 had opened such stores as Kahn Brothers Grocery. The year 1875 saw the opening of the first synagogue. As early as 1890, non-Mormons accounted for half of the city's 45,000 residents. Nevertheless, Mormons continued to entrench themselves in Utah. The Mormon Temple was finished in 1892, after 40 years of construction. Brigham Young Academy, established in 1875 in Provo, was rapidly growing into Brigham Young University.

The Territory of Utah was growing, and it wished to incorporate into the United States. However, there was something the U.S. government could not accept: Mormon polygamy. Territory leaders petitioned for statehood unsuccessfully five times before at last agreeing to ban plural marriages. In 1896 Utah became the 45th state. Although tension between Mormons and non-Mormons was still omnipresent, Salt Lake City began to take on the feel it has today. A trolley system was put into place, the cars housed in Trolley Square, today a modern shopping and dining center.

Over the next 30 years, Salt Lake City's population tripled. Mining continued to be one of the driving industries of the city, and the new railroad pumped prospectors into the valley as quickly as ore could be picked from the hills. It was during this time that the Victorian mansions along South Temple Street were built by miners with their newfound riches. Salt Lake City's Alta Club, a prestigious non-Mormon gentlemen's club, grew powerful in the Intermountain West among miners, ranchers, and businessmen of influence.

Resentment between Mormons and non-Mormons grew stronger. Two political parties formed: the non-Mormon Liberal Party and the conservative Mormon People's Party. Elections were decided on church/anti-church matters rather than national politics. Salt Lake's residents segregated themselves into Mormon and gentile neighborhoods. The city leaders even considered commissioning two separate partisan government buildings until the parties resolved to coexist in the Salt Lake City and County Building. Business was segregated, as the LDS church struggled to be a self-supporting enterprise in spite of globalization. Even the schools were divided. The Mormons had a stronghold on the public school system, forcing gentiles to establish their own private school system.

External pressure and simple reality eventually coerced the parties to "play nice." Businesses and clubs finally grew to include the other party. Symbiosis led to prosperity. Although the Great Depression stunted the city's growth, Salt Lake City's powerful mining companies saw a major revival during World War II due to their key involvement in the defense industries. A major player in this era was the Kennecott Copper Mine. Today this open-pit mine is the largest of its kind, at more than 2.5 miles across and 0.75 mile deep.

The momentum of the World War II economy carried Salt Lake City into the 1950s, when the city undertook a major modernization effort. During this time, many city parks were created or improved, and the suburbs began to grow. The airport gained another terminal.

A family statue at Temple Square   Jonathan Echlin

Storm drains and a sewage treatment plant were built. The suburbs of Murray, Holiday, and Sandy sprang up and became home to thousands of families. Toward the end of the century, Salt Lake City began acquiring talented artist groups, such as Ballet West.

Tourism was boosted by the country's economic stability. Utah became increasingly attractive in the 1960s with its many newly established national monuments and parks, including Capitol Reef, Arches, and Golden Spike. The New Orleans Jazz became the Utah Jazz in 1979, and people began traveling to experience Utah's legendary skiing.

In 1995 a fire was lit under Salt Lake City's economy. Upon winning the bid for the 2002 Winter Olympics, the city's infrastructure underwent a modernizing uplift, with the addition of the I-215 beltway, construction of entertainment facilities, and renovation of major stadiums. Salt Lake City proper gained national recognition for its urban regrowth and greening efforts.

All this would suggest that Salt Lake City has acquired a cultural thrust that compels the world to explore Utah. Onetime dilapidated switching stations are now chic art gallery rows with waiting lists for would-be renters. With the Mormon stereotype losing significance every day and the growing

Rice Eccles Stadium, University of Utah Jonathan Echlin

cultural and business opportunities, Salt Lake City is acquiring new residents at twice the
rate of the nation. It seems that people have come here to do what they love, whether religious, cultural, or recreational. The affordability of the city, its access to the mountains, and
the surrounding community make this rich lifestyle possible.

NEIGHBORHOODS

As most urban areas have, Salt Lake City originated as a solitary outpost and grew into an
expansive conglomerate. Located in a broad, flat valley, the only geographical barrier to the
city's growth was the Wasatch Range and foothills framing the city to the north and east.
Thus development was forced south and westward.

Salt Lake City proper actually has quite a small footprint when compared to the greater
metropolitan area. Even so, it has the most points of interest and the richest history. (Outlying townships such as Murray, Sandy, and Holladay were founded much later and function
primarily as residential suburbs.) Salt Lake City broke ground at the Mormon Temple and,
very much according to plan, has grown outward from there. Today Temple Square is still in
the heart of downtown, among a garden of modest skyscrapers that represent the main
finance section of town. Though not in the original Mormon city plans, this financial district has been rooted here since the 1870s. As with the rest of non-LDS Salt Lake City, the
financial district and Mormon Church have inextricably integrated into a unified way of

Utah Transit Authority's Trax, University of Utah Jonathan Echlin

life. The Mormon religion now fully embraces financial activity, and the Wasatch Front now bustles as an economic hub of the Rocky Mountain West. Today, the attractive buildings and clean streets of downtown are home mainly to business and church affairs, although some fine restaurants and entertainment venues have been smartly interspersed.

A few minutes northeast of downtown is the Avenues district. One of Salt Lake City's oldest neighborhoods, it peers down at the city from the hillside on which it is perched. The southern border of the Avenues is marked by North Temple Street. Many of the Victorian mansions here today were commissioned by miners in the 1860s. The neighborhood continues upward and only stops when the foothills become too steep for homes. Many celebrity homes are folded into the winding upper creases of this hilly neighborhood. In the lower avenues, several bed & breakfasts operate out of historic mansions. With walking proximity to downtown and the quiet of a stately neighborhood, the Avenues district is a perfect location for these guesthouses.

To the southeast of the Avenues is the University of Utah. With 25,000 students, it practically occupies its own city. Elevated on a bench, the U of U's campus was chosen in 1862 as the site of Fort Douglas, commissioned by President Lincoln to oversee Mormon activity. Today, this fort is commemorated by an on-site museum, while some of its original buildings are utilized for campus needs. This green 1,500-acre campus has many assets tucked into its dells and winding lanes, including a nine-hole golf course and the Utah Museum of Fine Arts. Much of today's understanding of cancer is forged at the Huntsman Cancer Institute, perched benevolently at the pinnacle of the campus, with its holistic patient facilities and cutting-edge research labs. Because of its northern abutment to the foothills, the Red Butte Gardens and many miles of the Bonneville Shoreline Trail are accessible from campus. The 2002 Salt Lake Olympics served to enrich much of the campus, leaving it with improved sporting facilities and dormitories. The renovated Rice-Eccles Stadium, home of the opening ceremonies in 2002, now hosts university football games and rock shows. As on most university campuses, parking here can be tricky and limited, so when visiting campus, call ahead for parking suggestions or ride UTA's Trax from downtown.

South of campus, nestled just beneath the benches, is Sugarhouse, a flourishing neighborhood packed with creative boutiques and remodeled brick homes. This district is cherished for its original shops and local flavor. Like most of Utah, Sugarhouse has undergone a most interesting past. Demarcated as "Sugarhouse Neighborhood" in 1853, it has been zoned industrial, called "Furniture Row" for its high number of furniture retailers, and reputed for depravity and profanity as recently as the 1980s. After a swift and perplexing turnaround, Sugarhouse is now one of the most sought-after areas in Salt Lake City, and real estate prices reflect just that. As a visitor, you can enjoy casual, yet high-end, burger and beer joints or shop at the coveted Patagonia and Sundance outlet stores. Because it is a hip and magnetic neighborhood, businesses and Realtors try to attach the name Sugarhouse to transactions so that the value may be increased.

Gateway Mall, downtown Salt Lake City Jonathan Echlin

Another region of interest is the up-and-coming art district. This would most likely be called West Downtown. Along the historic railroad lines, this district is transforming ghost-town industrial facilities into trendy think spaces. Presently, many old switching stations and warehouses are being flipped into hip gallery rows, studios, and alternative learning centers. You can peruse the artist studios during one of many cooperative gallery strolls, which include wine, hors d'oeuvres, and conversation. The Gateway Mall, a shopping staple, forms the northern end of this district. Practically a village, this two-level outdoor shopping center draws customers with high-end, artsy, and otherwise fun spe-

A view of the Oquirrh Mountains from an Avenues neighborhood |Jonathan Echlin

cialty stores, including the Apple Store and high-end boutique shops. Another West Down-town restoration, this complex is located at the site of the historic 1908 Union Pacific Depot.

Sandy, although by and large a suburb of Salt Lake City, is the town at the base of the Cot-tonwood Canyons; so if you visit the canyons to ski, hike, or climb you will probably wind up doing an après ski or a dinner there. Murray and Holladay, just west of Sandy, are almost purely residential, although Murray is home to the Fashion Place Mall and one of the area's two Costco stores. To the west is West Valley City. Stretching all the way to the Oquirrh Mountains on the western border of Salt Lake Valley, this is the second largest city in Utah, behind Salt Lake City and ahead of Provo. Historically, West Valley is a working-class ghetto and today it still has the highest crime rates in Utah. Truly a separate entity, West Valley does not seem to affect the safety of Salt Lake City, which earns acclaim for its very low crime rates and clean streets.

DRIVING IN THE CITY

With an understanding of the grid system, driving in the city should not be a hassle. Even if you do not master the methodology of Salt Lake City's street names, navigating the city is not challenging. A grid is intrinsically simpler and more forgiving than the convoluted spi-derweb streets of older cities, regardless of street names. The only obstacles you might encounter will be the frequent restrictions on left-hand turns in the downtown area. Parking here is, of course, limited, but a spot can usually be found in a reasonable amount of time. The Salt Lake City government covers all meters and allows up to two hours of free parking between Thanksgiving and New Year's Day.

Major north–south thoroughfares include 700 East, which runs the length of the city and has a speed limit of 40 to 50 miles per hour. State Street runs north–south as well, but has a slower speed limit. It connects Capitol Hill and Downtown to many of the major hotels to the south. Foothill Boulevard originates at the University of Utah campus, travels diagonally across town to the southeast, and terminates at I-80.

Major east–west roads include South Temple, which crosses through downtown and traverses the base of the Avenues Neighborhood, and 400 South, a jugular that crosses much of the valley, including West Downtown and the University of Utah. At the university, it dips 45 degrees toward the southwest and becomes Foothill Boulevard, eventually ending in I-80. A bit farther to the south, 1300 South, 1700 South, and 2100 South Streets are all major roads.

A major expeditor of travel is Salt Lake City's interstate beltway, a square-shaped expressway whose top side is I-80 and bottom three-quarters is I-215. At any point in the city, you are no more than 10 minutes away from the beltway. A multiyear construction project has been particularly concentrated on the I-80 portion of this expressway. Estimates are that the project should finish toward the end of 2010 or in 2011. Be advised that many exit- and on-ramps are closed during this project, and that ramps' statuses change fairly frequently.

University of Utah Library, Salt Lake City |Jonathan Echlin

Lodging

With as many business travelers as ski tourists, Salt Lake City has as many hotels as it does bed & breakfasts. Both have plentiful assets and varied options, so you will be perfectly satisfied with whichever choice you make. The many hotels in Salt Lake City are in large part what create its urban skyline. If staying in a top floor of one of these hotels, you will be afforded a priceless view of the mountains, valley, and Great Salt Lake. When staying in a historic bed & breakfast, you are often privileged to learn some of the quirky history of the building and experience unique decor and quirky service. With the vast majority of major hotels and bed & breakfasts located in or near downtown, chances are you will enjoy nearness to the airport and interstates, as well as a leisurely walking distance from your destination. Be sure to book your stay well in advance in the event that your visit falls in line with a major event in town. Most hotels and B&Bs offer package deals for extended stays and recreation, especially during peak ski season or major conferences, such as the LDS Semiannual Conference or the Outdoor Retailer Show.

Because of the extreme popularity of Utah's ski tourism, most hotels offer some sort of winter package deal. A common item is the **Superpass**, sold to guests for $48. This day pass is good at Alta, Brighton, Snowbird, or Solitude. Superpass holders can ride the Utah Transit Authority's Line 215 (to the base of the Cottonwood Canyons) at no charge. Special packages are subject to availability.

Regarding handicapped access, the options listed as accessible all have elevators where necessary, but are not necessarily fully equipped for all needs. Inquire for specific information.

Hotels and Motels

The majority of Salt Lake City's major hotels are concentrated downtown. Salt Lake City has an abundance of moderate, familiar chain hotels. A handful of hotels stand out as higher-end accommodations. Both the moderate and deluxe categories offer thousands of beds in comparable locations, enough to satisfy any taste. The hotels listed below are all located downtown, the nearest

Salt Lake City Tribune building, downtown Salt Lake City Jonathan Echlin

hotel district to the sights and activities in Salt Lake City. For hotels near the ski areas, see Chapter 4, Ski Country.

CRYSTAL INN
230 West 500 South
Salt Lake City, UT 84101
801-328-4466, 1-800-366-4466
www.crystalinnsaltlake.com
Price: Inexpensive to Moderate
Credit Cards: AE, Disc, MC, V
Handicapped Accessible: Yes
Pets: No
Special Packages: Ski packages at Alta, Brighton, Snowbird, and Solitude

At the Crystal Inn you won't find any frills, but the service is cordial and the rooms are always tidy. This is perfect for families with energetic children who would prefer not to fret over fine furniture. Guests enjoy a free airport shuttle, relaxed atmosphere, and wireless Internet. A hot breakfast buffet will help you get through your day, whether business or pleasure.

EMBASSY SUITES HOTEL
110 West 600 South
Salt Lake City, UT 84101
801-359-7800, 1-800-434-6835
www.embassysuites.com
Price: Moderate
Credit Cards: AE, Disc, MC, V
Handicapped Accessible: Limited
Pets: No
Special Packages: Superpass

Embassy Suites is a comfortable choice if you are looking for firm quality without unnecessary frills. The decor is handsome, yet the furniture is not extraordinary. Its nearness to downtown and to a Trax station make it a convenient spot for business travelers. This particular hotel has a pool, weight room, whirlpool, and even cooked-to-order breakfasts, yet the average price of a room does not exceed $150. With a self-check-in kiosk, you can show yourself to your own room and not have to worry about being cordial at the end of a long flight.

GRAND AMERICA HOTEL
555 South Main Street
Salt Lake City, UT 84111
801-258-6000, 1-800-621-4505
www.grandamerica.com
Price: Very Expensive
Credit Cards: AE, DC, Disc, MC, V
Handicapped Accessible: Yes
Pets: No
Special Packages: Ski packages at Alta, Brighton, Snowbird, Snowbasin, and Solitude

Richelieu furniture, Italian marble, and mahogany saturation are what define this classically luxurious boutique hotel—likely the finest major hotel in Salt Lake Valley. Located just south of downtown, this service-oriented establishment pampers you with concierge service, plush bathrobes and slippers, afternoon tea, round-the-clock in-house dining, and an outdoor pool. Thoughtfully decorated, the guest rooms and suites are equipped with jetted hot tubs, Bose sound systems, and plasma screen television sets. This 775-room hotel distinguishes itself with decadent details, indulging its guests with massage therapy, hand-blown glass chandeliers, leather-top desks, private balconies, in-room safes, English wool carpeting, and crystal you wouldn't want to break. Babysitting services are available with prior booking. Special packages include spa, business, romantic, and ski options. If you aren't able to book in this hotel for budget or occupancy reasons, be sure to check Little America Hotel (listed below), Grand America's less expensive and less lavish, yet still quite fine younger sibling, immediately to its west.

HILTON HOTEL
SALT LAKE CITY CENTER
255 South West Temple
Salt Lake City, UT 84101

A pool in front of the Grand America Hotel Jonathan Echlin

801-328-2000
www.hilton.com
Price: Expensive
Credit Cards: AE, DC, Disc, MC, V
Handicapped Accessible: Yes
Pets: Yes

Special Packages: Superpass, ski packages at Deer Valley and Park City Mountain Resort, shuttle, and food options

If you've had enough adventure on your vacation and want to return to a familiar setting at night, the Hilton can be just right.

With your bed just a few blocks south of downtown, you can spend your hours at Salt Lake's finest attractions and restaurants, returning in the evening to overfilled duvets and flat-screen televisions. Of course, if you check into one of the top floors of this Hilton, you'll wake every morning to the views of the sun cresting the 11,000-foot peaks of the Wasatch Range.

HOTEL MONACO

15 West 200 South
Salt Lake City, UT 84101
801-595-0000, 1-800-805-1801
www.monaco-saltlakecity.com
Price: Very Expensive

Credit Cards: AE, DC, Disc, MC, V
Handicapped Accessible: Yes
Pets: Yes
Special Packages: No

Traveling solo and feeling lonely? The indulgent Hotel Monaco lends its guests companion goldfish, the "bowl of love," for the duration of their stay. Overwhelmingly elegant with a flair for youthful eccentricity, this hotel is a must for those seeking luxury with a touch of fun. In keeping with the prestige of its namesake country, this fine hotel is filled with plush furniture, bold colors, and decorative flair. Part of the Kimpton International Luxury Hotel Group, this is a favorite choice for business travel-

The Grand America Hotel ballroom   Courtesy of the Grand America Hotel

Hotel Monaco lobby Courtesy of Hotel Monaco

ers and vacationers who have grown to trust their quality and service. Each room in the Monaco resembles a present, wrapped in luxury carpet and heavy drapes of unique patterns and color combinations. In a hotel frequently acclaimed as the best lodging in Salt Lake City, you and your pet will be outfitted with state-of-the-art accommoda- tions and excellent guest services. Beyond wireless Internet, guests enjoy complimentary evening wine service and in-room massage by arrangement. What's more, the Monaco is located within a five-minute walk of the Capitol Theatre, Salt Palace Convention Center, Salt Lake Art Center, The EnergySolutions Arena (formally known as the Delta Center), Temple Square, and the fascinating Mormon Family History Library.

LITTLE AMERICA HOTEL AND TOWERS

500 South Main Street
Salt Lake City, UT 84111
801-596-5700, 1-800-281-7899
www.littleamerica.com/slc
Price: Moderate to Very Expensive
Credit Cards: AE, DC, Disc, MC, V
Handicapped Accessible: Yes
Pets: No
Special Packages: Superpass, ski packages at Snowbasin, Alta, Brighton, Snowbird, and Solitude

With a quaint name and modest exterior, this luxury hotel has turned all of its improvements where it counts—inside. The Little America group of hotels started in 1934 on the Wyoming prairie as an oasis for cowboys and pioneers. Having grown from its modest roots, it now operates fine hotels across the Southwest. If you really need to settle into your vacation, this hotel has poolside service, men's and ladies' boutiques, and a day spa. With an on-site steakhouse and coffee shop, you can dine in before heading out to the symphony. The down pillows, landscaped gardens, and spacious suites will give you some repose on your trip to Salt Lake City without taking away your lunch money.

MARRIOTT–SALT LAKE CITY DOWNTOWN

75 South West Temple
Salt Lake City, UT 84101
801-531-0800
www.marriott.com
Price: Moderate to Expensive
Credit Cards: AE, DC, Disc, MC, V
Handicapped Accessible: Limited
Pets: No
Special Packages: Ski packages, special weekend and multiday discounts seasonally

If you are curious about what to do when you arrive in Salt Lake City, simply log on to Marriott's Web site and check out their city events section. Given the dates of your visit, the Web site will be able to pull up concerts, cultural happenings, and sporting events. While Marriott lacks some of the appeal of local establishments, a certain level of quality is assured. If the Marriott Downtown is full, go just a few blocks southeast to Marriott City Center (220 South State Street; 801-961-8700 or 1-866-961-8700), whose service and environs are just as good, and it is a negligible distance farther from downtown. Both Marriott Hotels in Salt Lake City are massive establishments, with more than 350 rooms apiece.

PEERY HOTEL

110 West Broadway (300 South)
Salt Lake City, UT 84101
801-521-4300, 1-800-331-0073
www.peeryhotel.com
Price: Moderate to Expensive
Credit Cards: AE, DC, Disc, MC, V
Handicapped Accessible: Limited
Pets: Yes
Special Packages: Dining and extended stay packages, as well as ski and other recreation packages, seasonally

Constructed in 1910, strategically just a few blocks from the city's railroad depots, the Peery was a well-deserved resting spot for successful boom miners and frontiersmen. Built on the belief that guests should be pampered by a lavish atmosphere, this tradition has given the hotel nearly a century of business. The 62 guest rooms are dressed in a European style with attention to quality rather than quantity. Each mattress is handpicked, and each bedsheet is made from 100 percent Egyptian cotton. This hotel still retains a hint of Old West essence. With base camp in the heart of historic downtown Salt Lake City, guests here are in the midst of the Utah Jazz games at the EnergySolutions Arena (formerly known as Delta Center), the international conventions of the Salt Palace, and the celebrated summer concert series of the Gallivan Center. Although the Peery offers meals from on-site restaurants Romano's Macaroni Grill and Christopher's Seafood and Steak House, it is located within walking distance of many more of Salt Lake's best dining opportunities. The special ski packages are available online and by phone. Calling for ski packages can save you as much as $60 a day, compared to packages booked online.

RADISSON HOTEL SALT LAKE CITY– DOWNTOWN

215 West South Temple
Salt Lake City, UT 84101
801-364-5800, 1-800-395-7046
www.radisson.com
Price: Moderate
Credit Cards: AE, DC, Disc, MC, V
Handicapped Accessible: Yes
Pets: Yes
Special Packages: Family and recreation packages, seasonally

The Radisson Downtown has more than 380 rooms and completed a $5 million renovation in 2006. It now has the cleanliness and polish of a new hotel, but the knowledgeable staff of an established one. Fully modernized, this hotel is ideal for business with its downtown location, immediate proximity to the Salt Palace Convention Center, 15,000 square feet of meeting space, and on-site DHL, FedEx, and UPS pickup. Its Web site adds convenience to business and pleasure trips by listing recommended health, beauty, entertainment, and spirituality resources.

RED LION HOTEL SALT LAKE CITY DOWNTOWN

161 West 600 South
Salt Lake City, UT 84101
801-521-7373, 1-800-325-4000
www.redlion.com
Price: Moderate to Expensive
Credit Cards: AE, DC, Disc, MC, V
Handicapped Accessible: Yes
Pets: Yes
Special Packages: Superpass

Although a large hotel with almost 400 rooms and suites, the Red Lion has a design that gives it a relatively homey feel. The Red Lion features a basic, yet pleasing decor. The rooms, spacious and bright, have an uncluttered feel that neither detract from, nor add to, your experience. Some guest rooms offer balcony access for peering out over downtown or the Great Salt Lake. With complimentary parking, a café, and restaurant, a lot of the worry of your trip will disappear. The Sky Bar, Salt Lake's only rooftop club, is located here, and often hosts nationally popular musicians and DJs.

SHILO INNS SUITES HOTELS– SALT LAKE CITY

206 South West Temple
Salt Lake City, UT 84101
801-521-9500, 1-800-222-2244
www.shiloinns.com
Price: Inexpensive to Moderate
Credit Cards: AE, DC, Disc, MC, V
Handicapped Accessible: Yes
Pets: Yes
Special Packages: Ski packages at Alta, Brighton, Snowbird, and Solitude

Self-described as a conference hotel, the Shilo has 200 guest rooms, seven distinct meeting areas, and ample banquet space. This hotel is also family-friendly, charging nothing for children under 12 and setting out fresh cookies daily in the lobby. The Shilo is a standard hotel with clean rooms and no frills. On the western edge of downtown, guests here enjoy hassle-free walking access to destinations as well as nearness to the airport and I-15. If your stay outlasts your fresh clothing, valet and guest laundry facilities are available.

Downtown Salt Lake City | Jonathan Echlin

Bed & Breakfasts and Inns

The whimsical turrets, lacy woodwork, and dramatic peaks of Victorian architecture make the 19th-century bed & breakfasts here a fanciful way to slumber on your vacation. Considering the quality and privacy of the B&Bs, they offer a surprisingly affordable way to stay in the area.

ANNIVERSARY INN FIFTH SOUTH

460 South 1000 East
Salt Lake City, UT 84102
801-363-4900, 1-800-324-4152
www.anniversaryinn.com
Price: Expensive to Very Expensive
Credit Cards: AE, Disc, MC, V
Handicapped Accessible: Limited
Pets: No
Special Packages: No

A collection of almost 30 luxury suites, the Anniversary Inn on Fifth South will tickle your imagination and leave you feeling pampered. Many of the suites have been outfitted within the realms of conservative tastes, yet a portion of the guest rooms is adventurously decorated to take you on a jungle safari, whisk you into Shakespeare's Romeo and Juliet, or induct you into the Swiss Family Robinson. The creativity of the inn is not an indicator of pure whimsy; it is equally matched by luxury. Though imaginative, each room retains adult dignity. Some are much more traditional than others, like the Mansion, the French Canopy, and the Presidential Suites. Because of the inn's popularity among locals and returning visitors, it is advisable to book your stay in advance.

ANNIVERSARY INN ON SOUTH TEMPLE

678 East South Temple
Salt Lake City, UT 84102
801-363-4950, 1-800-324-4152
www.anniversaryinn.com
Price: Expensive to Very Expensive
Credit Cards: AE, Disc, MC, V
Handicapped Accessible: No
Pets: No
Special Packages: No

Built in 1889, this mansion was originally home to Emmanuel Kahn. A Prussian immigrant and political activist, he operated a general store that catered to pioneers traveling through Utah. Another Anniversary Inn, this has been decorated for romantic getaways and fanciful retreats. The Inn on South Temple has gingerbread-house Victorian architecture, colorful gardens, and leafy green surroundings. Each room is wholly different from the last, ranging from an Egyptian motif to an enchanted garden theme. This bed & breakfast has a reputation as "most romantic" among local couples and is perfect for an intimate escape. The mansion has 14

luxury suites that should be booked well in advance, as you will be competing against vacationers and locals alike.

ARMSTRONG MANSION
HISTORIC BED & BREAKFAST

667 East 100 South
Salt Lake City, UT 84102
801-531-1333, 1-800-708-1333
www.armstrongmanor.com
Price: Moderate
Credit Cards: AE, Disc, MC, V
Handicapped Accessible: Yes
Pets: By discretion
Special Packages: Occasional

Just south of the Utah Governor's Mansion, this elaborately decorative 1893 Queen Anne home is filled with history, canopy beds, and lace. Linen napkins, crystal, and freshly baked pastries all accentuate the casual elegance of this bed & breakfast. Tall, angled ceilings and stately bold colors complement the hand stenciling, intricately carved wood, and marble guest room fireplaces. For the price and intimacy, this could be a great deal with a downtown location.

ELLERBECK MANSION
BED & BREAKFAST

140 North B Street
Salt Lake City, UT 84103
801-355-2500, 1-800-966-8364
www.ellerbeckbedandbreakfast.com
Price: Moderate
Credit Cards: AE, Disc, MC, V
Handicapped Accessible: No
Pets: No
Special Packages: Discounted extended stays, ski packages (inquire upon booking)

This historic Avenues mansion offers convenient nearness to downtown attractions. Guests enjoy personal service without compromised solitude. With plenty of privacy and quiet, you will only encounter other guests in passing. If you require assistance, the caretaker's apartment is tucked away in the basement. Each guest room is spacious, with unique decor ranging from the Winter Dreams Room to the Summer Hill Suite. In addition to affordable rates, they offer ski packages and 10 percent discounts to parties staying three or more nights. Children must be at least 10 years of age.

INN ON THE HILL
225 North State Street
Salt Lake City, UT 84103
801-328-1466
www.inn-on-the-hill.com
Price: Inexpensive to Moderate
Credit Cards: AE, MC, V
Handicapped Accessible: Very limited
Pets: No
Special Packages: No

The Inn on the Hill was refurbished in 2003 as a deluxe bed & breakfast, designed for vacationers and businesspeople alike. These improvements now establish the Inn as at least a notch more stately and formal than most of its peers in Salt Lake City. Though each room has been named after a regional highlight, you will find no themed decorations. Breakfast is individually prepared for each room. From its location on Capitol Hill, you peer out over downtown and watch the sunrise over the Wasatch.

MILLCREEK INN BED & BREAKFAST
5803 East Millcreek Canyon Road
Salt Lake City, UT 84124
801-278-7927

Located three miles up the cool, forested Millcreek Canyon just east of the University of Utah, this upscale B&B offers nearness to the city with rarified seclusion and peaceful surroundings. Though not within walking distance of downtown, this forested retreat is still just 15 minutes' drive from the heart of the city but is nonetheless completely sealed within the Wasatch Mountains and very near the canyon's many trails perfect

for hiking, trail running, mountain biking, and the like. The grounds of this B&B have been smartly embellished with flower beds, stone-laid terraces, and other greenery, marrying it to its wooded surroundings and blending well with its rustic-modern interior. Because of its fine ambience and special surroundings, this inn is highly in demand for occasions such as weddings, so call to ahead to be sure your visit isn't dominated by such an event.

PARISH PLACE BED & BREAKFAST
720 East Ashton Road (2340 South Street)
Salt Lake City, UT 84106
801-832-0970
www.parishplace.com
Price: Inexpensive to Moderate
Credit Cards: AE, Disc, MC, V
Handicapped Access:
Pets: No
Special Packages: Seasonal and extended stay packages

A bit farther south of downtown than many of the B&Bs in this guide, Parish Place is quite near the I-80 portion of the Salt Lake City beltway, and therefore much closer, time-wise, to the skiing and other mountain activities. In fact, the proprietors of the establishment are quite accustomed to ski vacationers and have dedicated a portion of their services to these guests, including in-room boot warmers, daily snow report print-outs, and a hot tub—with a listing on their Web site of all of the nine nearest ski areas with their mileage and traveling time from the estate. The rooms themselves are handsome with plush bedding, mature decoration themes, and furniture appropriate for the 1890 National Historic Register home.

WILDFLOWERS BED & BREAKFAST
936 East 1700 South
Salt Lake City, UT 84105
801-466-0600, 1-800-569-0009

High in Millcreek Canyon   Christine Balaz

www.wildflowersbb.com
Price: Inexpensive to Moderate
Credit Cards: MC, V
Handicapped Accessible: No
Pets: No
Special Packages: No

Wildflower gardens and bright colors engulf
this 1891 Victorian mansion. Well-lit rooms
and high ceilings give this B&B a sense of
pastoral living, and hot breakfasts of the
garden and southwestern variety help
guests to start the day in rare form. Guests
have purchased the artwork adorning the
walls—created by one of the Wildflowers'
hosts—to take home to their personal collections. Each of the five rooms is named

within the wildflower theme. The charm of
the Wildflowers Bed & Breakfast and hospi-
tality of the hostesses make you feel as if you
are staying with your favorite aunt.

RESTAURANTS

In Salt Lake City you play hard and eat well.
The restaurants here represent a surprising
variety of cuisine at a consistently high
quality. Salt Lake City is earning a reputation among the culinary circuit for gourmet
food at reasonable prices. The service here,
like the lifestyle, is a step more casual than
in other metropolitan areas. You can sample
Moroccan, Italian, Japanese, Thai, and even

Tibetan cuisine, without having to fret over formal apparel. Most residents here consider themselves "dressed up" with a nice pair of jeans or slacks. All the same, you can expect attractive decor by way of modish sushi bars or handsome steakhouses.

THE BAYOU

645 South State Street
South Downtown
801-961-8400
www.utahbayou.com
Serving: L, D
Open: Daily
Price: Inexpensive to Moderate
Credit Cards: AE, MC, V
Reservations: No
Handicapped Accessible: Yes

If you think Utah lacks full-strength beer, you have not been to the Bayou. A Cajun-style restaurant with nightly live music, this upscale (yet casual) restaurant offers 260 bottled and 32 draft beers. The bottled beer comes in from around the world and is just as strong as it was intended to be. However, if your selection is not available, do not be too disappointed, as ordering difficulties usually render the roster a bit incomplete. The proprietors of the Bayou also own a nearby brew supply shop, The Beer Nut (www.beernut.com), and are consummate experts in this delightful beverage. Free pool and a hip atmosphere make this a great casual evening out.

THE BOHEMIAN BREWERY & GRILL

94 East Fort Union Boulevard (7200 South Street)
Midvale
801-566-5474
www.bohemianbrewery.com
Cuisine: Casual American, Czech
Serving: L, D
Open: Daily
Price: Inexpensive to Moderate
Credit Cards: AE, Disc, MC, V
Reservations: Yes
Handicapped Accessible: Yes

Equipped for dining in any month, the Bohemian opens its patio in summer and lights the fireplace during the winter. Likewise, the Bohemian's beer is fit for drinking in any season. Most would agree that the beer is the highlight of the establishment, with seasonal specials and delicious resident brews. Located 10 minutes west of the Little Cottonwood Canyon bases, this is a great après ski or dinner spot for skiers lodging in the valley. The menu includes deluxe pub food as well as some traditional entrées.

CAFÉ TRIO

680 South 900 East
Sugarhouse
801-533-8746
www.triodining.com
Cuisine: Contemporary Italian
Serving: Brunch (Sun. only), L, D
Open: Daily
Price: Moderate to Expensive
Credit Cards: AE, Disc, MC, V
Reservations: Yes
Handicapped Accessible: Yes

Café Trio's bright, modish, and clean atmosphere perfectly complements its fresh, unpretentious cuisine. All meals are served à la carte, with an optional first course of locally grown mesclun greens, fresh oysters on the half shell, or the renowned flatbread and house tapenade. Appetizers can be followed by either another light course or a full entrée. Trio's emphasis is on quality, not quantity. When possible, vegetables served are in season and locally grown. The sauces and seasonings taste crisp and fresh, and the olive oil is first-rate. Trio's bartenders even incorporate fresh fruits into their specialty mojitos and martinis. For an après ski, try the larger Cottonwoods location (6405 South 3000 East; 801-944-8746), near the base of Big and Little Cottonwood canyons. Like the

Sugarhouse location, this outpost features "Halfy Hour." Every day between 3 PM and 5 PM appetizers are half price.

CAFFÉ MOLISE

55 West 100 South
Downtown
801-364-8833
www.caffemolise.com
Cuisine: Traditional Italian
Serving: L, D
Open: Mon. through Sat. L and D, Sun. brunch only
Price: Moderate
Credit Cards: AE, Disc, MC, V
Reservations: Yes
Handicapped Accessible: Yes

Caffé Molise is tucked discreetly into downtown. Perfect for a fresh meal after a day of sightseeing or before a show, it offers a selection of meat and vegetable dishes from Italy's Molise region. Visitors to the Gallivan Centeror Salt Palace Convention Center will find this location convenient, yet quiet.

CEDARS OF LEBANON

152 East 200 South
Downtown
801-364-4096
Cuisine: Middle Eastern
Serving: L, D
Open: Mon. through Fri. lunch and dinner; Sat. dinner only
Price: Inexpensive to Moderate
Credit Cards: Amex, MC, V
Reservations: Yes
Handicapped Accessible: Yes

Located very near downtown, this eccentric hole-in-the-wall is richly embellished with full-blown Middle Eastern adornments, from the decor to the music and the costumes of the staff. If you come for dinner on Friday or Saturday nights, there will even be belly dancers wandering between the tables. The dishes on the menu represent a spectrum of origins, from Lebanon to Morocco and Armenia to Israel, with vegetarian and meat dishes. Appetizers, main dishes, combination platters, à la carte options, and the possibility to book a floor-seating private Moroccan room make this a good option for a family-style group outing.

CUCINA TOSCANA

307 West Pierpont Avenue (250 South Street)
Downtown
801-328-3463
Cuisine: Italian
Serving: D
Open: Mon. through Sat.
Price: Moderate to Expensive
Credit Cards: AE, MC, V
Reservations: Yes
Handicapped Accessible: Yes

This elegant restaurant serves traditional Italian cuisine with house-made gnocchi, ravioli, risotto, and other pastas, intermixed with seafood and other fresh meats and sauces. Half portions and a sampler plate allow you to experience more of the menu. Because of the popularity of this serial award winner, reservations are strongly suggested. Early diners are rewarded with discounted meals.

FRESCO ITALIAN CAFÉ

1513 South 1500 East
Sugarhouse
801-486-1300
www.frescoitaliancafe.com
Cuisine: Italian
Serving: D
Open: Daily
Price: Expensive
Credit Cards: Amex, MC, V
Reservations: Yes

Located in a historic corner of Sugarhouse known as 15th and 15th, this little gem serves refined, gourmet contemporary and traditional Italian dishes in the small, intimately broken-up space of an early 1900s brick home. Knowledgeable waitstaff, a solid wine list, fireplace, and candlelight further enhance the comfort of this upper-echelon dining experience. In 2009, this restaurant was awarded "Best Overall Restaurant" and "Best Italian Restaurant" in Salt Lake City by Salt Lake Magazine and, in 2007, the AAA Three Diamond award and Wine Spectator Award of Excellence. If you arrive early enough, stop by The King's English, a locally owned bookshop located in the front half of this same structure.

THE GARDEN RESTAURANT AT TEMPLE SQUARE

15 East South Temple
Joseph Smith Memorial Building, 10th Floor
Downtown
801-539-3170
www.templesquarehospitality.com
Cuisine: American
Serving: L, D
Open: Mon. through Sat.
Price: Inexpensive to Moderate
Credit cards: AE, MC, V
Reservations: Yes
Handicapped Accessible: Yes

For a rooftop, heart-of-the-city dining experience that is affordable, yet elegant—and very much on the tour of downtown historic sites, visit the Garden Restaurant. Occupying the open-walled 10th floor of the Joseph Smith Memorial Building, this offers a diverse, yet quite reasonably priced menu of the American persuasion. During warmer months, a retractable roof makes the view even better. For the more upscale brother of this restaurant, visit The Roof (801-539-1911; Open Mon. through Sat., dinner only), on the same floor of the Joseph Smith Memorial Building.

HIMALAYAN KITCHEN

73 East 400 South
Downtown
801-596-8727
Cuisine: Northern Indian
Serving: L, D
Open: Mon. through Thurs. (lunch and dinner), Fri. through Sun. (dinner only)
Price: Inexpensive to Moderate
Credit Cards: AE, Disc, MC, V
Reservations: Yes
Handicapped Accessible: Yes

A modest dining room and unassuming appearance could not hide the Himalayan Kitchen's menu from local fame. Vegetarians and meat-eaters alike can choose dishes of outstanding quality from an extensive selection. Tender meats are served in tandoor dishes and intricate curries made from vegetable pastes and yogurts. Sweet, spicy, and tangy twists are given to each entrée, which can be mopped up with heaps of house naan. Even if buffets are not your thing, come for the legendary weekday lunch special. Copious amounts of delicious foods are set out for your sampling.

MACCOOL'S PUBLIC HOUSE

1400 South Foothill Drive
Foothill Village
801-582-3111
Cuisine: Irish
Serving: L, D
Open: Daily
Price: Moderate
Credit Cards: AE, MC, V
Reservations: No
Handicapped Accessible: Yes

Like its neighboring Foothill Village markets and boutiques, MacCool's far surpasses what one would expect to find in a shopping center. The cuisine includes traditional Irish favorites that satiate the largest appetite. Stews and roasts are enjoyed on massive wooden furniture handcrafted in Ireland. Notoriously tasty appetizers pair with beer to make a great light dinner. MacCool's is a casual deviation from the norm of downtown dining.

MARKET STREET GRILL

48 Market Street (350 South Street)
Downtown
801-322-4668
www.gastronomyinc.com
Cuisine: Surf and turf
Serving: B, L, D
Open: Daily
Price: Moderate to Very Expensive
Credit Cards: AE, DC, Disc, MC, V
Reservations: No
Handicapped Accessible: Yes (call ahead;
wheelchair accessible space is limited)

If you can, go to the Market Street Grill. The
freshness and variety of its seafood rivals
that of major port cities. Situated in the
heart of downtown, its location only adds to
its list of assets. The black-and-white tiles
and polished brass railings lend it the feel
of a New York deli, while the tiered seating
and wooden partitions divide the large dining room into more private sectors. Market
Street is the perfect example of Salt Lake
City's superior dining in a casual atmosphere. Comfortable in jeans or a suit, you
can order from a menu that contains Oregon Dungeness crab, Totten Inlet oysters,
and Baja Corvina sea bass, none of which
have ever been frozen. If that weren't
enough, the plates of prime rib, filet
mignon, and New York steak alone would be
enough to keep a restaurant in business for
decades. If spending your days skiing in the
Cottonwood Canyons, consider the **Market
Street Grill Cottonwoods** (2985 East Cottonwood Parkway; 801-942-8860), serving
the same menu but open for fewer early
meals. People visiting the University of Utah
can dine at the **Market Street Grill University** (260 South 1300 East; 801-583-8808).

The Market Street Grills are part of a
family of restaurants that includes two **Oys-
ter Bars**, one adjoining the Downtown Grill
(801-531-6044), and one at the Cottonwoods Grill location (801-942-8870). For
seafood lovers and social diners, these are
the go-to establishments in Utah. **The New
Yorker** (54 Market Street; 801-363-0166)
has the same flavor as the Grills, but is a bar
where patrons must be 21 or older.

MARTINE

22 East 100 South
Downtown
801-363-9328
Cuisine: Mediterranean
Serving: L, D
Open: Daily
Price: Moderate to Very Expensive
Credit Cards: AE, DC, Disc, MC, V
Reservations: Yes
Handicapped Accessible: Yes (downstairs)

Another superb, yet small, downtown
restaurant, this can be perfect for a lighter
meal or for a family-style occasion characterized by sampling and bite swapping.
Although the menu is brief, it covers a wide
range of food, from light to decadent, and
with selections for vegetarians as well as
omnivores. With many more pages than the
menu, the wine list will please and prompt
you to perhaps open your wallet a bit further
than you had expected.

MAZZA

1515 South 1500 East
East Sugarhouse
801-484-9259
www.mazzacafe.com
Cuisine: Middle Eastern
Serving: L, D
Open: Mon. through Sat.
Price: Inexpensive to Moderate
Credit Cards: AE, DC, Disc, MC, V
Reservations: No
Handicapped Accessible: Yes

Kick-start your meal with tabouli or
Lebanese salad. The dinner menu consists
of various entrées and sandwiches, with
familiar items like kabab, shawarma,
falafel, and sausages tying together some of
the less familiar ventures. Fresh vegetables,

fruits, and yogurts balance heavier stews and fried treats. Vegetarians will find more than enough choices. Modern decor and a professional staff render this walk-in experience a touch more genteel. For a nearly identical experience in a nearby location, try its sister branch (912 East 900 South; 801-521-4572), serving lunch and dinner Mon. through Fri. and lunch only on Sat.

THE NEW YORKER

60 West Market Street (350 South Street)
Downtown
801-363-0166
www.gastronomyinc.com
Cuisine: Gourmet contemporary
Serving: L, D
Open: Mon. through Sat.
Price: Expensive to Very Expensive
Credit Cards: AE, DC, Disc, MC, V
Reservations: Recommended
Handicapped Accessible: No

Combining an exquisite selection of seafood, domestic game, and USDA prime beef, the New Yorker creates each plate as a piece of culinary art. Beware the seductive appetizers, for Sonoma pheasant, Maine lobster, and veal scallopini are the headliners on the menu that require a hearty appetite. Although you will be served with a steak knife, you won't need to touch it for the utter tenderness of the entrées.

PARIS BISTRO AND WINE BAR

1500 South (Emerson Avenue) 1500 East
Sugarhouse
801-486-5585
www.theparis.net
Cuisine: American, Continental, and Mediterranean
Serving: D
Open: Daily
Price: Expensive to Very Expensive
Credit Cards: Amex, MC, V
Reservations: Required
Handicapped Accessible: Yes

Offering new American cuisine infused with continental and Mediterranean overtones, this fine boutique dining establishment pulls together the finest and freshest locally produced ingredients to form dynamic, seasonal menus characterized by rich, decadent dishes of fresh produce in combination with so-slowly cooked meats of the most tender variety. While food is considered here to be a matter of the soul, wine is, in European tradition, beheld as an equally important mate, and the pairing of the two can be suggested by the well-groomed waitstaff.

PORCUPINE PUB & GRILLE

3698 East Fort Union Boulevard
Sandy
801-942-5555
www.porcupinepub.com
Cuisine: Brewpub
Serving: B (Sat. and Sun. only), L, D
Open: Daily
Price: Inexpensive to Moderate
Credit Cards: AE, Disc, MC, V
Reservations: No
Handicapped Accessible: Yes

Located just below the base of Big Cottonwood Canyon, the Porcupine caters to thirsty skiers as well as it does to family diners. Housed in a two-story lodge, this restaurant and bar serves its gargantuan nachos half price between 3 PM and 5 PM daily. For those settling in for dinner, burgers, pasta, pizza, filet mignon, and ahi tuna are some of the many choices. The cuisine could best be called American, but southwestern selections are frequent on the menu.

RED IGUANA

736 North West Temple
North Downtown
801-322-1489
www.rediguana.com
Cuisine: Mexican

Serving: L, D
Open: Daily
Price: Inexpensive
Credit Cards: AE, Disc, MC, V
Reservations: No
Handicapped Accessible: Yes

This restaurant's burnt-orange and red exterior hint at the food and ambience inside. A fun atmosphere with "killer Mexican food," the Red Iguana is Salt Lake City's best Mexican experience. Feisty southern spices and high-quality ingredients have given this restaurant many best-of-Salt-Lake awards throughout its 20 years of business. The real gems of the Iguana are its seven Oaxacan-style moles, available for sampling upon request.

RUTH'S DINER

2100 Emigration Canyon
801-582-5807
www.ruthsdiner.com
Cuisine: American casual
Serving: B, L, D
Open: Daily
Price: Inexpensive to Moderate
Credit Cards: AE, Disc, MC, V
Reservations: Dinner only
Handicapped Accessible: Yes (rear entrance)

This is one of Salt Lake City's favorite breakfast locations. Every table is given a complimentary plate of nearly "mile-high" biscuits, and the excellent coffee is bottomless. The quality of every meal is reliably excellent, with fresh vegetables and fruit, flavorful seasonings, and 60 years of perfection. The diner, which opened in 1930 as Ruth's Hamburgers, has quite a bit of rebel history, including fistfights and sheltering girls of "ill repute" from police officers. Ruth, who boldly served beer and burgers to miners, ranchers, and other "gentiles," was practically run out of town in 1949. Not to be deterred, she bought and dragged a trol-ley car up Emigration Canyon, where the diner has been operating for six decades. Summer perks include patio dining and live acoustic music. If you have plans to cycle when you are in Salt Lake City, take a ride to the top of Emigration Canyon and on your way back to town, stop off at Ruth's Diner.

SAWADEE

754 East South Temple
East Downtown/Avenues
801-328-8424
Cuisine: Thai
Serving: L, D
Open: Mon. through Sat.
Price: Inexpensive to Moderate
Credit Cards: AE, Disc, MC, V
Reservations: Yes
Handicapped Accessible: Yes

Sawadee offers a comfortable blend of modestly elegant atmosphere and affordable, high-quality entrées. This small, downtown restaurant serves traditional Thai curries and wok dishes, as well as many progressive salads and desserts. Though many of the dishes here share the same name with those that you would see on most American Thai menus, the meats and vegetables are much fresher and more generously served than in most other establishments—all in all, a notch higher in quality, flavor, and presentation than most of its Salt Lake City peers.

SQUATTERS

147 West Broadway
Downtown
801-363-2739
www.squatters.com
Cuisine: Contemporary
Serving: B (Sat and Sun only), L, D
Open: Daily
Price: Inexpensive to Moderate
Credit Cards: AE, Disc, MC, V
Reservations: No
Handicapped Accessible: Yes

With a downtown location and simply the best pub menu in town, Squatters attracts lunch and dinner crowds as well as night crawlers. This restaurant serves its own tasty beer, along with diverse cuisine ranging from seared ahi tuna to green curry and fish & chips. Each is created with fresh, first-rate ingredients. Offering a choice of tofu, chicken, or beef on many of its dishes, Squatters satiates vegetarians and omnivores alike.

TAKASHI

18 West Market Street (350 South Street)
Downtown
801-519-9595
www.takashisushi.com
Cuisine: Japanese
Serving: L, D
Open: Mon. through Sat. (dinner only on Sat.)
Price: Moderate to Expensive
Credit Cards: V, Disc, MC, AE
Reservations: Very limited
Handicapped Accessible: Yes

Takashi is located squarely in the restaurant hot spot of downtown. Among seafood and fondue greats, it holds its own with inventive, contemporary Japanese cuisine and a hip atmosphere. The sushi menu appears to be normal in length, but has some strikingly unique and delicate inventions. Rolls share the company of entrées and nightly specials. Family-style sharing makes the experience at Takashi even better by expanding the number of dishes you can sample.

THAI SIAM

1435 South State Street
801-474-3322
www.thaisiam.net
Cuisine: Thai
Serving: L, D
Open: Mon. through Sat.
Price: Inexpensive
Credit Cards: AE, MC, V
Reservations: Yes
Handicapped Accessible: Yes

Thai Siam is one of the best dining values in Salt Lake City. Each dish comes with a choice of meat, plenty of vegetables, and flavorful sauces. However, even with the lack of showy atmosphere and speedy service, many customers choose to lunch here. Miraculously, many of the main courses, which are loaded with fresh ingredients, cost less than $10 and are large enough for two people. This is possibly the best take-away option in the valley.

TIN ANGEL CAFÉ

365 West 400 South
West Downtown
801-328-4155
www.thetinangel.com
Cuisine: American
Serving: L, D
Open: Mon–Sat
Price: Moderate
Credit Cards: Amex, MC, V
Reservations: Yes
Handicapped Accessible: Yes

The Tin Angel, tucked quite out-of-the-way and west of downtown, is one of Salt Lake City's most quirky, artsy, and home-grown seeming restaurants that still manages to draw a dignified clientele. Meals here walk the line between gourmet and home-style cooking, are created with garden-style ingredients and local meats. The seeming contradictory juxtapositions of this establishment are what give its charm; linen-draped tables decked with mismatched flatware; well-trained waitstaff sporting tattoos and piercings, and middle-aged couples seated next to provocative art. Thursday, Friday, and Saturday most weeks see live music.

Attractions

With as many ski vacationers as LDS tourists, Sundance entourages, and conference-goers, Salt Lake City can entertain an array of guests. Located centrally in the populated Wasatch Front, it has all the amenities of a major metropolitan area, including museums, film societies, and shopping centers. Naturally the 2002 Winter Olympics had a major impact on Salt Lake City and left behind many state-of-the-art athletic and entertainment facilities, as well as infrastructure improvements. The Sundance Film Festival, which takes place every year in Park City, has outgrown its host town and now spills into Salt Lake City. As the mecca of the Mormon religion, Salt Lake City is infused with celebrations of faith and an obsession with its pioneer history. Fantastic natural surroundings shape everything here, from the summer events calendar right down to people's bodies. Many of the outdoor concerts and LDS historical tours are completely free and within leisurely walking distance of each other.

Museums and Galleries

Many of Salt Lake City's museums are expectedly in line with Mormon history. Others, related to the University of Utah, are in the fine arts and educational vein. Still others seem like wild cards, adding variety to your experience here. Many museums and galleries offer free admission, although donations are always encouraged.

CLARK PLANETARIUM

110 South 400 West
West Downtown
801-456-7827
www.clarkplanetarium.com
Open: 10:30–9 Mon. through Thurs.; 10:30–11 Fri. and Sat.; 10:30–8 Sun.; Closed Thanksgiving and Christmas
Admission: Variable for shows, free for exhibits
Handicapped Accessible: Yes

With an IMAX theater and music venue (the Hanson Dome Theater), the Clark Planetarium is a daytime or evening destination for space enthusiasts. With more than 15 exhibits, including an Earth Globe, Marsscape, Moonscape, and a full-room photographic diary from the Hubble Telescope, this could easily stand alone as a museum. The "Reason for Seasons" exhibit provides a great explanation to kids, and the Clark Observatory has telescopes that guests can experiment with. Filled with high-tech gadgets and space-age decor, this museum inspires your inner astronomer. All of the exhibits are free.

DAUGHTERS OF UTAH PIONEERS MUSEUM

300 North Main Street
Salt Lake City
801-538-1050
www.dupinternational.org
Open: 9–5 Mon. through Sat.; closed Sun. (open 1–5 Sun. in summer)
Admission: Free; fee for special exhibits
Handicapped Accessible: Yes

Established by direct descendants of the early Utah pioneers and dedicated to honoring these individuals, this down-home museum is pleasantly quaint, yet considered one of the nation's foremost collections of Intermountain West pioneer artifacts. Items in the collection include ordinary belongings such as photographs, handcarts, pianos, furniture, and clothing. Other historically significant articles, such as early hand-sewn flags from the Brigham Young estate and interpretive paintings of the early Mormon struggle, appear as well. This museum has six floors of galleries.

DISCOVERY GATEWAY

444 West 100 South
West Downtown
801-456-5437
www.childmuseum.org
Open: 10–6 Tues. through Thurs. and Sat.; 10–9 Mon. and Fri.; 12–6 Sun.
Admission: $ 8.50 adults, $6 seniors (65 and up), free 1-year-old and under
Handicapped Accessible: Yes

Completely revitalized by its 2006 relocation, Discovery Gateway (formerly known as **Children's Museum of Utah**) is a great detour during a shopping trip at the modern, outdoor Gateway Mall. Contemporary and colorful, the museum is filled with interactive exhibits and hands-on projects for kids of all ages. Bright doodads and full-size simulations transport kids to a world of their own. The museum was created in 1978 to help children to connect more deeply to their world with creative learning.

FAMILY HISTORY MUSEUM

35 North West Temple Street
Downtown
801-240-2584, 1-866-406-1830
www.familysearch.org, www.visittemplesquare.com
Open: 8–5 Mon.; 8–9 Tues.–Sat.; closed Sun.; special holiday schedule as listed online
Admission: Free
Handicapped Accessible: Yes

Because family is one of the most sacred concepts in the Mormon religion, the Family History Library was created in 1985 to aid in genealogical research. Located adjacent to Temple Square, the library is by far the largest of its kind in the world. With over two billion names on file and millions of records in books and on microfiche, this has become one of Salt Lake City's most popular destinations. Information here extends well outside Utah to Africa, Asia, Australia, the British Isles, Canada, Europe, and Latin America. You can dig up census, court, property, probate, and cemetery records, and even emigration and immigration lists, genealogy trees, and written family histories. The library is staffed by literally hundreds of employees and volunteers who can assist you if you choose to do a search of your own. If you are truly interested in doing serious research, visit the Web site ahead of time and utilize the online tools designed to help you prepare for your visit.

HELLENIC CULTURAL MUSEUM

279 South 300 West
Downtown

801-328-9681
www.pahh.com
Open: Wed. 9–12; Sun. "for 1 hour after church," by appointment
Admission: Free
Handicapped Accessible: Yes

Did you know that Salt Lake City has been considered a hub of Greek and Greek Orthodox culture since the early 1900s? A Trip to the Hellenic Cultural Museum will give you some insight into the finance, mining, and railroad history of Utah, as well as a glimpse into the experience of non-LDS minority groups. In 1905 the church of Holy Trinity was opened in Salt Lake City. It was considered the Greek "mother church" of the Intermountain West, and today Salt Lake's Hellenic community still operates a Greek language school. The museum, which was the first of its kind in the country, becomes very popular in September during the annual Greek Festival. The personal stories of immigrants and pioneers are conveyed by artifacts, photographs, and written histories.

MUSEUM OF CHURCH HISTORY AND ART

45 North West Temple Street
Downtown
801-240-4615
www.lds.org/churchhistory/museum
Open: 9–9 Mon.–Fri.; 10–7 Sat. and Sun.; special holiday schedule as listed online
Admission: Free
Handicapped Accessible: Yes

The Museum of Church History and Art is exactly what you would expect from its name, but it's a fascinating experience for faithful Mormons and curious non-Mormons alike. Exhibits with commemorative religious art illustrate LDS pioneers and leaders, as well as scenes from the Book of Mormon. Common themes are paintings of Jesus Christ and Joseph Smith, as well as paintings depicting the famed and strenuous handcart treks that brought horseless Mormons to Utah.

SALT LAKE ART CENTER

20 South West Temple
Downtown
801-328-4201
www.slartcenter.org
Open: 11–6 Tues. through Thurs. and Sat.; 11–9 Fri.; closed Sun. and Mon.
Admission: Free
Handicapped Accessible: Yes

Dating to before the Great Depression, the Salt Lake Art Center has a history of educating and challenging Salt Lake's residents with social and political art. With three different primary galleries and large spaces, the collections and exhibitions include huge sculpture installations and photographic series. More than just a gallery, the center is committed to engaging the community in the arts, and has an art school that offers classes to children and adults.

SALT LAKE PUBLIC LIBRARY
210 East 400 South
South Downtown
801-524-8200
www.slcpl.lib.ut.us
Open: 9–9 Mon. through Thurs.; 9–6 Fri. and Sat.; 1–5 Sun.
Admission: Free
Handicapped Accessible: Yes

The combination of Salt Lake Public Library's award-winning, environmentally friendly architecture and free gallery make this destination a must. The spectacular, modern library is beautiful both on a large scale and in the details, with imaginative shape given to the whole campus and functionality incorporated into every unique nook. A rooftop garden, five-story glass lobby, and solar lighting are some of the features of this great, curving structure. To access the free gallery, step inside and ride the glass elevator through the soaring lobby to the third floor. Though small, it features sculptures, handicrafts, and paintings done by artists from Utah to Africa. Underground parking directly beneath the library is free for the first 30 minutes.

UTAH MUSEUM OF NATURAL HISTORY
1390 East President's Circle
University of Utah
801-581-6927
www.umnh.utah.edu
Open: 9:30–5:30 Mon. through Sat.; 12–5 Sun.
Admission: $7 adults, $3.50 seniors, $3.50 youth (ages 3–12), free 3 and under
Handicapped Accessible: Yes

If you are curious about Utah's Native American history, geology, or dinosaurs, this can be a one-stop educational experience for you. With a working paleontology lab and a mere 150-mile proximity to Dinosaur National Monument, the museum has a heavy emphasis on pre-historic life. Other objects of interest are fully assembled dinosaur skeletons, an interactive "Discovery Hall," and special temporary exhibits. The spacious rooms are filled with large, colorful displays that entertain and educate children. Special attention is paid to families here, and currently the first Monday of each month admission is free, and the museum remains open until 8 PM. Located on the University of Utah campus, parking can be tricky. Limited free parking exists in front of the museum. If these spots are taken, you might try parking off-campus, as the museum is on the western edge of the campus.

UTAH MUSEUM OF FINE ART
410 Campus Center Drive
University of Utah
801-581-7332
www.umfa.utah.edu
Open: 10–5 Tues.–Fri.; 10–8 Wed.; 11–5 Sat. and Sun.; closed Mon. and holidays
Admission: $5 adults, $3 seniors, $3 students and youth, free 6 and under
Handicapped Accessible: Yes

Housed in a sleek brick and glass building with a tidy, geometric interior, the Utah Museum of Fine Art strives to maintain a diverse collection of old classics and fresh contemporaries with special consideration for local history. While most of the pieces in the gallery are paintings, the style and content vary wildly. A special collection of 19th-century Utah art helps you imagine what the valley was like before it was home to two million people. A large main room often houses larger-than-life traveling works and featured installations. Because of its University of Utah location, be sure to tell the desk person the number of your parking space in order to avoid a parking ticket. The museum is fully wheelchair accessible and offers services to the hearing and vision impaired.

Gardens, Parks, and Zoos

Salt Lake City has just one zoo. What it lacks in exotic animals, it makes up for with colorful flowers. Thousands of flower beds cover Temple Square alone. Other gardens have been planted around the city to commemorate fallen soldiers and explore plant diversity.

Brigham Young Historic Park (State Street and 2nd Avenue) is a tribute to early Mormon leader Brigham Young. It is a pleasant, green retreat just north of downtown. The memorial portion of this square contains commemorative statues and a waterwheel that spins under the flow of City Creek. Located on land once farmed by Young, this rather unadorned green space is a venue for Tuesday and Friday evening concerts during the summer months.

Gilgal Garden (749 East 500 South) is a small sanctuary of interpretive sculptures and stone installations created by LDS artists. Mormon faith and values are emphasized in the sculptures, which enlighten the curious and comfort the faithful. Themes include family relations, craftsmanship, and scenes from the Book of Mormon.

Hogle Zoo (2600 East Sunnyside Avenue; 801-582-1631; www.hoglezoo.org), located on the bench just beneath Emigration Canyon, is home to hundreds of animals and insects ranging from snakes and spiders to giraffes. The resident roster includes camels, orangutans, rhinoceroses, and bears, plus terrariums full of exotic creepy-crawlies. With many more animals on display in the warm months, a visit to the zoo would best be planned in the summer or early fall. Especially pleasing to children is the miniature train that tours the zoo's campus.

Jordan River Parkway (801-533-4496, golf: 801-533-4527) is located parallel to and west of I-15. The parkway contains an intermittent system of trails that parallels Salt Lake Valley's bisector, the Jordan River. The park spans from Salt Lake City down to the southern border of the county. Perks include miles of bike and jogging paths, wildlife viewing, bathroom facilities, picnic areas, and even paddleboat and canoe marinas. Other attractions within the park are a nine-hole golf course and **the International Peace Gardens** (900 West 900 South). Because the park is so vast and fragmented, call ahead for specific information if your exact destination is important to you.

Liberty Park (900–1300 South and 500–700 East) is one of Salt Lake City's largest parks and one of its oldest. Originally Pioneer Farm, it had a flour mill that was owned in part by Brigham Young. Liberty Park's 110 acres are today filled with shade trees, various recreational opportunities, and museums. For play, the park, which is lined with wood-chipped and paved running trails, has tennis courts, a swimming pool, volleyball courts, a playground, and a pond with paddleboat rentals. **Tracy Aviary** (801-596-8500; www.tracyaviary.org), home to more than 400 birds spanning 135 species, is hardly noticeable within this huge park, but can be found on the southwest corner. The **Chase Home** (801-533-5760), built in 1853, was for years a favorite haunt of Brigham Young, and a popular gathering place for musicians and dancers. Home to the **Museum of Utah Folk Art**, the Chase Home today is filled with handicrafts, music, and creative people. Traveling with your dog? **Herman Frank's Park** (700 East 1300 South), located immediately to the east of Liberty Park, is a haven where dogs are free to run off-leash.

Memory Grove (135 East North Temple) is yet another shady retreat within reasonable distance of downtown. With historic plaques and peaceful landscaping, this tree-lined nook is dedicated to all of Utah's soldiers who fought and died in World War I, World War II, and Vietnam. Folded into the base of City Creek Canyon, this is an excellent access point for the Bonneville Shoreline Trails. Every June, the **Wahsatch Steeplechase** (www.wahsatchsteeplechase.com) starts and finishes here. Competitors run a total of 18 miles, climbing up the foothills to the top of Black Mountain, and returning down City Creek Canyon.

Red Butte Garden and Arboretum (300 Wakara Way, University of Utah; 801-581-4747; www.redbuttegarden.org) is carved into the foothills at the northeastern end of the University of Utah campus. Open year-round, this garden, with its 200 plant species and harmonious surroundings, is a favorite place for people to walk, read, and paint. Every summer the garden hosts an outdoor concert series. Recent performers have included John Hiatt, Herbie Hancock, North Mississippi Allstars, and the Indigo Girls.

Sugarhouse Park (2100 South–I-80 and 1300 East–1700 East) is another favorite destination for joggers and families within the city. Home of the Utah State Prison until 1951, this park now has a pond and a meandering 1.8-mile roadway around its perimeter, as well as a baseball diamond, basketball court, soccer field, and two playgrounds. Access to the park is along its northern border (2100 South Street).

Temple Square Gardens (Temple Square, North Temple–South Temple and Main Street–100 West Street) couldn't have a more convenient location for downtown visitors, and is highly recommended to be a part of your visit. These well-manicured gardens blanket the square and church buildings in brilliant colors, and are an integral, flowing part of its design. Informational tours include horticulture's place in LDS history, as well as tips for gardening at home. The gardens are comprised of 250 beds with 160,000 plants representing 750 species. Although the flowers die off in the winter, extensive holiday lighting brightens the square between Thanksgiving and New Year's Day.

Amusement Parks

If you are willing to take a short drive, the kids will thank you. Although Salt Lake City has a few recreation centers, Farmington (17 miles north of Salt Lake City) is home to Utah's major amusement park, Lagoon. Although you will encounter lines, they will be substantially less than in other amusement parks.

LAGOON
375 Lagoon Drive
Exit #322 from I-15 Northbound, 17 miles north of Salt Lake City
Farmington
801-451-8000
www.lagoonpark.com

Open: Varied and seasonal
Admission: $25.95 plus tax (more for select rides), $7 parking fee
Handicapped Accessible: Limited

Just 17 miles north of Salt Lake City, Lagoon is a full-sized, national-caliber amusement park able to please kids and adults. Pools, waterslides, and splash rides abound, making this a perfect summer cool-down. With a standard arsenal of bumper cars, a Tilt-A-Whirl, a merry-go-round, the less brave will have plenty of entertainment while their daring family members take a flight on the Rocket, a 200-foot tower of blast-off and free-fall terror, or the 45-mph Jet Star Roller Coaster. The ultimate thrill here has to be the Sky Coaster, which requires a voluntary step off a 143-foot platform onto the end of a 120-foot pendulum cable.

NIGHTMARE ON 13th HAUNTED HOUSE
300 West 1300 South
801-467-8100
www.nightmareon13th.com
Open: Varied and seasonal
Admission: $15 (more for select thrills)
Handicapped Accessible: No

Nightmare on 13th is a fun evening for teenagers and fun-seeking young adults during the Halloween season. A large warehouse darkened and filled with meandering walls and spiderwebs, this is an innocent way to get your heart rate up. However, if you are staying in one of the historic bed & breakfasts, you might not need any more haunted houses in your life.

RAGING WATERS
1200 West 1700 South
801-972-3300
www.ragingwatersutah.com
Open: 10:30–7:30 Mon. through Sat.; 12–7:30 Sun. (summer only)
Price: $20 adults, $16 under 11
Handicapped Accessible: Very limited

Raging Waters is Salt Lake City's favorite cool-down during the summer months. This park has created about as many different water activities as one could imagine. Most involve a swift descent down a slide, but other areas feature rope swings, water-sled skimming, and raft rides through tunnels. Mellow areas were created for younger children, including the toddler pool with a colorful fountain and dinosaur pool.

Historic Buildings and Sites
Many of the preserved and promoted historic buildings and sites in Utah are LDS-related. While these are beautiful and fascinating, there is more on Salt Lake Valley's historical register than Temple Square.

CAPITOL BUILDING
Capitol Hill
400 North State Street
801-538-3000

Built in 1915, this stately government seat overlooks the city from Capitol Hill, just north of downtown. The 40 green acres, located among some of Salt Lake City's finer homes, offer an unimpeded view of the Wasatch and Oquirrh ranges across the valley. If you have a hankering to tour another historic building while on Capitol Hill, visit **Council Hall** (300 North State Street). Originally located at 120 East 100 South, this served for 30 years as Salt Lake City's seat of government upon its completion in 1866. Over the years the building has assumed many roles, and in 1961 it was dismantled and reassembled at its current location. Today it is home to the **Utah Travel Council** and **Utah Film Commission**, among other organizations. During the summer months, the Capitol Building's lawn is the site of "Movie Under the Stars" nights, which take place two or three times a month; call for information.

CATHEDRAL OF THE MADELEINE
331 East South Temple
Downtown/Avenues
801-328-8941
www.saltlakecathedral.org

By 1899 the Catholic community of Salt Lake City had grown prominent enough to facilitate the construction of this grand cathedral. Completed in 1909, this structure combines a Romanesque exterior with a boldly colorful Gothic interior. Gargoyles perched on the cathedral's ornate Gothic spires peer down 185 feet at the sidewalks below. High, vaulted ceilings, stained glass, and brilliant murals make for a vivid and ornate interior. Intricate wood carvings and sculpted shrines of charity add to the decorative richness. The cathedral hosts evening concerts each Sunday during the summer months, and is home to year-round choral and organ performances (see online for details).

FORT DOUGLAS
32 Potter Street
University of Utah
801-581-1251

In the beginning of the Civil War, Colonel Patrick Connor and the California-Nevada Volunteers were sent to Utah to prevent possible secessionist activity. They arrived in October 1862 and erected Fort Douglas high on the eastern bench so that they could oversee the activity below. When the Mormon behavior turned out to be less threatening than they had imagined, the soldiers set about prospecting in the hills. Their findings helped spark the mining industry in Utah. Fort Douglas saw many changes throughout the years. During the Indian Wars it was used as a military supply center, and even served as a POW camp during the two world wars. Designated a National Historical Landmark in 1970, the fort's remaining original buildings now house the Fort Douglas Military Museum on the University of Utah campus. Though there is no formal tour and these buildings are currently in use for modern university purposes (aside, of course, from the museum), a stroll around this old fort is a worthwhile stop for those interested in Utah's not-so-distant past.

GOVERNOR'S MANSION
603 East South Temple
801-538-1005

Born in Canada and raised in Nebraska, Thomas Kearns came to Park City in 1893 to try his hand in mining. His career had humble beginnings, and his first job, mucker, was the worst available. Ambition turned his fortune around, and by 1902 he had made himself wealthy enough to spend $350,000 to build this French château–style mansion. Kearns's careers included a term as senator and ownership of the Salt Lake Tribune. The home was deeded by Kearns's widow to the state of Utah in 1937. Today the mansion is the official (and actual) residence of the governor and his family. Free tours are available. Call for times.

PIONEER TRAIL STATE PARK
2601 East Sunnyside Avenue
801-584-8392

The **Old Deseret Village** (open Memorial Day to Labor Day) is a living history museum with period artifacts and a cast that reenacts the lives of Utahans between 1847 and 1869. Each building, carriage, and costume in this village has been carefully restored or designed to accurately convey what life would have been like for these pioneers. With more than 40 buildings and 150 staff members, the village engulfs you in history. Also on these grounds you will find **This is the Place State Park** (open year-round). This marks the end of the 1,300-mile Mormon Trail and celebrates Brigham Young's declaration on July 24, 1847, that Utah was to be the new home of the Mormons. After your visit, you can take a hike or jog on the Bonneville Shoreline Trail system, a major entrance point for which is immediately to the east of this park.

WASHINGTON SQUARE
Salt Lake City and County Building
Between State Street–200 East and 400 South–500 South
801-535-7605

The Salt Lake City and County Building was opened in 1894, amazingly after only three years of construction. Of imposing size and stately Richardsonian Romanesque architecture, this is where many of the city and county offices are. The building's early history was filled with controversy, for its size and structure were thought to mock the LDS temple. Symbolic details can be spied throughout the building, including the carvings depicting Utah history above doorways. The greater square is a pleasant place to take a green stroll or enjoy flipping through a good book.

TEMPLE SQUARE AND ENVIRONS
Mainly between West Temple–State Street and North Temple–South Temple
801-539-3101 or 1-800-453-3960
www.visittemplesquare.com

The oldest and most richly historic block of town, Mormon Temple Square, enthusiastically welcomes all visitors. Free guided tours are more difficult to avoid than find, and the staff and volunteers will joyfully and informatively share with you their history and (in a gentle way) their spirituality. Temple Square itself is enclosed by stone walls, but many related museums and historical sites exist in the immediate proximity. The famous **Temple Square Gardens** with over 250 beds and 165,000 plants are an unforgettable part of this complex. After the flowers die in the fall, the square is elaborately lit for the holiday season (beginning the first Friday after Thanksgiving and ending New Year's Day). Two visitors centers on Temple Square, the North Visitor Center (50 West North Temple) and the South Visitor

Latter-day Saints office building Jonathan Echlin

Center (50 West South Temple), are each open 9–9 daily to provide more in-depth orientation free of charge.

Assembly Hall is a dramatically Gothic 1877 building with severely pointed spires and stained-glass windows. Every Friday and Saturday evening, free concerts are held within these walls. Additional concerts are held Tuesday and Wednesday during the Christmas season. (A minimum age of eight is required; located at 50 West North Temple)

Beehive House dates back to 1854 and is available for viewing by way of free 30-minute guided tours. Home to Brigham Young during the first years of his presidency of the Mormon Church and term governor of the Territory of Utah, this building is extremely well preserved. Rooms include the "Family Store" and "Fantasy Castle." Located east of Temple Square at 67 East South Temple, this house is adorned with a beehive, the Mormon symbol of industry.

Brigham Young Monument, located at the intersection of South Temple and Main streets, is an 1893 bronze monument to pioneer and religious leader Brigham Young, who led the pilgrimage of Mormons into Utah in 1847. Also commemorated by the sculpture are the Native Americans and fur trappers who resided here before the Mormons arrived. At the same intersection stands the **Eagle Gate**. This symbol originally marked the entrance of Brigham Young's City Creek Canyon house. Not the original gate, this replica stands 76 feet wide and supports a 2-ton eagle with a 20-foot wingspan.

The **Deuel Pioneer Log Home** (35 North West Temple) was one of many slipshod homes thrown together immediately upon arrival in Utah, so that pioneers might survive their initial winter here. One of only two of these provisional houses still remaining, the Deuel Pioneer Log Home has been carefully restored. It is decorated with period furnishings and artifacts. Admission is free.

The **Joseph Smith Memorial Building** (15 East South Temple), formerly called Hotel Utah, has a fascinating interior design and emblematic murals. With a theater, two restaurants, and luxury reception halls, this is a popular destination for tourists and locals alike. Both rooftop restaurants offer expansive views and tasty cuisine. Of the two, **The Garden** is slightly more casual and well suited for a lunch break.

Family History Library (35 North West Temple; 801-240-2584 or 1-866-406-1830; www.familysearch.org) is the largest library of its kind in the world, with millions of records containing genealogical information that spans the globe and extends as far as Asia, Africa, and Australia.

The **LDS Church Office Building**, completed in 1972, is located at 50 East North Temple, and is the global headquarters of the financial sector of the Church of Jesus Christ of Latter-day Saints. With 28 stories, this is the tallest building in Salt Lake City and has a 26th-floor observation deck open to the public. The building is surrounded by some of the Temple Square Gardens, which are completely redesigned twice a year.

Lion House (63 East South Temple) is yet another of Brigham Young's houses, commissioned in 1856 to be a private residence. Named "Lion House" partly for Young's nickname, Lion of the Lord, and partly for the lion that adorns the front porch, the house today is home to a restaurant and banquet facilities.

Mormon Pioneer Memorial Monument (140 East First Avenue) commemorates the 6,000 Mormon pioneer lives lost during their migration westward and is the actual **grave site of Brigham Young** and other early Mormon pioneers. Eliza Snow, who penned many LDS poems and hymns, is also buried here.

The **Museum of Church History and Art** (45 North West Temple) offers another opportunity to understand Mormon heritage through iconic art depicting religious scenes and the trials of the pioneer trek westward. Admission is free.

The **Relief Society Building** (76 North Main Street) is home to the all-female Relief Society that has been a part of Mormon society since 1842 when it was founded in Nauvoo, Illinois. Built in 1956, the building today contains a resource center with volunteers assisting visitors.

Salt Lake Temple on Temple Square is a neo-Gothic granite building that was 40 years in the making. Despite adverse circumstances, including starvation and cumbersome quarrying methods, no aspect of the building, from the research to the decorations, was cheaply or carelessly done. Dedicated in April 1893, it is the mother church of the entire LDS religion. Astrology and religious symbolism are incorporated into every brushstroke and tower placement. The angel Moroni, represented by a 12.5-foot sculpture covered in copper and gold leaf, adorns the tallest spire (210 feet) on the Temple.

Seagull Monument on Temple Square celebrates Utah's beloved state bird. The California gull is so honored because of its 1848 rescue of the Mormon crops from hordes of hungry crickets.

The **Tabernacle** on Temple Square, with its fully self-supporting domed roof, was designed by Brigham Young and was under construction from 1863–75. The odd, egglike shape of the building and its organ of 11,623 pipes are perhaps the most famous traits of the Tabernacle. Home to the world-famous Mormon Tabernacle Choir founded in 1849, the Tabernacle is the site of weekly free concerts every Sunday at 9:30 AM. The Sunday concerts are the source of the *Music and the Spoken Word* live broadcast airing since July 15, 1929. If you wish to attend, you must arrive and sit by 9:15. Informal rehearsals take place Thursdays at 8:00 PM.

A free shuttle takes visitors from Temple Square to **Welfare Square** (780 West 800 South). Welfare Square was founded during the Great Depression with the purpose of extending aid to the unfortunate and providing the unemployed with work opportunities. It has grown significantly since its inception and now is comprised of a bakery, cannery, employment center, grain elevator, milk-processing operation, and even a thrift store.

Sports Teams

Utah's most nationally recognized sports team is the **Utah Jazz** (801-325-2500; www.nba.com/jazz). The Jazz have called Salt Lake City home since their 1979 move from New Orleans. John Stockton and Karl Malone are the most notable figures in Jazz history. They came to the team in the mid-1980s, turning the team's success around and earning fame over the next dozen years. The Jazz play their home games in the EnergySolutions Arena (301 West South Temple), formerly the Delta Center.

Regionally, the **University of Utah Utes** (http://utahutes.cstv.com) are the most fervently followed teams. Ute teams have a die-hard following of students, alumni, and their families. The Utes' largest home facility is the Rice-Eccles Stadium (400 South Street, Southwest Campus) where track & field meets and football games are held. The Jon M. Huntsman Center (Wasatch Drive, East Campus) holds basketball games and gymnastics competitions. Soccer is played at the Ute Fields (Wasatch Drive, Northeast Campus). Other University of Utah sports are baseball, golf, skiing, swimming and diving, cross-country, softball, and volleyball.

Salt Lake hockey fans have the **Utah Grizzlies** (www.utahgrizzlies.com), an East Coast

Salt Lake Bees baseball game with Wasatch backdrop Christine Balaz

Hockey League (EHCL) team. Though the name would suggest otherwise, the teams of the ECHL are now scattered throughout Utah. They are based in West Valley in the Maverik Center (801-988-8000; www.maverikcenter.com). The **Salt Lake Bees** (www.slbees.com) are Salt Lake City's baseball team, and a part of the Pacific Coast League. They play home games at the Franklin Covey Field (77 West 1300 South; 801-485-3800). These beautiful facilities are new and clean, and the lush, green diamond has a perfect Wasatch backdrop. A Bees game is highly recommended for a casual, yet entertaining, evening outside; during the summer months, "Thirsty Thursdays" feature half-price beers. Inexpensive and fun for families, date nights, or friends.

You may find it surprising that Salt Lake City has its own roller derby team. The **Salt City Derby Girls** (www.SaltCityDerbyGirls.com) play just as rough and wicked as any other team in the Women's Flat Track Derby Association. If you are unfamiliar with roller derby, you should know that no matter how cute the participants may be, the sport is fairly brutal.

Nightlife

Though Salt Lake City is not known for its nightlife, there is more fun to be had here than urban legend would suggest. A recent—and major—change to the night scene took place in the summer of 2009; bars, formerly "private clubs" requiring membership to enter, finally became free, and open to anyone (21 and up) without any kind of membership purchase required. With this died one of Utah's biggest and scariest urban legends. Also, Utah's decision to go smoke-free has made going out all the more pleasant.

Though bars have now been opened to the public, you should know that they are still distributed fairly widely throughout the city, and there is no real "party" zone. The key to enjoying your evening in Salt Lake is planning ahead. Because there is no central crawl, you might only visit one or two establishments in an evening. Because of the dispersed nature of the city's pubs, a great amount of Salt Lake City's after-hours energy is concentrated in concerts and other events. Between June and October, you cannot find a better time than Thursday nights at the **Gallivan Center Twilight Concert Series** (239 South Main Street; 801-535-6110). Free weekly concerts turn this outdoor pavilion into a beer garden and dance floor at 7 PM. Twilight Series headlining artists in the past have included Spearhead, Martin Sexton, Earl Scruggs, Clap Your Hands Say Yeah, Bon Iver, Sonic Youth, and Soullive, to name a few.

During the winter, people go indoors to venues like **The Depot** (400 West South Temple; 801-456-2800; www.depotslc.com), **In The Venue** (279 South 500 West; 801-359-3219; www.inthevenue.com), and **Burt's Tiki Lounge** (726 South State Street; 801-521-0572). Many even put an extra layer on and attend free outdoor concerts in Park City—yes, in the winter (as well as in the summer). **The Canyons** (www.thecanyons.com) and **Deer Valley** (www.deervalleyresort.com) often sponsor free shows in conjunction with World Cup Freestyle Skiing events and the Sundance Film Festival. Check resort and venue Web sites before your visit to scope out any shows you might want to attend.

The closest you will come to finding a park-and-walk bar district in Salt Lake City is the hotel district downtown. Inside the Hotel Monaco is **Club Bambara** (202 South Main Street; 801-363-5454), a swanky little number perfect for sipping cocktails. **Club Piastra** (220 South State Street; 801-961-8700) is Marriott's contribution to the bar scene, enjoyed for its modern, high-end atmosphere. **Kristauf's** (16 West Market Street; 801-366-9490) is another hip little spot to top off your dining experience at any of the many nearby restaurants, like the Market Street Grill. An extensive martini list and a quiet atmosphere allow you to enjoy the company of friends without competing for bar service. The **Mynt Martini Bar** (63 West 100 South; 801-355-6968) has a niche among high-end cocktail sippers and offers live music. For wine and tapas sampling, go to **Panache** (299 South Main; 801-535-4311; www.panache.net). You can opt for the restaurant, café, or wine bar. Here you will find **The Red Door** (57 West 200 South; 801-363-6030; www.behindthereddoor.com), where the bartenders mix their many, many liquors into some of the best and most creative cocktails in town. With a trendy, upscale atmosphere and exposed brick, this bar can get busy.

For less posh downtown socializing, go to **Murphy's Bar & Grill** (106 South Main Street; 801-359-7271). A motley crowd appreciates this bar for its simplicity and relatively quiet atmosphere. Smoking is allowed here. **The Tavernacle Social Club** (201 East 300 South; 801-519-8900) employs a pun to suggest the "duelin' pianos" you'll find here. The interactive performances require that you come in the mood to be entertained.

Also keep your eyes open for the downtown brewpubs, **Squatters** (147 West 300 South;

801-363-2739) and **Red Rock Brewing Company** (254 South 200 West; 801-521-7446), just a block apart. Each brews fantastic beers and has a fun, pleasant atmosphere. Squatters draws a slightly larger crowd, though it's never rowdy or uncomfortably full. Less "bars" and more dining facilities, these make for good group and family outing spots.

If you decide to venture slightly farther away, you might try **The Bayou** (645 South State Street; 801-961-8400; www.utahbayou.com). With more than 230 different beers, front stage, and free billiards, the Bayou is a great place to enjoy a Cajun dinner and live jazz. The Bayou is smoke free. Other State Street bars have adopted a younger crowd and Irish theme.

One of Salt Lake's most beloved and clever establishments is **Brewvies Cinema Pub** (677 South 200 West; 801-355-5500; www.brewvies.com). As you might guess, Brewvies is a beer joint and movie theater rolled into one. They have also added a sitting area, pub menu, and free pool tables to the front lounge, making it hard to leave after the film is done. Watch the schedule for old favorites and new ski or rock climbing films. Keep an eye on their Web site for special events such as these.

If you decide to enjoy your evening in, you may decide to visit one of Salt Lake's **Utah State Liquor Stores**. Hard alcohol and wine are sold exclusively in these government-run stores, as is "real" beer. Most liquor stores are very similar, with the exception of the two Utah State Wine Store (255 South 300 East; 801-533-6444) and the newer location (1605 South 300 West; 801-977-6800). This boasts the state's best wine selection and is fortu-itously located downtown.

Salt Lake City 2002 Winter Olympic Facilities

A fun addition to your trip might be a visit to any of the remaining facilities from the 2002 Winter Olympics and Paralympics. At the **Olympic Cauldron Park** (451 South 1400 East,

A sign at Utah Olympic Park   Jonathan Echlin

University of Utah) is a plaque telling the 17-day story of games in Utah, the geodesic Hoberman Arch under which athletes were awarded their metals, and of course the 72-foot Olympic Cauldron. Also on the university campus is the onetime Athlete Village that has since been transformed into student dormitories. With a 3,500-resident capacity, the village sits just south of historic Fort Douglas. If you can spare a 30-minute drive from downtown Salt Lake, you should consider visiting the **Utah Olympic Oval**, formerly known as the Oquirrh Park Oval (5662 South 4800 West, Kearns; 801-968-6825; www.olyparks.com). At once a ice playground and serious training facility, it has two speed-skating ovals, a rink for ice hockey and curling, a soccer field, and a running track. Five dollars will get you a pair of speed skates and admission. You'll go much faster than you'd expect. More Olympic leftovers are found in **Park City at the Utah Olympic Park** and the **Alf Engen Ski Museum**. See Chapter 2, Park City, for more information.

Arts and Entertainment

Venues

Maurice Abravanel Concert Hall (123 West South Temple; 801-355-2787) is one of the premier fine arts venues of Salt Lake City, known for its impeccable, bright acoustics. Home to the Utah Symphony, Abravanel Hall wears many hats and occasionally hosts an extreme skiing film. Built in 1979 as "Symphony Hall," it has a modish, soaring lobby and a classically beautiful concert hall. It is still one of Salt Lake's architectural gems today.

Capitol Theater (50 West 200 South; 801-355-2787) dates back to 1913 and is one of the older functioning concert halls in historic downtown. It has been home to vaudeville troupes, opera companies, dance companies, and even early film screenings. With its changing functions and owners, it has assumed many different faces. Most recently, an $8.6 million grant in 1978 restored it to maximum beauty and functionality.

The Depot (400 West South Temple; 801-456-2800; www.depotslc.com) is a two-tiered music venue where you'll find yourself among a livelier crowd than in Abravanel Hall. You can dine on French cuisine at the **Butterfly Restaurant** downstairs before entering the two-tiered, U-shaped concert hall. Each stadium-seating level has its own bar, so you won't have to go far for libations. Plenty of room is found behind the seating for milling around and dancing. While the capacity is too small for a Rolling Stones concert, you will still be able to catch artists like the Young Dubliners, Ziggy Marley, or even the Nitty Gritty Dirt Band.

In The Venue (279 South 500 West; 801-359-3219) is a oh-so-slightly renovated warehouse building simply partitioned by blocks of speakers, dancing stages, bars, and curtains. During the summer months the balcony level is expanded to include an outdoor patio with a full bar. Because of the industrial nature of the building, it attracts harder music and a younger crowd than other locales.

Jon M. Huntsman Events Center (1825 East South Campus Drive; 801-581-8849; www.utahutes.com) is a 1969 colossal dome structure that hosts events like University of Utah Utes basketball games and gymnastic competitions. With a capacity of 15,000, it has hosted several record-sized audiences for its events.

Rose Wagner Performing Arts Center (138 West 300 South; 801-323-6977; www.slccfa.org) is a fine arts venue whose architecture itself is attractive, though functional. It arose from Salt Lake City's great demand for more performing arts space and has grown to be a hub for artists of all kinds. Within the Center are three theaters and one gallery, all completed between 1997 and 2002. **The Leona Wagner Black Box Theatre**, **The Jeanné Wagner Theatre**, and **The Studio Theatre**, each of a different seating capacity, are home to numerous groups, ranging from children's dance troupes to international pianist societies, theater companies, and Sundance Film Festival screenings.

Film

The **Salt Lake Film Center** (210 East 400 South, Library Square, Salt Lake Library; 801-746-7000; www.slcfilmcenter.org) was created in 2002 by Academy Award–winning producer Geralyn Dreyfous, who recognized the disconnect between the Sundance Film Institute and the community around it. With offices located in the courtyard of the stunning Salt Lake Public Library, this organization manages to screen as many as five films a week at little or no cost, many with a panel assembled from relevant community groups.

Although the Utah offices of the **Sundance Institute** (801-328-3456; www.sundance .org) are based in Park City, there is a tangible impact on Salt Lake City. The institute is a brainchild of film star, activist, and philanthropist Robert Redford, whose passion for independent films inspired him to establish a foundation that would foster grassroots filmmakers. Since its inception in 1981, it has grown to world predominance. Every January the Sundance Film Festival descends on Park City, bringing with it hordes of filmmakers, celebrities, groupies, and even major rock groups. While the center of the festival is Park City, Salt Lake now hosts much of the event that has outgrown its parent town. If you intend to experience any part of the festival, it is recommended that you begin preparation several months in advance; admission is very limited and sometimes accessible only by luck.

Music

SALT LAKE CHORAL ARTISTS
1375 East Presidents Circle
801-587-9377
www.saltlakechoralartists.org

Led by Artistic Director and Conductor Brady Allred, the Salt Lake Choral Artists is an assemblage of three groups. A 155-piece concert choir, 57-voice women's choir, and 38-member chamber choir provide this group versatility. It gives many concerts alone, but often partners with other local troupes. The Choral Artists split their time between recording and performing, usually mustering six productions a year.

SALT LAKE SYMPHONY
Columbus Center
2531 South 400 East
Sugarhouse
801-463-2440
www.saltlakesymphony.org

Directed by Robert Baldwin, the Salt Lake Symphony is the premier all-volunteer, non-profit Wasatch Front orchestra. With community outreach as a major objective, the orchestra offers inexpensive, informal renditions of old classics and experimental pieces to audiences of all ages. Since 1976, this group has combined over 10,000 volunteer hours to produce approximately 15 concerts annually.

UTAH OPERA COMPANY
Capitol Theater
50 West 200 South
801-533-6683, 1-888-451-2787
www.utahopera.org

Easily accessed by Trax (at the Main Street stop between 200 and 300 South), the Capitol Theater is home to the Utah Opera Company. Annually, the opera offers productions of assorted vintages to a combined audience of 150,000 people, more than half of whom are students. Striving to keep opera contemporary and accessible to the widest possible audience, the company constantly adjusts and revitalizes its colorful sets and innovative performances. The Utah Opera Company has been a valley institution since 1978, is an integral part of the annual, summer Deer Valley Music Festival, and often works in conjunction with the Utah Symphony.

UTAH CHAMBER ARTISTS
801-572-2010
www.utahchamberartists.org

Conducted by Barlow Bradford and Rebecca Durham, this small group by its very nature can play in many diverse locations. For each season they prepare a new concert. These are often comprised of full-length pieces, a choice that deviates from the more common compilations of short chamber pieces usually performed by similar groups. For concert listings, call or watch at various venues around town.

UTAH SYMPHONY
Abravanel Hall
123 West South Temple
Downtown
801-533-5626
www.utahsymphony.org

Led by new director Thierry Fischer, this is a fully professional troupe producing more than 200 polished concerts annually, all while upholding a rigorous recording schedule. Although their home is Abravanel Hall, they frequently perform in outdoor concert series during the summer and travel to other regional cities and Europe. Their season lasts from September through May, and includes four productions in the Capitol Theater with the Utah Opera Company, as well as the Deer Valley Music Festival during the summer in Park City.

Theater
Unlike Salt Lake City's mostly professional music and dance scenes, the theater circuit is dominated by active community troupes and very casual, less-refined offerings. With the University of Utah, Westminster College, and Salt Lake Community College, the student theater groups have a dominant share of the limelight. A good many of the performances take place in the Capitol Theater (50 West 200 South, 801-355-2787) and Kingsbury Hall (1350 West 200 South; 801-581-7100), as well as on the University of Utah campus.

Desert Star Playhouse (4861 South State Street, Murray; 801-266-2600) combines bright colors, straightforward sets, and fun in their productions. A lighthearted theater, the Desert Star offers dinner-theater shows, during which meals are served. Expect a child- and family-friendly, very down-home type experience at the Desert Star.

The Lab Theater (240 South 1500 East; 801-581-6448) of University of Utah is known for its modern staging and performances filled with allusion and subtle themes. Many of the plays performed by the Lab are written by student-actors. Productions here can lack sophistication, but are usually filled with compensatory vigor.

Off Broadway Theater (272 South Main Street; 801-355-4628) will be your best bet for downtown comedy. Within these walls, you can see parodies and comedies à la Broadway. Every Friday and Saturday the **Laughing Stock Improv Comedy Troupe** goes onstage for some belly laughs.

Plan B Theatre Company (353 West 200 South; 801-201-9791; www.planbtheatrecompany .org), without a theater to call their home, presents an alternative to many easy-to-swallow, conservative troupes around Utah. Their productions take place on various stages around the valley and often comment on local and global politics.

Pygmalion Productions Theatre Company (48 West Broadway; www.pygmalionproductions .org) strives to create compelling theater that celebrates the beauty of humanity from a feminist viewpoint.

Salt Lake Community College's **Grand Theatre** (1575 South State Street; 801-957-3322; www.the-grand.org) combines professional and amateur actors in each of their five yearly productions. The resulting dynamic between the polished professional and hungry amateur is what drives the theater's performances. This is one of the most active theater troupes in town, and their performances are well-advertised.

Performance and Dance

Although Salt Lake City has only three major dance groups, its prowess as a dancing hub is recognized internationally, in symbiosis with the University of Utah's renowned dance programs. Founders, directors, and dancers, past and present, have come from outstanding backgrounds and have had an impact on the global dance community. Salt Lake City is gifted with a thriving dance legacy that includes both modern and classical dancing.

In 1963, after establishing the first university ballet company in the United States at the University of Utah, San Francisco Ballet cofounder William F. Christensen helped create **Salt Lake City's Ballet West** (50 West 200 South; 801-323-6900; www.balletwest.org) in 1963. Since its inception, Ballet West has had a stream of preeminent directors and dancers, making it one of Salt Lake City's jewels. Although the group travels extensively, it still gives many performances on its home stage.

Ririe-Woodbury Dance Company (138 West Broadway; 801-297-4241; www.ririewoodbury.com) turns classical theater inside out and upside down, using dynamic form and full body paint, inventive light displays, and multimedia sets to distort the senses and engage the audience. Often featuring the works of the internationally acclaimed, late Alwin Nikolais, this company gives its audiences exclusive opportunities to witness these unique dances. The performances delight children as much as they challenge adults.

Repertory Dance Theatre (138 West 300 South; 801-534-1000; www.rdtutah.org) was founded in 1966 as a modern dance company. Fully professional since its initiation, this

High Wasatch in early summer Christine Balaz

company has evolved to be a uniquely democratic organization that strives to share the arts with a large array of people.

Recreation

The Canyons and Nearby Areas

Perhaps Salt Lake City's finest asset is what exists outside the city limits. With the valley floor at 4,400 feet, the peaks of the Wasatch Range at 11,000 feet, and over seven canyons pouring out into the city, you have hundreds of square miles of recreational opportunities at your convenience. Each canyon varies dramatically from the next in flora and geology. Because of a strong refrigeration effect, these canyons tend to be about 10 to 15 degrees cooler than the valley below.

The **Bonneville Shoreline Trail System** is an immensely extensive network of unsigned trails crisscrossing the grassy foothills north of the city. Because of the low-profile vegetation, you will easily keep your bearings and not get lost. This system has its western origin above Capitol Hill's Memory Grove Park, and is a spiderweb that spans the northern foothills, dwindling only when it reaches the east end of the University of Utah and This is the Place Heritage Park. Although there are many trailheads, some of the most convenient access points are at City Creek Canyon/Memory Grove, Red Butte Garden, and the parking lot on Sunnyside Boulevard east of This is the Place Heritage Park.

The Salt Lake City Wasatch Front's northernmost canyon is **City Creek Canyon**, which can be accessed by Bonneville Boulevard between the Avenues and Capitol Hill or by the trail from Memory Grove Park below. A paved road runs up the base of this rather steep canyon and is closed to cars on odd-numbered days, making the canyon great for runners and road bikers. The pavement deteriorates toward the top of the canyon, but is still pass-able by road bike. From City Creek Canyon you can also access the Bonneville Shoreline Trail System, which branches east from the parking lot gate. **Black Mountain**, visible from downtown Salt Lake City, can be accessed by the trail at the terminus of the canyon road.

Emigration Canyon is the next canyon, moving south along the Wasatch. It is a moder-ately rolling canyon whose road achieves a surprisingly rewarding view at its apex. Emigra-tion Canyon is easily reached by taking Sunnyside Boulevard (800 South Street) up and east out of the city, directly into the mouth of the canyon. Although this road services many canyon residences and connects to **East Canyon**, it sees only moderate traffic and is the most popular road bike route near the city. To gain the view of East Canyon, stay on the main road up the canyon until you encounter a major fork about 5 miles above the mouth of the canyon. Follow signs toward East Canyon and I-40 that will direct you to take a sharp right-hand switchback. A few cafes (including Ruth's Café, listed in Salt Lake's Dining sec-tion of this chapter) line the road.

Parleys Canyon was chosen as I-80's route through the Wasatch and so does not see as much recreational use, yet a few very pleasant trails (good for mountain bikers and hikers) are tucked within the canyon, and are accessed by the East Canyon Reservoir. **Mountain Dell Golf Course** (and Nordic ski trails) and **East Canyon** can both be accessed via Exit 134. East Canyon has a switchbacking road that offers a nice out-and-back road ride or provides easy access to the top of the mountain bike trail that connects back with the road at the bot-tom of the canyon.

Millcreek Canyon is among the most popular canyons for summer recreation. Road bikers enjoy the grind to the top of the 10-mile road, and mountain bikers especially enjoy the **Pipeline Trail** and the vast system of trails that start at the top of the road. Millcreek Canyon is a fee canyon, $3 per vehicle. The lower part of the canyon stays warm in all sea-sons and is a trail-running option in the winter. Dog owners love the canyon for its policy that allows dogs to run off-leash on odd-numbered days. Owners must carry plastic bags with which to remove solid waste. Receptacles are located at the base of major trailheads. Appreciative for this opportunity, the community strictly abides by this policy.

Travel farther south and you will find **Big Cottonwood Canyon**. Although rock climbers, road bikers, and some hikers enjoy recreation here in the summer, this canyon is most popular in the winter when snow covers the slopes of Brighton, Solitude, and the back-country.

Little Cottonwood Canyon is the southernmost of the major canyons adjacent to Salt Lake City. A strikingly deep glacial "U" of white granite, it attracts gravity freaks all year long. The boulders and cliffs are a playground for rock climbers, and the world-famous Alta, Snowbird, and Little Cottonwood backcountry terrain summons skiers. Additionally, the **LDS Granite Mountain Storage Vault** can be seen on the northern side of the canyon just a few miles above the mouth.

Running and Inline Skating

For a quick jog on flat terrain, try either Sugarhouse Park (1300 East 2100 South) or Liberty Park (700 East 1300 South). Both offer trails and road loops with plenty of shade and opportunities for inline skating. Another similarly pleasant destination is the University of Utah, a campus with little traffic and few major throughways. The campus is only mildly hilly, but enough so to make for a more challenging run.

A short drive will get you to the **Jordan River Parkway**, a state park with miles of pavement for skaters and cyclists, as well as unpaved trails for knee-friendly running. Jordan River Parkway extends for miles on the western edge of Salt Lake City, and there are several different parking lots and trailheads. For advice on finding the most convenient access point for your needs and location, call the **Jordan River State Park** (801-533-4496) or the **Salt Lake Running Company** (801-484-9144).

For those seeking more elevation gain, **Memory Grove** and **City Creek Canyon** are two adjoining parks that have as much elevation gain as anyone could want. Memory Grove, a peaceful memorial park dedicated to fallen Utah veterans, sits a few hundred wooded yards below the City Creek Canyon parking area. You can access Memory Grove by parking just east of the **Capitol Building** (400 North State Street) and walking down the paths into the park. A trail from Memory Grove cuts upward and northward through the woods, connecting it to the base of City Creek Canyon. This higher parking area can be accessed along Bonneville Boulevard between Capitol Hill and the Avenues. Here you will find a paved roadway and trail system that ascend City Creek Canyon and the surrounding foothills.

From this trailhead you can gain the summit of **Black Mountain** or explore the **Bonneville Shoreline Trail**. This is a vast network of trails that crisscrosses the actual former shoreline of ancient Lake Bonneville around the northeastern perimeter of Salt Lake City. The Shoreline Trail System lets you choose between broad and rolling, rugged and steep, and allows you to customize your distance and difficulty.

Utah has many running events, but most runners know Utah for its grueling September **Wasatch Front 100-Mile Endurance Run** (www.wasatch100.com). As the name suggests, this run is not only a century, but has almost 27,000 feet of vertical gain and 26,000 vertical feet of loss. Many people opt for the "easy" way out, participating in the **Salt Lake City Marathon** (www.saltlakecitymarathon.com), **July 24th Marathon**, or 18-mile **Wahsatch Steeplechase** trail run (www.wahsatchsteeplechase.com).

Golf

With a choice of 25 golf courses in the metropolitan Wasatch Front alone, you will find no lack of terrain variety or course flavor. Reservations are recommended at all courses, because the demand is as high as the supply. March sun warms the valley and marks the beginning of golf season. While the Wasatch are still deep in snow, many locals and savvy visitors top off a day of skiing with nine holes of golf. Listed below are Salt Lake City's public courses.

Bonneville Golf Course (954 Connor Street; 801-583-9513): 18 holes, par 72, 6,824 yards; wide fairways, hilly, challenging greens, few water hazards, driving range, scenic

Fore Lakes Golf Course (1258 West 4700 South; 801-266-8621): 9/9 holes, par 31/27, 2,285/1,350 yards; many sand bunkers and lakes, difficult executive course, driving range

Forest Dale Golf Course (2375 South 900 East; 801-483-5420): 9 holes, par 36, 3,126
 yards; many trees, water hazards, sand bunkers, flat

Glendale Golf Course (1560 West 2100 South; 801-974-2403): 18 holes, par 72, 6,939
 yards; narrow fairways, large greens, many water hazards

Jordan River Golf Course (1200 North Redwood Road; 801-533-4527): 9 holes, par 27,
 1,070 yards; many trees, narrow fairways, flat, scenic

Meadowbrook Golf Course (4197 South 1300 West; 801-266-0971): 18 holes, par 72,
 6,800 yards; many water hazards, sand bunkers, trees, scenic, driving range

Mick Riley Golf Course (421 East Vine Street; 801-266-8185): 9/9 holes, par 36/27,
 3,056/1,401 yards; scenic, easy executive course, driving range

Mountain Dell Golf Course (Exit 134 on I-80, Parleys canyon; 801-582-3812): 18/18 holes,
 par 72/71, 6,787/6,710 yards; steep canyon course, narrow fairways, many water hazards,
 many trees, scenic; no children under the age of six

Murray Parkway (6345 South Murray Parkway Drive; 801-262-4653): 18 holes, par 72,
 6,794 yards; many water hazards, many trees, driving range

Nibley Park Golf Course (2780 South 700 East; 801-483-5418): 9 holes, par 34, 2,895
 yards; Utah's oldest, flat, many sand bunkers

Old Mill Golf Course (6000 South Wasatch Boulevard; 801-424-1302): 18 holes, par 71,
 6,731 yards; challenging, many trees, hilly, streams, scenic, driving range

Riverbend Golf Course (12800 South 1040 West; 801-253-3673): 18 holes, par 72, 6,876
 yards; many sand bunkers and water hazards, Jordan River location, scenic, driving
 range

Rose Park Golf Course (1386 North Redwood Road; 801-596-5030): 18 holes, par 72,
 6,696 yards; many sand bunkers and trees, narrow fairways, driving range

University of Utah Golf Course (102 Central Campus Drive; 801-581-6511): 9 holes, par
 33, 2,500 yards; hilly, few trees, easy, scenic

Wingpointe (3602 West 100 North, Salt Lake International Airport; 801-575-2345): 18
 holes, par 72, 7,101 yards; water and tall grass hazards, Great Salt Lake location

Biking and Bike Rentals

Salt Lake Valley's extremely dry weather, long biking season, superb trails, and challenging
canyon roads make cycling a popular sport with die-hard contestants and recreational
enthusiasts.

Mountain Biking

For anyone with an inkling of curiosity and an athletic tendency, Utah mountain biking is a
must. Utah has endless mountain biking trails for every ability level. The mountain biking
season in the Wasatch region begins as early as March, when the intense Utah sun melts the
snow on south-facing mountain slopes. By June, bikers are out en masse, eating up the
miles of trails in Millcreek and East Canyons, even linking and looping around several different canyons in one day. Though deep summer is too warm near the valley floor (except
early in the morning), higher elevation rides are perfect for July and August. Fall is the
golden season for biking nearer the valley, when the trails are dry and the heat has relented
a bit. Local favorites include the **Millcreek Pipeline Trail** in Millcreek Canyon, the **Albion
Basin Summer Road** at Alta, **Grizzly Gulch** of Little Cottonwood Canyon (with the abandoned Prince of Wales Mine en route), the service roads and singletrack at **Snowbird**, and
the **Wasatch Crest Trail**. These include the full spectrum of difficulty and scenery. For

Salt Lake City summer bike commuting Christine Balaz

more information and trail recommendations, visit the Web site **www.utahmountain biking.com**. This site catalogs rides by city and is illustrated with pictures and videos. For more suggestions, call or visit **Wasatch Touring** (702 East 100 South; 801-359-9361; www.wasatchtouring.com), a beloved downtown shop where locals convene to talk shop. Peruse their Web site for upcoming in-store film screenings.

Road Biking

If you decide to hit the road, an escape into any of the many nearby canyons will offer you the most peaceful and challenging experience. Because of the fact that road biking in the actual city is generally unpleasant and chaotic, the majority of miles pedaled by Salt Lake cyclists are on mountain canyon routes. A scenic exception to this rule is a ride to and around **Antelope Island State Park** (Syracuse, UT; 801-652-2043; www.stateparks.utah .gov), also a pleasant place to spend the day on a mountain bike. This is a surreal desert island in the middle of the Great Salt Lake, where every July an organized moonlight ride is held. The ride out to the island on its causeway can be quite brutal in case of a strong west wind, so check the weather. The Wasatch mountains, rimming the city on its north and east side, offer many winding, paved climbs. From north to south, the bike-friendly canyons near Salt Lake City are **City Creek**, **Emigration**, **Millcreek**, **Big Cottonwood**, and **Little Cottonwood** canyons. Each has its own distinct flavor, from gently rolling Emigration Canyon to punishing, exposed, and steep Little Cottonwood Canyon. The canyon scenery varies drastically as well, from the cool deciduous creek bottom of Millcreek Canyon to the cubist quartzite formations of rugged Big Cottonwood Canyon. More information and

Autumn in Millcreek Canyon   Christine Balaz

intimidating elevation profiles can be found on the comprehensive and excellent Web site **www.saltlakecycling.com**.

Rentals

Utah Ski and Golf (34 West 600 South; 801-355-9088; www.utahskigolf.com), an all-seasons rental company, and one of the Wasatch region's biggest and most well-rounded, offers road bike rentals and a wide range of mountain bikes, including full-suspension frames. Nearer to the Cottonwood Canyons is **Canyon Sports** (844 Fort Union Boulevard; 801-942-3100; www.canyonsports.com), also renting road and mountain bikes.

Hiking and Snowshoeing

The Salt Lake area has more miles of hiking than you could ever walk, and because of the mammoth altitude range of the canyons, you are rarely limited by season. Nearest to town, and lowest in elevation, is the **Bonneville Shoreline Trail System**. Hikes here get the most of the valley's sun and warmth and can range from casual to moderate, depending on your motivation. The easiest points of access for the Bonneville Shoreline Trail are adjacent to This is the Place State Park, Red Butte Gardens, and at the mouth of City Creek Canyon. Because of the oft-gradual gradient, broad girth, and choice-rich plentitude of this network, it is popular for trail runners. Only 20 minutes from downtown is **Millcreek Canyon**. By far one of the most popular hiking canyons in the Wasatch, it has trails low enough to remain passable through most of the winter. Warm summer temperatures render the upper canyon more desirable. With dozens of trailheads literally on the roadside, you can depart from anywhere the urge strikes. Dogs are allowed to run off-leash on odd-numbered days. Millcreek Canyon is located on the east side of 3800 South Street, and is most easily accessed by the 3900 South exit off I-215, and there is a $3 per day entrance fee.

Recommended destination hikes include the **Lake Blanche Trail** of Big Cottonwood Canyon, a steep 3.3-mile trip one way to a scenic lake deserving of the effort. In Little Cottonwood Canyon, a hike in the **Albion Basin** of Alta will show you the most alpine scenery for your effort. You can stroll the few miles through the glacial basin to Cecret Lake, or continue upward, gaining the top of Devil's Castle (an 800-foot limestone buttress with panoramic views) via the saddle ridge just above the lake. On the return trail, you will encounter historic mine shafts from the rowdier days of Alta. Trail-specific information can be attained by calling the **Salt Lake Ranger District** (801-733-2660).

Rock Climbing

Dry weather and proximity to dozens of world-class rock climbing areas make Utah a major North American hub for climbers of all breeds. Climbing season in the immediate Salt Lake area comfortably begins as soon as April and lasts through October. Most climbers here insist that it lasts longer, but have invented elaborate ways of keeping themselves warm and cheat by making weekend trips to Indian Creek, St. George, or Ibex.

For traditional climbing in the immediate area, the glaciated walls of **Little Cottonwood Canyon** are tops. Although the walls appear fragmented and low-angle, they actually can produce very long routes of great difficulty, and even some pitches of an overhanging aspect. Many moderate classics can be found here, among which Becky's Wall and Satan's Corner are famous.

Sport climbers must travel to the quartzite of **Big Cottonwood Canyon** or the blocky limestone of **American Fork Canyon** (east of Lehi) for true cragging. Be advised that the

Rock climber in American Fork Canyon Christine Balaz

sport climbers of Salt Lake City are a fearsome bunch; it is rare to find a climb rated less than 5.11. The major exception to this rule is the Escape Buttress of American Fork, which is a grid wall of fun 5.10.

Boulderers could spend a lifetime on the hundreds of granite boulders in **Little Cotton-wood Canyon**. Strewn throughout the length of this canyon, these boulders have been cleaved from some of the finest granite, and offer hundreds of varied problems. Steep and slabby, burly and technical, these boulders have it all. Many of the boulders even have a perfectly flat landing to boot.

If you get the chance to sneak away, the **Uinta Mountains**, **Maple Canyon**, **Ibex**, **St. George**, **Indian Creek**, and the **City of Rocks** are all within five hours or less of Salt Lake City and are visited by people from around the world. In town, **The Front Climbing Club** (1450 South 400 West; 801-466-7625; www.frontslc.com) and **Rockreation Sport Climbing Center** (2074 East 3900 South; 801-278-7473; www.rockreation.com) can keep you fit or introduce you to the sport. Located in the same complex as the Black Diamond factory and store, this is also a good place to stop for equipment. A new addition to the (southern part of the) valley is **Momentum Climbing** (220 West 10600 South, Sandy; 801-990-6890; www.momentumclimbing.com), one of the nation's best rock climbing gyms. In a spacious, pleasantly designed building, this cleverly integrates impressive amounts of lead climbing at steep and vertical angles, as well as vertical toproping, a bouldering room, and a fitness room. Excellent route setting and very realistic splitter cracks put the icing on the cake. The Front is a bouldering-only gym, so no ropes or confusing apparatus will be involved. Rockreation primarily caters to sport climbers, but does have a bouldering cave. Momentum does it all.

Air Adventures

The predictable afternoon winds and miles of Wasatch foothills make the area perfect for paragliding. **Point of the Mountain**, just 10 miles south of Salt Lake City on I-15, has a reputation among paragliders as being the best training site in the nation. If curious, you might give it a try. Lessons are surprisingly affordable and available through a handful of companies in the area. **Cloud 9 Soaring Center** (12665 South Minuteman Drive, Draper; 801-576-6460; www.paragliders.com), **SuperFly Paragliding Academy** (8683 Sandy Parkway, Sandy; 801-255-9595; www. superflyinc.com), and **Two-Can Fly Paragliding** (474 East Tonya Drive, Sandy; 801-971-3414; www.twocanfly.com) will take you out.

Fishing

Although you won't catch more in the Great Salt Lake than brine shrimp, many superior freshwater fishing experiences exist within driving distance of Salt Lake City, and many guide services would like to take you there. Although most are at least two hours away, a full day in the golden sun might be the icing on your trip. **Western Rivers Flyfisher** (1071 East 900 South; 800-545-4312; www.wrflyfisher.com) and **Destinations Inc. Fly Fishing** (2578 Dimple Dell Road, Sandy; 801-816-0790) are the favorite outfitters in Salt Lake City, operating trips to the famous Flaming Gorge area of the Green River, the Provo River, and to other small streams.

If you have come equipped to fly-fish and require no guide, the Green and Provo Rivers are among the best in Utah. For lake fishing, take your reel to **Strawberry Reservoir**, **Pelican Lake**, **Starvation Reservoir**, **Jordanelle Dam**, **Deer Creek Dam**, **Provo River**, **Utah Lake**, or **Deer Creek Reservoir**.

Canoeing, Kayaking, Rafting, and Sailing

Although Utah has plenty of whitewater, most is found in dangerous mountain creeks or on the big rivers in southern Utah. Salt Lake City's **Sidsports** (265 East 3900 South; 801-261-0300; www.sidsports.com) does not offer guiding service, but has the most knowledgeable ownership and staff around, particularly with regards to whitewater. This is the go-to shop for supplies and to discuss conditions.

For local flat-water paddling, visit the gentle waters of **Jordan River State Park** (801-533-4496) or **Antelope Island State Park** (801-652-2043). For sailing, you can find everything you need at the full-service marinas of **The Great Salt Lake Marina** (801-250-1898) and the **Antelope Island Marina** (801-773-2941).

If you are serious about boating and have the desire to paddle the Green or Colorado Rivers, consider **Adrift Adventures** (9500 East 6000 South, Jensen, UT 84035; 1-800-824-0150; www.adrift.com), **Dinosaur River Expeditions** (P.O. Box 3387, Park City, UT 84060; 1-800-345-7238; www.dinoadv.com), or **Sherri Griffith Expeditions** (P.O. Box 1324, Moab, UT 84532; 1-800-332-2439; www.griffithexp.com).

Scuba Diving and Snorkeling

You would not believe it, but year-round warmwater diving exists just 50 miles west of Salt Lake City. The Bonneville Seabase (I-80 West to Exit 84, 5 miles south on UT 138; 435-884-3874; www.seabase.net) is a set of three geothermally heated small bays that maintain a constant temperature of around 80 degrees F (26 degrees C) all year long. Within the temperate waters of these pools swim stocked exotics like French angelfish, nurse sharks, porkfish, puffers, lowdown jacks, and many others that may be completely new to you.

SHOPPING

Boutiques and Fine Arts

If boutiques are your fancy, the **Sugarhouse** district of town is one of your best bets. With the most original shops as well as many familiar chain stores, this will be the most efficient area to park and walk from the bookstore to the burger joint, the liquor store, and the shoe store. Fortunately for all Salt Lake residents, the Patagonia Outlet Store (2292 South Highland Drive; 801-466-2226; www.patagonia.com) makes its home right in Sugarhouse. All of the goods at less of the cost make this a fun indulgence. Inspired by the taste of Robert Redford and his resort, the Sundance Catalog Outlet (2201 South Highland Drive; 801-487-3400; www.sundancecatalog.com) is just across the street from the Patagonia shop. On the quirky side, Game Night Games (2030 South 900 East; 801-467-2400; www.gamenightgames.com) is a store for people who absolutely love board games. If this is your fancy, stop by for their Wednesday night games. Along the way are many bookstores, coffee shops, and restaurants. Finally, do not forget to make a trip to the Utah State Liquor Store (1154 East Ashton Avenue; 801-468-0320; www.thecityofsaltlakecity.com/liquor), just south of Patagonia.

Just a few miles north at **9th & 9th** (900 East 900 South), you will find another small collection of fun shops, including the **Coffee Garden** (870 East 900 South; 801-355-3425) to give you a boost and the **Children's Hour** (914 East 900 South; 801-359-4150; www.childrenshourbookstore.com) where some of the most funky, yet luxurious women's

Jonathan Echlin

and children's clothing in Salt Lake City is sold. Also stop by **Great Harvest Bread** (905 East 900 South; 801-328-2323; www.greatharvest.com) for some breakfast buns or coffee and receive a generous complimentary sample of bread, on which you can smear butter and honey. A handful of popular restaurants (see Dining, this chapter) offer visitors to this area some of the tastiest bites in town.

The **Downtown** of Salt Lake City is more of a financial district than a shopping square, but still a few worthy shops have their storefronts here. **Ken Sanders Rare Books** (268 South 200 East; 801-521-3819; www.kensandersbooks.com) is a find for the Edward Abbey–loving Desert Southwest fan. With more than 100,000 books on the geology, indigenous people, and the pioneer history of the region, as well as locally inspired fiction, the store has many desert sunsets that you can take home. These people know and love books, and Ken is an expert in regional history and is likewise a political spokesperson. **Utah Artist Hands** (61 West 100 South; 801-355-0206; www.utahhands.com) promotes the colorful paintings of local artists, ranging from still life to landscape studies. **Sam Weller's Zion Bookstore** (254 South Main; 801-328-2586, 1-800-333-7269; www.samwellers.com) opened in 1929 and currently has more than 150,000 Mormon books on the shelves.

The Gateway Mall Jonathan Echlin

South of downtown is the local favorite, the **Beer Nut** (1200 South State Street; 801-531-8182; www.beernut.com). Salt Lake City's beer supply store, it nurtures eager brewers and educates them to be craftspeople. Because of the lowered alcohol in much of Utah's beer, brewing is an overwhelmingly popular hobby of locals.

Gourmet Shops and Farmers Markets

Though unassuming, Liberty Heights Fresh (1300 South 1100 East; 801-583-7374; www.libertyheightsfresh.com) has an impressive ability to locate and import fine cheeses and charcuterie that much larger shops cannot. The other shelves and baskets of the store are brimming with artisan breads and organic fruits from local farms. A small shop with a rich and potent collection of delicious, whole, though high-priced foods. The Scandia Kaffe House (1693 South 900 East; 801-467-0051) is an import store with a Scandinavian accent. You can enjoy their raspberry-filled pastries and other fine baked goods in the quaint dining area. Very popular among a loyal customer base.

During the summer months you can shop at the **Downtown Farmers Market** in **Pioneer Park** (300 West 300 South). Every Saturday you will find the wares and fruits of the area's laborers, with early summer peas giving way to August raspberries. You may even catch a winemaking demonstration given by the **Beer Nut** (1200 South State Street; 801-531-8182; www.beernut.com).

Malls and Squares

The Gateway Mall (50 North–200 South and 400 West–500 West; 801-456-0000; www.shopthegateway.com) is the newest outdoor shopping center in Salt Lake City. With winding lanes and two levels, this is home to restaurants, clothing shops, furniture shops, and a movie theater. Part of the compound is the restored 1908 Union Pacific Depot. More than just shops, the Gateway is a community center. It is home to many events, marking the end of the Salt Lake City Marathon, and hosting concerts and the Quicksilver Skate Competition, among others. This very modern, bright, and cheery open-air establishment takes the tackiness, recycled air, and moldy carpet out of the "mall" concept. **Foothill Village** (1300–1700 South Foothill Boulevard; 801-487-6670; www.foothillvillage.com) is another outdoor square whose high-end shops and restaurants are the attraction. Fine sporting goods, imported shoes, and a Neiman Marcus are right in line with their peer establishments. Do not be repelled by its outwardly drab appearance. **Trolley Square** (500–600 South and 600–700 East; www.trolleysquaremerchants.com) is a modern mall inside the former switching station of the Salt Lake Trolley Company of the 1920s and '30s. Two favorites here are the brewpub Desert Edge Brewery (801-521-8917) and the Trolley Wing Company (801-538-0745), where you can get beers and wings in an original trolley car with outdoor seating.

PARK CITY

Park City is an island in the mountains—geographically and culturally. This is what defined Park City upon its founding, and it is what fosters its growth today. Tucked half a mile above, and a mountain pass away from, Salt Lake Valley, this was where Utah miners first founded a city of their own away from Mormon settlements. Folded snugly into the peaks of Summit County, it now abounds with outdoor enthusiasts. No matter where you are in Park City, you are surrounded by unlimited world-class skiing, mountain biking, hiking, and photography. You should not be surprised, then, that Park City is a destination for all of these.

Summit County has 39 of Utah's tallest peaks. Its eastern side is comprised of the Uinta Mountains, and its western half is rumpled by the Wasatch Range. Surprisingly, it has historically been the path of choice through Utah. From early nomadic peoples to the first transcontinental railroad and I–80, this has been a portal for much of Utah's history.

An early mining town, Park City started with a bang. Just over 90 years later, it was nearly dead. Officially registered as a ghost town in 1963, Park City was again rekindled by fledgling ski resorts. Today Park City skiers have their pick of three major ski areas: Deer Valley, The Canyons, and Park City Mountain resorts—each of which would stand alone as a vacation destination. In the summer, after the 350 inches of winter snow melt away, a wild-flower-lined spiderweb of trails seduces mountain bikers and hikers back to the slopes. For those less into gravity sports, the town's historical mining sites and Main Street's boutique galleries provide ample entertainment.

Your evenings can begin with a meal at one of the nation's best restaurants, and finish with an outdoor concert at The Canyons. Park City's winter months are punctuated by World Cup Ski Racing and Freestyle events, the Sundance Festival, and glitz. The summer season passes serenely with gallery strolls and fly-fishing.

Park City is a vibrant town whose history and culture have everything to do with its surrounding peaks and canyons. Though many of Park City's visitors come for outdoor sports, this mountain culture can be just as easily enjoyed through vivid western photography, mining museums, and elk steak served at grills. You can shop, dine, and be pampered at one of many local day spas. Because of its open spaces and surrounding fields, you will spot all sorts of animals, from cattle on ranches to deer and elk grazing in meadows and parks. Because Park City is home to the U.S. Ski and Snowboard Association, odds are great that you will bump elbows with a U.S. Ski Team coach or athlete while enjoying an après ski beer.

Perched 7,080 feet above sea level, Park City has historically had, and continues to have, a distinctly different climate and different customs than most Utah cities and towns. Salt Lake City and Provo bake in the summer and remain temperate in the winter; Park City has

OPPOSITE: *Snowy rooftops near Park City Mountain Resort* Jonathan Echlin

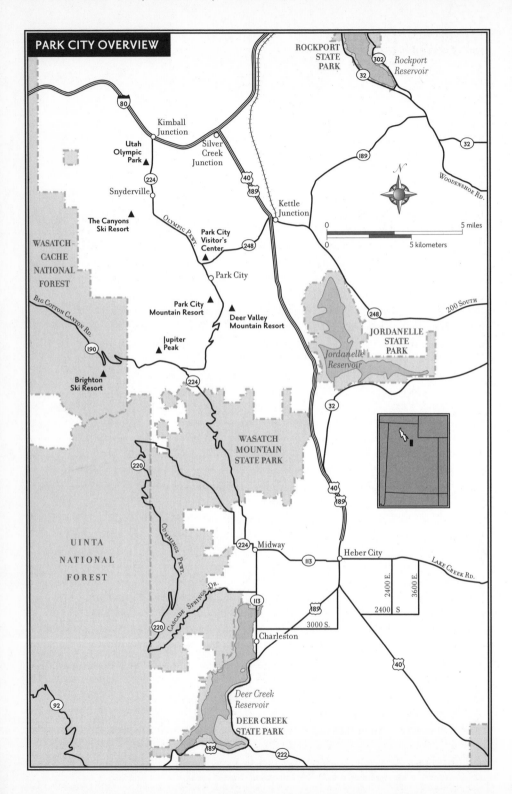

PARK CITY OVERVIEW

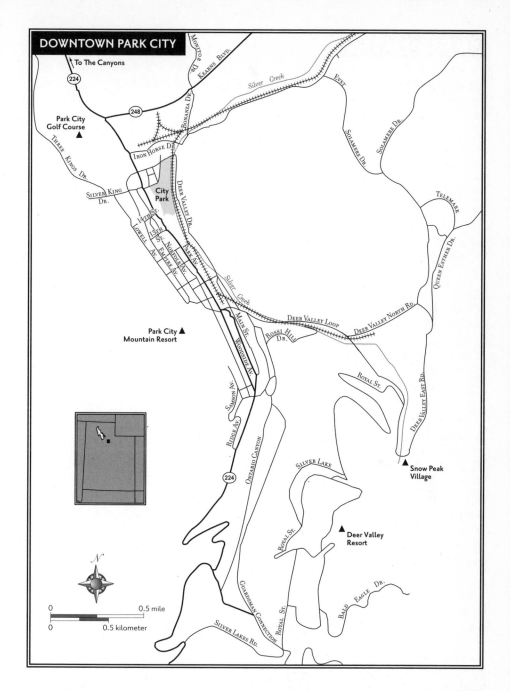

DOWNTOWN PARK CITY

a strong cycle of four seasons. It has a genuine "white Christmas" winter that melts through spring into a pleasantly warm summer, which then glides into a colorfully rich fall. While most civic energy in Utah is dedicated to faith, family, and industry, Park City's liveliness is channeled into outdoor recreation, fine cuisine, and nightlife. Historic monuments in other Utah towns are rightly dedicated to various Latter-day Saint (LDS) leaders, and most historical buildings were built by early Mormon pioneers. However, Park City's preserved buildings and sites illustrate its renegade mining history.

Affluent and trendy, modern Park City has grown to be vastly different than when it was founded in 1872. If you check out the Old Miner's Hospital or stand slope-side at a freestyle skiing competition, you will see that it still retains its renegade roots and thrives on its people's vivacity. It seems wholly appropriate that Park City was founded on the Fourth of July. Now a safe haven for celebrities and ski bums, Park City ignores most of the covenants of its parent state (within legal limits).

Local History

To the northeast of Park City is Echo Canyon, one of the most easily passable sections of the formidable Uinta Mountains. This canyon connects the grasslands of Wyoming to the salt flats of Utah, and is the portal from New England to California. This has always been a route of travel for animals and people alike, and much history has been made possible by this route. Kamas Valley, on whose floor Park City sits, was traversed by nomadic indigenous peoples and animals because of its proximity to Echo Canyon. The lands of modern-day Summit County, rich with wildlife, were a hunting and fishing area for Northern Shoshone and Ute Indians for centuries. However, although Echo Canyon let them in, the cold weather forced them out. Because of its high alpine environment and cold winter months, the valley was not inhabitable as a permanent home to these Native American tribes.

The 1820s brought the first European American visitors to the area. They too were nomadic, traveling wherever the fur trapping and trading were best. Among these were western legends William Ashley and party, Jim Bridger, Kit Carson, and Jedediah Smith. Traveling in small groups or alone, they left little, if any, impact on the area. However, their documentation brought knowledge of Utah to future settlers.

In 1847, Echo Canyon saw the first Utah-bound Mormon pioneers and the beginning of the Mormon Trail, which would eventually serve as the passageway for 80,000 Mormon pioneers and the porthole for a burgeoning religion. Passing the Kamas Valley, they continued westward, through Parleys canyon and down into Salt Lake Valley. In his studies of the American West, Brigham Young had identified the Great Basin as an undesirable location where his followers could be left alone to live peacefully. Spotting the Great Salt Lake, he recognized this as his goal and declared Salt Lake Valley "The Place." An influx of Utah immigrants ensued.

During the 1850s the Overland Stage was a means of travel for people heading to the Intermountain West and California. An all-purpose transcontinental organization, much of its business was also derived by transport of mail and other goods. The Overland Stage passed through Utah by way of Echo and Parleys canyons. It did a good deal of business in the area because of its good relations with Brigham Young, then President of the Church of Jesus Christ of Latter-day Saints and Governor of Utah Territory. This was a cumbersome complex of horses, carriages, and restocking stations located every 10 miles. The Overland Stage lasted only a decade, and was finally replaced by the streamlined Pony Express in the 1860s.

In 1857 President James Buchanan was witnessing his country growing rapidly apart and simultaneously enduring slander that he supported polygamy. So he cut Utah's mail supply off without warning and sent 2,500 troops to oversee the Mormon activities and replace Brigham Young with Alfred Cumming as governor. Though most Mormon dissent was peaceful, there was some reactionary violence. The next two years were filled with the battles of the Utah War. Disruptive and costly, the war accomplished little, though it certainly served to create tensions between Utah's Mormons and the United States federal government and non-Mormon general population. .

With the Civil War in sight, the U.S. government took interest in the possibility of a transcontinental telegraph line. Congress offered support and subsidy to any company willing to undertake this construction effort. In 1860 the Western Union Telegraph Company submitted a winning bid and construction began in Salt Lake City, extending outward to the east and west. In 1861 the Pacific Telegraph line was completed, connecting the former gap between Omaha, Nebraska, and Carson City, Nevada. Delivery of a message, that would have taken more than 30 days by Overland Stage or 15 days by Pony Express, was now virtually instant.

Colonel Patrick E. Connor was sent to Utah in 1862 to build a fort on the foothills above Salt Lake City. His mission was to assure the U.S. government that the Mormons had no intention of secessionist activity. In fact, the Mormons did not, and Connor sent some of his men out to seek precious metals in the nearby canyons and hills. His hopes were that their discoveries would lure prospectors and miners to Utah Territory and dilute the LDS population.

The year 1869 was pivotal for Park City and Utah alike. The Young American lode was discovered in modern-day Park City, and the area was instantly distinguished as a mining district, attracting thousands of prospectors. On May 10, 1869, the first transcontinental railroad joined the Union Pacific and Central Pacific railroads. Would-be miners now had state-of-the-art access to these rich mountains.

Mormon polygamist George Snyder built a boardinghouse near the Town Lift at present-day Park City Mountain Resort, so that he could profit from the mining in Utah. On July 4, 1872, an American flag sewn by George's third wife Rhonda was raised over the Snyder home. The miners declared, "We shall call this place Parley's Park City," after Mormon prophet Parley Pratt. The name Parley was quickly dropped, along with the Mormon presence in Park City. Shortly after the Young American was unearthed, hungry picks exposed the Buckeye, Flagstaff, McHenry, Pinon, Walker, and Webster mines. However, it was the much larger Ontario Mine that catalyzed the ensuing silver mining boom. The rights to the mine were sold to San Franciscan George Hearst for only $27,000. Over the next few decades, it would produce an alleged 50 million dollars' worth of silver ore.

With the Transcontinental Railroad complete, laid-off railroad workers came from Promontory Point to Park City to start a new career in mining. As the first buildings in Park City went up and the mines became more prolific, people from outside Utah set out by rail for one last chance at mining. The booming '49ers era was all but gone most everywhere else. At times, more than 300 individual mines were in operation in Park City. By 1879 there was a significant village in the lower canyon, where Park City stands today. However, mostly made of wood, the town saw its first devastating fire in the bitterly cold month of December 1882.

The mining village was rebuilt and continued to grow. Boardinghouses sprang up alongside theaters and saloons. Park City's path was very similar to other western mountain mining districts, and entirely unlike the rest of the Mormon's Territory of Utah. The residents came from widely varied backgrounds and classes. Irish, Scandinavian, Scottish, and other displaced American miners worked alongside the many Chinese brought here by rail work. Established mining magnates, wealthy from previous decades in California and

Nevada, leveraged more than their share of wealth out of the miners' labors. A complex hierarchy developed, based on ethnicity, faith, and wealth. The citizens aligned themselves within fraternity groups like the Elks, Masons, and Odd Fellows.

In 1884 Park City incorporated and immediately endured another small structure fire in 1885. The fires did little to hinder the magnetism of the new city. Although a disproportionate few retained the bulk of the wealth, and distinct classes remained segregated, the wealth of the mines trickled down through the ranks. The original cabins and shacks were replaced by real homes, and miners sent for their families to join them in Park City. As the town matured, theaters and brothels gave way to schools and proper city infrastructure. New mining companies like Silver King came into power. An opulent town grew in around them and their multimillion-dollar ore exports.

Although the town was regularly damaged by fires, the gusto of booming Park City dulled the people's sense of caution and they continued to erect wooden structures. The town grew larger and the structures more numerous and nearer each other. On June 19, 1898, Park City's Main Street was consumed by fire yet again. This fire, to date the worst in Utah's history, destroyed roughly 200 buildings and 75 percent of the town.

The driving urge for wealth rebuilt Park City quickly. With Utah connected to the nation by the railroad and a reputation for tremendous opportunity, Park City continued to prosper. By the 1910s, travelers began passing through on the Lincoln Highway. This was the first transcontinental highway, which had developed piecemeal over several years. Not surprisingly, it passed through Echo Canyon and Salt Lake City.

As late as the 1920s, major new ore deposits were discovered and exported to the rest of the nation. Mining companies by this time were large conglomerates, and the Park Consolidated Mining Company was the nation's most prolific silver producer in 1928. As skiing caught on around the nation, people gleefully took to the snowy hills to try their luck. The miners used "long board snowshoes" fashioned from barrel slats. Directed skiers used more developed technology. The Park City Ski Club built large ski jumps with intricate scaffolding at old mine sites and dumps. Serious competitions took place, and participants were flying as far as 200 feet by 1940. The Denver & Rio Grande Western Railroad created special lines to carry winter sports enthusiasts from Salt Lake City to Park City in 1936, and later from as far away as Ogden. Legendary Alf Engen, after whom Park City's ski museum is named, was a record-breaking ski jumper in his day. Brigham Young University held winter carnivals at Ecker Hill, now the location of Olympic Sports Park ski jumps. Though none of the early chairlifts and ski jumps have endured, they sewed the seeds for Park City's future.

Unfortunately, Park City's mining industry was petering out, and local enthusiasm for skiing alone could not keep the city afloat. With the Great Depression and World War II, Park City's mines were plagued by strikes, and the prosperity bubble burst. The number of workers dwindled to a few hundred and, as the town died, mine owners fled with their wealth. Despite this, Park City's first ski lift was built at Snow Park (now Deer Valley) in 1946. However, by 1950 Park City was all but dead.

The 1960s saw the city's low point, as well as the beginning of yet another boom—this time perhaps more sustainable than the last. In 1963, Park City was officially listed as a ghost town on the national register. The last remaining mine, United Park City Mines, was given federal aid to convert its property to a ski area in the hopes that this would revive the town's dying economy. Here skiers rode deep into the mountain on a train through the old Spiro Tunnel. After deboarding they rode the Thaynes Hoist, a mine elevator that lifted

Snowy roofs on Park City condos Jonathan Echlin

passengers 1,750 feet to the top of Park City Mountain Resort's modern-day Thanes Lift.

The last mining activity of any kind to take place in the hills around Park City was in 1982. Simultaneously, greater Utah tourism was boosted by the nation's relative economic stability and the addition of the national monuments Capitol Reef, Arches, and Golden Spike. The New Orleans Jazz became the Utah Jazz in 1979. US 40 was gradually converted over 30 years into I-80, whose path is roughly that of the old Lincoln Highway. Salt Lake City International Airport was expanding, and people began traveling to ski Utah's infa-

Park City neighborhoods from above   Christine Balaz

mous resorts, not the least of which were located in Park City. Because of its unique combination of non-Mormon history and premium Utah outdoor recreation, Park City became
the most attractive destination for tourists and second homes.

In 1985, just 22 years after it was declared a ghost town, Park City stumbled into a chance
to host its first World Cup ski races. When another ski resort canceled at the last minute,
Park City Mountain Resort jumped at the chance and threw a memorable event that
included skydivers, speed skiers, and rock bands. This success earned Park City the honor
of hosting many future ski events and professional ski tours, not the least of which were
other World Cups and much of the 2002 Winter Olympics. Today the U.S. Ski Team and
National Ability Center call Park City home.

Park City's enthusiasm, festivity, and beautiful environs prompted the Sundance Film
Festival to find its home here each January, starting in 1984. The festival resulted from the
pairing of Robert Redford's Sundance Institute and the struggling U.S. Film Festival. With a
first-year roster of A-list celebrities and innovative films, the revitalized event was an
instant hit, drawing film enthusiasts, groupies, and fans. Glitz and glitter have ensued, with
major rock bands playing private parties and party girl Paris Hilton accessorizing the event.
Roughly 20,000 people come to this event annually.

Modern Park City has grown far from its small mining village into three major ski resorts, Kimball Junction, Jeremy Ranch, and beyond. Its ski and tourism business give it great prosperity. The natural beauty of the area has attracted its wealthy residents; the prosperity of the town has given it beautiful homes and clean streets. The population, though of a different profession than mining, still enjoy a slightly renegade lifestyle. Once a mining boomtown, now a flourishing ski town, Park City still has its trademark enthusiasm.

NEIGHBORHOODS

Park City sits beneath the hills and high canyons that were once home to mines and now have been manicured into ski trails. It is now a collection of villages, having grown out from its original Main Street in podlike growths, as dictated by topography. Unlike gridded Salt Lake City and Provo, Park City has a somewhat convoluted system of roads. Growth has

Main Street Jonathan Echlin

Park City Mountain Resort in summer Christine Balaz

pushed many subdivisions high on the hills surrounding the valley. This varied topography begets winding and switchbacking lanes. Developers have divided the town into manifold neighborhoods and gated communities. The best advice for driving in Park City, particularly in the outlying neighborhoods, is to carefully follow a map.

At the center of town is the historic Main Street, where most of the gallery shopping, dance floors, and restaurants are found. Main Street is paralleled by several other side streets, along which are homes and access to parking. Park City Mountain Resort is the closest resort to Main Street, with the Town Lift actually touching down in downtown, although best access to the resort for day skiers and new arrivals is at the resort center.

To the north of town, between Park City and Kimball Junction, is The Canyons Resort. This has its own, clearly signed access road. To the northeast of Main Street, along Kearns Boulevard, are some of the older neighborhoods, dating back to the 1960s. Deer Valley is found to the southeast of downtown. It is slightly offset from the rest of town. Because of its minor distance from Park City's center and vast adjoining neighborhoods, it feels nearly like its own town.

Just north of Park City are Snyderville and Silver Springs. These towns, filled with homes and town houses, feel like more neighborhoods of Park City than distinct town-ships. Farther north, adjacent to I-80, is Kimball Junction. Yet another residential extension of Park City, Kimball Junction is home to box stores and famous outlet shops. Many hip clubs, restaurants, and pubs are sandwiched between these stores.

DRIVING IN PARK CITY

Park City is located along UT 224, 5 miles south of the Kimball Junction exit on I-80, and 2 miles west of US 40 by way of Kearns Boulevard. Park City's historic Main Street forms its downtown area, with all of the upscale shopping and country taverns within walking distance of each other. With the southern end of Main Street climbing a hillside, the roads here are narrow, sloped, and reminiscent of pre-automobile mining towns. Pedestrian traffic is heavy, and street junctions come suddenly. The easiest way to maneuver in this compact district is by foot. To park in the downtown area, follow signs to parking garages, which are wedged under buildings or tucked behind them. You may luck out and be able to park along the street in metered spaces, but do not rely on it.

The Canyons Resort's turnoff is on the western side of UT 224, between Kimball Junction and Park City. A traffic light and signs mark its entrance. Park City Mountain Resort, also easily discernible by signage, is reached by the well-traveled, clearly marked Empire Avenue, departing west from UT 224 just north of Main Street and its congestion. Of the three resorts, Deer Valley is the most southerly. Traveling south by Main Street, Park Avenue, or any parallel street, you will eventually come to a roundabout. If you continue in your southerly, upslope direction, a divided, spacious boulevard will eventually dump you right on Deer Valley's front steps.

In general, the easiest way to navigate Park City, once you've parked your rental, is with the free bus system. The town has cleverly created a public bus network that sweeps the greater area year-round, leaving little need for congestion-causing personal automobiles. Though bus stops and the buses themselves are visually obvious, you can easily get more information (such as schedules and exact locations) online at www.parkcity.org.

LODGING

Park City is a small town with big draw. Although the city itself has roughly 8,000 residents, the town's guests can double its population, and sometimes more than that. The importance of early reservations cannot be emphasized enough, especially during peak ski season or the Sundance Film Festival. During ski season, you should allow yourself a few months' advanced booking to ensure you get the style of lodging you prefer; for the Sundance Film Festival, you may even consider booking a year or more in advance to get any room at all.

Although Park City is much smaller and more compact than Salt Lake City, its lodging options are much more complicated for many reasons. Whereas Salt Lake City is one contiguous grid of straight roads, the various neighborhoods of Park City are geographically separated from each other and are connected by winding, hilly roads. Each of these neighborhoods is distinct. Downtown is unlike Deer Valley, Park City Mountain Resort, and The Canyons, and these are all very different from outlying Kimball Junction. Although rates fluctuate wildly with the season, you should always anticipate a higher price than in Salt Lake City or Provo. Due to Park City Center's compact nature, most large hotels will be found on the expansive ski slopes or in nearby locations, such as Kimball Junction.

Park City has the bed & breakfast and hotel accommodations of a larger town, and the infinite vacation rentals of a ski resort.

You can stay in a budget or deluxe room in town or in a slope-side condominium. Because of the varied and competitive nature of Park City's lodging, you may consider consulting with a booking service. With regard to private home and condo-

Park City Mountain Resort Village Jonathan Echlin

minium rentals, such advice can be extremely useful and will usually yield competitive package deals. **Resort Quest's Central Reservations of Park City** (435-649-6606 or 1-800-401-9913; www.resortquest parkcity.com) specializes in condominiums, villas, and other private vacation homes. **Deer Valley Lodging** (1-888-976-2732; www.deervalleylodging.com) can assist you with premier accommodations at Deer Valley and in Park City proper. **Resorts West** (435-665-7097 or 1-800-541-9378; www.resortswest.com) has information on vacation rentals at Park City Mountain Resort, The Canyons, and Deer Valley.

The Canyons Resort and Park City Mountain Resort are fairly simple resorts to navigate, each with one primary nucleus. At Deer Valley, there are three separate villages: Snow Park Village at 7,200 feet above sea level, Silver Lake Village at 8,100 feet, and Empire Pass at 8,145 feet. Each is accessible by road and in close proximity to chairlifts. If planning a trip to Deer Valley, you will be best served by calling the resort itself (1-800-558-3337; www.deervalley resort.com) for in-depth advice. Known as the crème de la crème of fine lodging, Deer Valley has the most expensive lodging in perhaps all of Utah. Naturally, Park City Mountain Resort, The Canyons, and downtown lodging will be expensive during times of high demand, although they offer a more complete spectrum of prices. With each establishment fighting for your business, your stay in Park City is almost guaranteed to be excellent.

Because Park City has such an extensive array of lodging, only a minute portion is included here. The lodging listed below offers a range of quality and location, including outstanding resort lodging. Regarding handicapped access, the options listed as accessible all have elevators where necessary, but are not necessarily fully equipped for all needs. Inquire for specific information.

Hotels, Lodges, and Condominium Hotels

BEST WESTERN LANDMARK INN
6560 North Landmark Drive
Park City, UT 84098
435-649-7300; 1-800-548-8824
www.bwlandmarkinn.com
Price: Inexpensive to Moderate
Credit Cards: AE, Disc, MC, V
Handicapped Accessible: Yes
Pets: Small, by discretion
Special Packages: Ski packages at The Canyons, Deer Valley, and Park City Mountain Resort
Location: Kimball Junction

With more than 100 hotel rooms, this Kimball Junction option puts you about 10 minutes from Main Street, but drops a zero or two from the end of your hotel fees. Although the price of this establishment is many tiers lower than that of others nearby, it still has the cleanliness and reliable basic quality of a standard hotel. Although you may be farther from the skiing, you will be much nearer the outlet shops. If this hotel has no vacancies, try the **Best Western Holiday Hills** (200 South 500 West, Coalville; 435-336-4444; www.bwstay.com), a similar establishment 10 minutes east on I-80. Although not quite as convenient, this reasonable option may be the nearest vacancy during heavy travel periods.

CHATEAU APRÈS
1299 Norfolk Avenue
Park City, UT 84060
435-649-9372; 1-800-357-3556
www.chateauapres.com
Price: Inexpensive to Moderate
Credit Cards: AE, Disc, MC, V
Handicapped Accessible: No
Pets: No
Special Packages: Discounted lift tickets at Park City Mountain Resort
Location: Park City Mountain Resort

With an ideal mountainside location and

the coziness a ski lodge, the Chateau Après is a unique fixture of Park City. Its very simple decor and matching low prices seem a throwback to the "old days" when Park City hadn't yet grown into its modern-day glitz. Its very humble furnishings and quirky Austrian style make your stay here highly casual, yet provide you with basic comfort and cleanliness—perfect accommodations for those who put skiing and dining higher on the priority list. The exterior resembles a gingerbread house, with garlands in winter and flower boxes in summer. It has 30 hotel rooms with private baths, complimentary cocoa, and continental breakfasts. If you want to reduce your cost even further, spend a night bundled in the dorm bunks reminiscent of summer camp. This is the most affordable lodging anywhere near Park City, and it is only 150 yards from Park City Mountain Resort.

GRAND SUMMIT HOTEL

4000 The Canyons Resort Drive
Park City, UT 84098
1-866-604-4171
www.thecanyons.com/grand_summit
Price: Very Expensive
Credit Cards: AE, Disc, MC, V
Handicapped Accessible: Yes
Pets: No
Special Packages: Ski packages at The Canyons
Location: The Canyons

The Grand Summit is a quintessential example of large-scale, resort-side hotels, built into the folds of the surrounding hills and bathed in warm lights during the dark winter hours. Thick timbers support the many roofs of its cozy, lodge-style segments. The rooms are simply decorated, yet have a chalet feel, with pine headboards and adornments. The lobbies are open, multi-level spaces incorporating stones and raw timbers to welcome you to the hotel. Although the lodge is enormous, the inter-

rupted paint theme and intermittently displaced walls seem to diminish the enormity of this aesthetic ski-in, ski-out hotel. Daycare is available upon request. This is nearest to the Flight of the Canyons Gondola.

HOTEL PARK CITY

2001 Park Avenue
Park City, UT 84060
435-200-2000
www.hotelparkcity.com
Price: Very Expensive
Credit Cards: AE, Disc, MC, V
Handicapped Accessible: Limited
Pets: No
Special Packages: Ski packages at The Canyons, Deer Valley, and Park City Mountain Resort; spa and equipment rental packages
Location: Park City Center

The Hotel Park City in downtown Jonathan Echlin

The Hotel Park City has 54 suites, each with a king-sized bed, high ceilings, and separate living room. C. M. Russell prints and lightly stained wooden furniture give each suite a western ambience. Special attention was given in the design to ensure that each suite has mountain views and a private patio or balcony. Because of its location on Park City Golf Course, all views are largely unobstructed. Its clever layout makes you feel as if you have rented an entire condominium.

THE LODGES AT DEER VALLEY

2900 Deer Valley Drive East
Park City, UT 84060
435-649-4040; 1-800-782-4813
www.lodges-deervalley.com
Price: Moderate to Very Expensive
Credit Cards: AE, DC, Disc, MC, V
Handicapped Accessible: Limited (inquire)
Pets: No
Special Packages: Ski packages at Deer Valley
Location: Snow Park Village at Deer Valley

Decorated in southwestern themes, pine, sandstone, and marble, the condominium-style hotel, Lodges at Deer Valley, will surprise you with some of the lower prices at Deer Valley Resort. Built in 1999, each unique unit folded into the timbers of this hotel has custom cabinetry, high ceilings, and tastefully colorful paint schemes. Although not a ski-in, ski-out hotel, you are within 0.5 mile of the Snow Park Lodge and four major lifts. Rooms range from hotel rooms to three-bedroom suites. Although prices are classified as expensive, a night here in low season can cost as little as a few hundred dollars. This is significantly less than the few thousand dollars you can expect to part with at many other Deer Valley accommodations. Tucked into the many peaks and partitions of this lodge are bike, fly-fishing, and ski rental shops, as well as five major conference rooms.

LOFT AT MOUNTAIN VILLAGE

Park City Mountain Reservations
1386 Lowell Avenue
Park City, UT 84060
435-647-5440 or 1-800-331-3178
www.parkcitymountain.com
Price: Moderate to Very Expensive
Credit Cards: AE, MC, V
Handicapped Accessible: Yes
Pets: No
Special Packages: Packages created for guests (inquire)
Location: Park City Resort Center

These moderate condominium units range in size from one to three bedrooms. Each unique unit is equipped with a full kitchen, common room, and fireplace, and has access to laundry facilities. Underground parking is free, which can be a serious bonus for slope-side lodging at Park City Mountain Resort.

MARRIOTT'S MOUNTAINSIDE

1305 Lowell Avenue
Park City, UT 84060
435-940-2000
www.marriott.com
Price: Moderate to Very Expensive
Credit Cards: AE, DC, Disc, MC, V
Handicapped Accessible: Limited
Pets: No
Special Packages: Ski packages at Deer Valley and Park City Mountain Resort
Location: Park City Mountain Resort

In the heart of Park City's Mountain Village, bordering the groomed trails of the Pay Day Lift, this Marriott has the ultimate ski-in, ski-out location. While some of the doors open directly onto the slopes, others lead to Park City Mountain Resort's rental shops, ticket offices, and proper après ski facilities. To treat your sore muscles, slip on your bathing suit and robe and head for the luxurious outdoor patio pool and steamy hot tubs. Although this Marriott has 364 rooms, its ideal location makes them disappear quickly. Guests have access to free public bus shuttles.

RED STAG LODGE
Deer Valley Central Reservations
2550 Deer Valley Drive East
Park City, UT 84060
1-800-558-3337
www.deervalley.com
Price: Expensive to Very Expensive
Credit Cards: AE, DC, Disc, MC, V
Handicapped Accessible: Yes
Pets: No
Special Packages: Ski packages at Deer Valley
Location: Snow Park Village at Deer Valley

The Red Stag was built in 2005 with a style reminiscent of classic European hunting lodges, but with luxurious modern conveniences. Whether your stay here is for business or vacation, the wet and dry spas, lap pools, fireplaces, and underground parking will make it a pleasurable experience. For its business clients, the Red Stag has four meeting rooms. Not to be outdone by any other Deer Valley accommodation, this lodge has furnished its condominiums with leather upholstery and king-sized beds. Located within Deer Valley's base area, Snow Park Village, the lodge is within a few minutes' walk of the mountain.

RESORT PLAZA CONDOMINIUMS AT PARK CITY MOUNTAIN RESORT
Park City Resort Village
Park City Mountain Reservations
Park City, UT 84060
435-647-5440; 1-800-331-3178
www.parkcitymountain.com
Price: Expensive to Very Expensive
Credit Cards: AE, MC, V
Handicapped Accessible: Yes
Pets: No
Special Packages: Packages created for guests (inquire)
Location: Park City Mountain Resort Center

These resort-center condominium units range from one to three bedrooms. Each condominium has its own decor and quality, but all are cozy and come with a kitchen, living room, and fireplace. All fit squarely within the ski condominium stereotype. The units are spread throughout three separate buildings that adjoin the Park City Mountain Resort's Main Plaza and its retail, rental, dining, and après ski options.

SILVER KING HOTEL
1485 Empire Avenue
Park City, UT 84060
435-649-5500; 1-888-575-2775
www.silverkinghotel.com
Price: Moderate to Very Expensive
Credit Cards: AE, Disc, MC, V
Handicapped Accessible: Yes
Pets: No
Special Packages: Special summer recreation and Olympic Park packages
Location: Park City Mountain Resort

The Silver King Hotel is located at the base of Park City Mountain Resort. The rooms are appointed with simple furniture that create an inviting ambience, and leave ample free space for luggage and gear. Naturally, this would not be a Park City hotel without a sauna, pool, fireplace, and two-minute walking access to Park City Mountain Resort. The guest rooms range from one-bedroom suites to three-bedroom condominiums.

SILVER QUEEN BOUTIQUE HOTEL
632 Main Street
Park City, UT 84060
435-649-5986; 1-800-447-6423
www.silverqueenhotel.com
Price: Moderate to Very Expensive
Credit Cards: AE, Disc, MC, V
Handicapped Accessible: Yes
Pets: No
Special Packages: No
Location: Park City Center

A sculpture in downtown Park City Jonathan Echlin

The Silver Queen, a small hotel of 12 varying suites, is Park City's ultimate in convenience. Tucked immediately among fine Main Street shops and fun bars, you are within walking distance of almost all of Park City's urban attractions. If that weren't enough, the Silver Queen has its own liquor license. Every suite is decorated in a hand-some, modern fashion, and has a washer and dryer and kitchen. Winter parking passes are given to guests free of charge, and eliminate the parking hassle of this central location. Visit the Web site for photographs as well as birds-eye schematics of each unit.

STEIN ERIKSEN LODGE
7700 Stein Way
Park City, UT 84060
435-649-3700; 1-800-453-1302
www.steinlodge.com
Price: Very Expensive
Credit Cards: AE, Disc, MC, V
Handicapped Accessible: Yes
Pets: No
Special Packages: Ski packages at Deer Valley
Location: Silver Lake Village at Deer Valley

If you wish to skip straight to five-diamond slope-side resort lodging, the Stein Eriksen Lodge should be your first choice. Though expensive, the rates here are actually comparable to some of the other less luxurious accommodations at this top-dollar resort. Located in the hills of Deer Valley's Silver Lake Village, it is situated immediately next to the Sterling and Viking Chairlifts. The Eriksen is not just for skiers; guests have access to advice on fishing, hiking, tennis, and horseback riding. The rooms are very private, but the hotel and surrounding Silver Lake Village is very populated, making socializing effortless. The lodge offers guests complimentary shuttle service to and from Park City in luxury sedans, with no reservations necessary.

SUNDIAL LODGE
4000 The Canyons Resort Drive
Park City, UT 84098
1-866-604-4171
www.thecanyons.com/sundialhome.html
Price: Expensive
Credit Cards: AE, Disc, MC, V

The lobby of the Sundial Lodge at The Canyons Resort Jonathan Echlin

Handicapped Accessible: Yes
Pets: No
Special Packages: Ski packages at The Canyons
Location: The Canyons

With underground parking, child care services, and staff available for assistance 24 hours a day, this Canyons lodge has plenty of comforts. All of the Canyons Village activities are within walking distance of the 150 rooms and condominiums. One of the best hidden perks is certainly the rooftop hot tub and its close proximity to the Sunrise Lift and Flight of the Canyons Gondola.

WESTGATE RESORT

3000 The Canyons Resort Drive
Park City, UT 84098
435-940-9444 or 1-877-819-4050
www.wgparkcity.com
Price: Very Expensive
Credit Cards: AE, Disc, MC, V
Handicapped Accessible: Yes
Pets: No
Special Packages: As available
Location: The Canyons Resort

For Canyons skiers and summer vacationers, the Westgate is an ideal choice for relaxation and convenience. The building itself is a massive modern lodge marked by thick timbers, stonework, and soaring glass lobbies. Skiers enjoy the ski-in, ski-out access and summer visitors appreciate the proximity to hiking trails and the golf course. The mountain surroundings can be appreciated throughout the year, as with the nearby nightlife and fine dining. The popular Westgate Grill, located on the premises, attracts not only guests but also customers from Salt Lake City and other surrounding towns. The Westgate has on-site child care. Guest villas range in size and amenities.

Bed & Breakfasts and Inns

1904 IMPERIAL HOTEL

221 Main Street
Park City, Utah 84068
435-649-1904
Price: Moderate to Expensive
Credit Cards: AE, Disc, MC, V
Handicapped Accessible: Limited (inquire)
Pets: By discretion
Special Packages: No
Location: Park City Center

A stay in the Imperial is a brush with history. This 1904 hotel was built as a bunkhouse for miners shortly after the devastating 1898 Main Street fire in the heyday of Park City's mining boom. Once a hospital and bordello, it is now a B&B. Its Main Street location cannot be topped for daytime shopping and nightlife. Each of the 10 rooms has its own private bath, and hot breakfast is served daily. Furnished simply with quaint period antiques, the Imperial's draw is its history, ambience, and location.

BLUE CHURCH LODGE AND TOWNHOMES
424 Park Avenue
Park City, UT 84060
435-649-8009; 1-800-626-5467
www.thebluechurchlodge.com
Price: Moderate to Expensive
Credit Cards: AE, MC, V
Handicapped Accessible: No
Pets: No
Special Packages: No
Location: Park City Center

Originally built in 1898 as Park City's first Mormon Church, the Blue Church Lodge and Townhouses now form their own lodging compound with a spa, fitness room, and free parking. Each town house has one to four bedrooms and is cozily outfitted in the way one would expect a B&B to be. Enjoy continental breakfast with other guests by the fireplace in the church lounge.

GOLDENER HIRSCH INN
7570 Royal Street
Park City, UT 84060
435-649-7770; 1-800-252-3373
www.goldenerhirschinn.com
Price: Expensive to Very Expensive
Credit Cards: AE, MC, V
Handicapped Accessible: Yes
Pets: No
Special Packages: Ski packages at Deer Valley
Location: Silver Lake Village at Deer Valley

With respect to skiing's alpine heritage, the four-diamond Goldener Hirsch decorates each guest room and suite with imported Austrian design. Recently renovated, each of the 20 rooms and suites is furnished with hand-carved, hand-painted Austrian furniture. A taste of the rustic without the sacrifice of comfort, these rooms each have a king-sized bed, mini bar, down bedding, and available fireplaces. This slope-side inn offers both an outdoor and indoor hot tub. In the Silver Lake Village of Deer Valley, guests here are immediately next to the Sterling and Viking Lifts. After a three-month face-lift in the fall of 2009, the Goldener Hirsch Inn and its restaurants will reopen in even grander style than before.

MARY E. SULLIVAN HOUSE
146 Main Street
Park City, UT 84060
435-731-0333; 1-800-803-9589
www.thistlesprings.com
Price: Moderate to Expensive
Credit Cards: AE, MC, V
Handicapped Accessible: No
Pets: No
Special Packages: No
Location: Downtown Park City

This guesthouse deviates from the Park City bed & breakfast norm. Instead of heavy pine furniture and southwestern schemes, it is decorated with delicate colors and lines suggestive of the Victorian era. Each guest room is themed with subdued uniqueness. Guests enjoy the shared formal parlor as well as sitting room. This home has survived Park City's passing eras since its construction in 1892.

OLD TOWN GUESTHOUSE
1011 Empire Avenue
435-649-2642; 1-800-290-6423
www.oldtownguesthouse.com
Price: Moderate to Expensive

Credit Cards: AE, MC, V
Handicapped Accessible: No
Pets: By discretion
Special Packages: No
Location: Park City Mountain Resort/Park City Downtown

The rooms of the Old Town Guesthouse have each been uniquely and quaintly decorated, as you would your family's favorite, old-fashioned ski lodge. Ample windows cast light onto the pine furniture, quilts, and braided area rugs. The effect is cozy, and it creates an atmosphere that feels more like home than this town's many done-up, modern hotels. Perched above town on Empire Avenue, guests have a view out over the rooftops of Park City. Perfect for casual vacationers, the Old Town's prices have a relatively low ceiling even in the height of ski season.

STAR HOTEL
227 Main Street
Park City, UT 84060
435-649-8333
www.rixey.net/starhotel
Price: Inexpensive to Moderate
Credit Cards: AE, Disc, MC, V
Handicapped Accessible: No
Pets: No
Special Packages: No
Location: Park City Center

Dubbed a hotel, the Star actually is much more like your grandmother's house, complete with breakfast, lunch, and dinner. However, it is located on the main street of one of the best ski towns in the country. The rooms are filled with quilts and photographs, and the halls with potted plants and paintings. This is perhaps the most affordable downtown Park City lodging, and certainly the homiest. Meals are served family-style.

WASHINGTON SCHOOL INN
543 Park Avenue
Park City, UT 84060
435-649-3800
www.washingtonschoolinn.com
Price: Moderate to Very Expensive
Credit Cards: AE, MC, V
Handicapped Accessible: No
Pets: No
Special Packages: Discounts on advanced booking
Location: Park City Center

If you are looking for the fullest historical experience on your vacation, stay at the Washington School Inn. One of the only surviving buildings of the 1898 fire, this school held its first class on November 18, 1889. In 1984 it was modernized and dramatically converted into the tasteful inn that it is today. The guest rooms, with four-poster beds and overstuffed down duvets, are each named after former teachers. For those who believe in ghosts, there is quite the lore of friendly encounters at the Washington School Inn.

WOODSIDE INN
1469 Woodside Avenue
Park City, UT 84060
435-649-3494; 1-888-241-5890
www.woodsideinn.com
Price: Moderate to Very Expensive
Credit Cards: Disc, MC, V
Handicapped Accessible: Yes
Pets: No
Special Packages: No
Location: Park City Mountain Resort/Park City Center

Although this is the closest bed & breakfast to Park City Mountain Resort, it is no more than a few minutes from The Canyons, Deer Valley, and Park City Center via the free city shuttle service. Built in 2000, the Woodside has the coziness of a B&B, but perks of modern design, such as double Jacuzzi tubs in each guest room and off-street, secured parking. Mornings begin with a full breakfast, and evenings are started with après ski refreshments.

Park City roofs in summer   Christine Balaz

Vacation Rentals

Park City's abundance of hotel and B&B accommodations is eclipsed by its vast selection of vacation rentals and lodging agencies. You may wish to begin your search with the reservations agents listed at the beginning of this section. These agents have a comprehensive understanding of all the lodging options within Park City, including the more fragmented sector of private rentals. Because many of these rentals are listed individually by private owners, the best source of collective information is a rental agency. If you are certain that your stay will be in a private rental, contact a vacation booking service. Most offer competitive rates, package offers, and one-stop shopping. Some even offer guided trip services.

Affordable Luxury Lodging (1-866-786-3755; www.affordableluxurylodging .com) takes pride in extending its clients the most affordable options possible, and will match any proven rate. They also assist with airfare searches. Although part of Park City Mountain Resort, **Park City Mountain Reservations** (435-649-8111 or 1-800-331-3178; www.parkcitymountain.com) has a breadth of knowledge that extends beyond just the mountain, and can assist you with virtually any reservation in the area. This company has a connection to 90 percent of Park City's accommodations. **Snow Valley Connection** (435-645-7700; www.snow

valleyconnection.com) is a local company that helps you find rentals based on your requirements for lodging space and location. **Utah Travel Connection** (801-453-1128; www.utahtravelconnection.com) can help you integrate a Park City trip into a larger tour of the Wasatch Region. Like many other companies of the region, Utah Travel Connection winter vacations focus mainly on ski vacations. Summer vacations extend into horseback riding, ranch, biking, and other western experiences as far away as Wyoming and Arizona. **Western Leisure** (1-800-532-2113; www.western leisure.com) offers complete vacation services that extend far beyond lodging to guided fishing, hiking, and even snowmobile tours and massage therapy. You are picked up at the airport and escorted to your hotel and all your destinations.

While some agencies offer general knowledge, others have specific domains. **The Canyons Central Reservations** (1-866-604-4171; www.thecanyons.com) can assist you with any Canyons accommodations, as well as help you navigate dining and other recreation options. For Deer Valley–specific reservations, go directly to the source: **Deer Valley Central Reservations** (435-649-1000 or 1-800-558-3337; www .deervalley.com). Although Deer Valley is but one resort, it has three separate villages, each with hotels and vacation rentals. **Park City Mountain Resort** (1-800-331-3178; www.parkcitymountain.com) has its own specialists that will make your trip as seamless as possible. Guests vacationing at Park City ski free on the first day of their stay.

RESTAURANTS

For as much as Park City can work up your appetite, it can satiate it. Park City will expand your expectations of small-mountain-town cuisine. With much more discretionary income than the "average"

community, the people of Park City can afford to demand fresh and exotic fare. While some restaurants honor their frontier heritage by serving elk loin, the menus of others pay tribute to the alpine history of skiing with Austrian cuisine. But Park City's worldly population would not be satisfied without Japanese, French, Thai, contemporary American, Italian, and Middle Eastern cuisine. You can expect a full range of formality as well, from proper wine service at Bangkok Thai to a juicy burger on the deck of the Pig Pen Saloon while still wearing ski gear. It seems that the most popular food in Park City is perhaps sushi and deluxe steak, as these items appear on the menu in establishments where you may not expect them.

Because of Park City's close quarters and mining history, many of your meals will be enjoyed in buildings dating back to the Main Street fire of 1898. Of course, with more than 100 restaurants in the area, many of these establishments have chosen locations in the spacious shopping centers of Kimball Junction and on the slopes of the ski resorts. Many restaurants enable you to continue your celebration of the outdoors with patio dining. If you have an urge to eat out, but cannot overcome the comfort of your hotel room, **Mountain Express Deliveries** (435-649-6368; www.mountainexpressdelivery .com) delivers from more than 20 restaurants, Tues. through Sun., for a modest fee.

350 MAIN STREET
NEW AMERICAN BRASSIERE

350 Main Street
Downtown Park City
435-649-3140
www.350main.com
Cuisine: Contemporary American
Serving: D
Open: Daily
Price: Expensive
Credit Cards: AE, Disc, MC, V
Reservations: Recommended
Handicapped Accessible: Yes

350 Main Street is home to some of Park City's staple contemporary American cuisine. With a menu that relies on the freshness and utmost quality of its ingredients, the selection here is always changing. Generally, you can expect a variety of meats and fish interpreted in many different ways. The theme tends toward fresh fish and Japanese preparations. Venison medallions are listed next to ono-ono, and sides range from edamame to mushroom pâté and four-cheese ravioli. Though the meals are all derived from healthy, whole foods, you can check the calorie content of each starter on the online menu.

ADOLPH'S

1500 Kearns Boulevard
Park City
435-649-7177
www.adolphsrestaurant.com
Cuisine: Swiss Continental
Serving: D
Open: Daily
Price: Expensive
Credit Cards: AE, MC, V
Reservations: Recommended
Handicapped Accessible: Yes (inquire)

The menu is divided into major categories of veal, seafood, and many entrées and chef's specials, including duckling à l'orange, Swiss bratwurst, and elk tenderloin. The plates are drizzled in house béarnaise, glacé, and other delicate sauces. The fresh vegetables are braised to tenderness. Adolph's proudly features a full bar and extensive wine selection, which will only add to your experience here. This establishment is perfect for those who seek a formal affair, yet also offers less formidable bar and patio seating with a separate menu.

BACCHUS WINE BAR

442 Main Street
Park City
435-940-9463

Cuisine: Contemporary Eclectic
Serving: D
Open: Daily
Price: Moderate to Expensive
Credit Cards: AE, MC, V
Reservations: Yes
Handicapped Accessible: No

With all of the excellent restaurants in Park City, it is very possible that you may eat a bit more than you will play. If this is the case, you may appreciate a detour away from large decadent plates and toward smaller portions interrupted by tastes of wine. Many of the wines may be new to you, as the emphasis here is on boutique wineries. Artisan cheeses complement their flights of wine. If you aren't into fermented grapes, the Bacchus has a full bar. Dessert can be taken as a sweet treat or as any of their fine coffees or teas. The atmosphere is a bath of decadent reds featuring lounge couches with intermittent high-backed bar stools. If you wish to spend your evening at one of the many outdoor summer concerts, the Bacchus will even prepare a basket packed with their finger food and wine.

BAJA CANTINA

1284 Empire Avenue
Park City Mountain Resort Center
435-649-2252
www.bajaparkcity.com
Cuisine: Mexican
Serving: L, D
Open: Daily
Price: Inexpensive
Credit Cards: AE, Disc, MC, V
Reservations: No
Handicapped Accessible: Yes

To keep its doors open in Park City's real estate market as a Mexican restaurant, the Baja Cantina must be doing something right. Located right at the base of the Park City Mountain Resort, this is a perfect summer or winter stop for ravenous appetites and alcoholic head rushes. The restaurant's atmosphere, filled with jungle-like colors and three-dimensional plant simulations, carries the spirit of fun, while the menu, filled with venerable family recipes, expertly satiates the most bottomless pit. Baja uses the healthiest ingredients appropriate for Mexican food in order to create its refreshing dishes.

BANGKOK THAI ON MAIN

605 Main Street
Park Hotel, First Floor
Downtown Park City
435-649-8424
www.bangkokthaionmain.com
Cuisine: Thai
Serving: D
Open: Daily
Price: Expensive
Credit Cards: AE, Disc, MC, V
Reservations: Yes
Handicapped Accessible: No

This is the locals' go-to Thai restaurant, and an upscale one at that. The food is of the highest quality and served with a gourmet presentation. The main dining area is highly formal and accordingly pricy; the bar side of the restaurant serves a limited selection of the full menu—at a more casual price—in a much more relaxed atmosphere. Its Main Street location and selection of over 500 different wines are a huge boon. In 2008, Bangkok Thai was the winner of Utah's Best in State Best Fine Dining Establishment.

BLIND DOG

1781 Sidewinder Drive
Prospector Square
435-655-0800
www.blinddoggrill.com
Cuisine: Surf and turf, sushi
Serving: D
Open: Daily
Price: Expensive to Very Expensive
Credit Cards: AE, Disc, MC, V
Reservations: Yes
Handicapped Accessible: Yes

Just a short departure from Main Street, the Blind Dog on Sidewinder Drive can reunite you with your New England seafood favorites. Under the same roof, you can also choose from a steak selection or Japanese menu. The lobster, blue crab, and fresh ocean fish are served whole, as well as in egg rolls and soups. They are complemented on the menu by land-dwelling offerings and, of course, a sushi bar. The restaurant offers two dining options: a more formal dining room, as well as a kicked-back sushi restaurant. The menu is categorized by "The Butcher Shop," "Fish Market," and "Produce." Although the decor is high-end with elegant lighting, wood paneling, and white linens, lighthearted paintings brighten the atmosphere.

THE CABIN

4000 The Canyons Resort Drive
Grand Summit Resort Hotel, The Canyons Resort
435-615-8060
http://www.thecanyons.com/dining.html
Cuisine: Contemporary American
Serving: B, L, D
Open: Daily (hours change seasonally)
Price: Expensive to Very Expensive
Credit Cards: AE, MC, V
Reservations: Recommended
Handicapped Accessible: Yes

This regional cuisine specialist combines the coziness of western American dining with the excellence of a culinary master. Each plate has simplistic regional themes with gourmet details and presentation. Inspiration is drawn from the surrounding areas, and ingredients are harvested locally when possible. The masterpiece is in the details, and in the delicate preparation of the foods that lets them speak for themselves. Fresh, regional herbs and vegetables accent the dishes. The Cabin's venison loin has been honored as the best dish in Utah. In keeping with seasonal appropriateness, ingredient availability, and the chef's inventiveness, the menu changes frequently and features many daily specials.

CHENÉZ

710 Main Street
Marriott Summit Watch Plaza
Downtown Park City
435-940-1909
www.chenez.com
Cuisine: French
Serving: D
Open: Daily
Price: Very Expensive
Credit Cards: AE, MC, V
Reservations: Required
Handicapped Accessible: Yes

Chenéz boasts Park City's most deeply traditional French dining experience, with an elegant atmosphere and a chef who compares eating to romantic encounters. Food is considered a fine art here, and items appearing on the menu include quail, rabbit, and elk loin. Centuries' worth of French culinary delights are accompanied with sauces and sides like demi-glace, hollandaise, mustard, capers, and mushrooms.

CHEZ BETTY

1637 Short Line Drive
Copperbottom Inn
435-649-8181
www.chezbetty.com
Cuisine: Contemporary American and French
Serving: D
Open: Daily Dec. through Mar.; Thurs. through Mon. from May through Nov.
Price: Expensive
Credit Cards: AE, Disc, MC, V
Reservations: Yes
Handicapped Accessible: Yes

The menu is comprised of dishes made from the freshest available ingredients, gracefully seasoned and carefully paired, extracting the natural flavors of the food. Items include decadently tender steaks, native red trout, and house-made pastas with fresh herbs. Tender baby greens and seasonal assortments of vegetables accent each plate. Chez Betty is an excellent choice for groups that include vegetarians. A Park City institution since 1991.

CHIMAYO

368 Main Street
Downtown Park City
435-649-6222
www.chimayorestaurant.com
Cuisine: Contemporary southwestern
Serving: D
Open: Daily
Price: Moderate to Very Expensive
Credit Cards: AE, Disc, MC, V
Reservations: Yes
Handicapped Accessible: Yes (call ahead)

This is southwestern fare cooked with grace of a gourmet establishment. Take a leave from rice and beans and savor fresh regional game. Meats are delicately cut and touched with citrus and spice. Sour cream is replaced with crème fraische. Enchiladas drizzled with honey are served alongside chili-cured duck and sugarcane elk satays with chipotle crème. Main courses feature larger cuts of red meat and delicate seafood creations. The atmosphere is filled with Mexican American flair, but maintains the elegance one would expect from a genuine highbrow Mexican eatery. Rarely has southwestern cuisine seen such intricate care and skilled exploration. The wine list holds up against the cuisine selection.

EATING ESTABLISHMENT

317 Main Street
Downtown Park City
435-649-8284
www.theeatingestablishment.net
Cuisine: American, barbecue

Serving: B, L, D
Open: Daily
Price: Inexpensive to Moderate
Credit Cards: AE, Disc, MC, V
Reservations: Yes
Handicapped Accessible: Yes

Utah—in the traditional down-home, big-family sense—comes to Park City. For a more casual dinner, or an escape from serial continental breakfasts, journey to Main Street's Eating Establishment. This is a perfect lunching venue for families with fun, simple items for children and more adventuresome, regional fare for adults. Lunch and dinner include items from Alaskan halibut and Rocky Mountain trout to straightforward burgers of the meat and garden varieties. Breakfast is served all day, and lunch extends into the evening, providing options to kids or adults seeking a less elaborate meal. As the oldest full-service restaurant in Park City, the Eating Establishment has found a niche among locals and tourists alike. Having a liquor license probably helps.

GRAPPA ITALIAN CAFE

151 Main Street
Downtown Park City
435-645-0636
www.grapparestaurant.com
Cuisine: Italian
Serving: D
Open: Daily
Price: Moderate to Very Expensive
Credit Cards: AE, Disc, V
Reservations: Yes
Handicapped Accessible: No

More of an Italian experience than a restaurant, Grappa surrounds guests with traditional stone fireplaces inside, and vines weaving through the wrought iron of the patio's perimeter outside. While some of the items may seem familiar from other Italian American dining experiences, many of its traditional dishes can usually only be experienced in Italy. Wine preparations, flaky pastries, earthy herbs, and of course fresh pastas all complement the featured meat and vegetables of each dish.

KAMPAI

586 Main Street
Downtown Park City
435-649-0655
Cuisine: Japanese and Asian fusion
Serving: L, D
Open: Daily
Price: Moderate to Expensive
Credit Cards: AE, MC, V
Reservations: Dinner only
Handicapped Accessible: Yes (via back entrance)

Perhaps it is the rarified air of Park City's mountains or the pervasive good health of the people. Whatever it is, Park City is stacked with restaurants serving the delicate, fresh foods of Asia. Kampai fits right in at the top of these exceptional establishments, serving what many consider to be the best sushi in town. Not only are the rolls in contention to be the most authentic, the selection is the most extensive and often creative of any sushi restaurant in town. If someone in your party does not particularly favor nori or uncooked yellowtail, the Asian fusion menu offers savory dishes such as miso-marinated sea bass. People who love Salt Lake City's Takashi Restaurant find this to be its Park City cousin.

LOCO LIZARD CANTINA

Kimball Plaza
Kimball Junction
435-645-7000
www.locolizardcantina.com
Cuisine: Mexican
Serving: B (Sat. and Sun. only), L, D
Open: Daily
Price: Moderate to Expensive
Credit Cards: AE, MC, V
Reservations: No

Handicapped Accessible: Yes

With its slightly remote location in Kimball Junction, secluded outdoor patio, and casual atmosphere, the Loco Lizard is the perfect place for a summer pitcher of beer after a long bicycle ride. Removed from downtown, with easier parking and less competitive crowds, this is a place where you can stretch your legs and linger while you digest. Although the appetizers are delicious, the main course portions are classically enormous. The waitstaff keeps your basket full of house chips and salsas, in case of ravenous hunger. Tucked behind the Wells Fargo Bank, the Loco Lizard is not visible from the main road, so a glance at a map or explicit directions from a local will make your search vastly easier.

MAIN STREET PIZZA & NOODLE

525 Main Street
Downtown Park City
435-645-8878
www.mainstreetpizzanoodle.com
Cuisine: Casual American
Serving: B, L, D
Open: Daily
Price: Inexpensive
Credit Cards: V, MC
Reservations: No
Handicapped Accessible: No

Not every meal must be elaborate, but every meal should be good. This is a beloved lunch spot in Park City, known for its fast service, fresh ingredients, and generous proportions—a great detour from formal, three-course meals. Pizza and pasta are the staple here, with a serious selection within each category—but sandwiches and burgers can be had as well. All of the reliable standards appear on the menu alongside many tasteful deviants that are sure to please a more adventurous palate. For the less ravenous individuals, soups and salads await your attention.

THE MUSTANG

890 Main Street
Downtown Park City
435-658-3975
www.mustangparkcity.com
Cuisine: Mixed American, Asian, and Mexican
Serving: D
Open: Daily Dec. through Mar.; Thurs. through Mon. from May through Nov.
Price: Expensive to Very Expensive
Credit Cards: AE, DC, Disc, MC, V
Reservations: Yes
Handicapped Accessible: Yes

Among mixed company or simply can't decide on your cuisine before you arrive at a restaurant? The Mustang can please almost any appetite in gourmet style. Known for unusual combinations and a blending of styles and ingredients, it will expand your horizons. Duck chile relleno, papaya mixed greens, and lobster with grapefruit salsa are some examples of their deliciously atypical cuisine. The atmosphere is a modern addition to Park City's Main Street. Mustang has a full bar.

RED ROCK BREWERY

1640 West Redstone Center Drive
Kimball Junction
435-575-0295
www.redrockbrewing.com
Cuisine: American and Italian
Serving: B (Sat and Sun), L, D
Open: Daily
Price: Inexpensive to Expensive
Credit Cards: AE, MC, V
Reservations: Yes
Handicapped Accessible: Yes

Tucked back in one of Kimball Junction's outdoor malls, Red Rock can most easily be found by consulting with a local. A brewpub serving its own beers, the Red Rock takes its restaurant side seriously and serves many full entrées and daily specials that often feature fresh regional fish and produce. The menu here tends toward Italian American cuisine with wild mushroom pizza and many pasta dishes, although grilled sandwiches and filet mignon also make the list. A children's menu is available. Red Rock Brewery consistently wins awards for its beers and restaurant alike, most notably America's Best Large Brewpub of the Year at the 2007 Great American Beer Festival.

RIVERHORSE CAFÉ

540 Main Street
Downtown Park City
435-649-3536
www.riverhorsegroup.com
Cuisine: Contemporary American
Serving: D
Open: Daily
Price: Inexpensive to Expensive
Credit Cards: AE, MC, V
Reservations: Yes
Handicapped Accessible: No

The Riverhorse is yet another nationally acclaimed Park City gem. Named one of the top restaurants in North and Central America, this restaurant has been prestigious since its opening in 1987. The dining room is a chicly redone industrial space with soaring ceilings and tall windows that overlook Main Street. Jazz and other live music accompanies meals most every evening. An award-winning wine list and fine regional game will help finish any day properly. The menu integrates the cuisine of many cultures. During summer months, try to get a table on the open balcony over Main Street.

SHABU

333 Main Street
Main Street Mall, Second Floor
Downtown Park City
435-645-7253
www.shabupc.com
Cuisine: Asian
Serving: D
Open: Daily

Price: Expensive
Credit Cards: AE, MC, V
Reservations: Dinner only
Handicapped Accessible: Yes

In keeping with Utah's emerging tradition of outstanding cuisine, Shabu was listed as one of the best 12 new restaurants in the United States by Condé Nast Traveler. Naturally, this is considered one of Park City's finest restaurants. Dishes are the result of adventuresome, modern interpretations of traditional Asian dishes. Adding to the experience is a sake martini bar and live dinner music every Thursday, Friday, and Saturday.

THE STEW POT

1375 Deer Valley Drive
Deer Valley Plaza
435-645-7839
Cuisine: Casual American
Serving: L, D
Open: Daily
Price: Inexpensive
Credit Cards: AE, Disc MC, V
Reservations: Yes
Handicapped Accessible: Yes

Considering Park City's many physically demanding activities, lunch can be as important a meal as dinner. The Stew Pot offers healthy, simple fare made with fresh ingredients in satiating quantities. The soups and stews change daily according to season and available ingredients. These can be paired with the many sandwiches and burgers. Although the sandwiches tend to fall in line with a traditional selection, their subtle twists and fresh ingredients make them interesting. In the summer months, take advantage of their lakeside deck.

WASATCH BREW PUB

250 Main Street
Downtown Park City
435-649-0900
www.wasatchbeers.com

Cuisine: Casual American
Serving: L, D
Open: Daily
Price: Inexpensive to Moderate
Credit Cards: AE, MC, V
Reservations: No
Handicapped Accessible: Yes (on main level)

For a quick dinner during peak dinner hours, the Wasatch Brew Pub is a good option. With one of the juiciest burgers around, as well as a healthy selection of salads and other sandwiches, the menu is simple and fast. If you get caught waiting at the front door, you can go upstairs to their full bar.

ATTRACTIONS

Museums

ALF ENGEN SKI MUSEUM
2990 Bear Hollow Drive
Utah Olympic Park
435-658-4233
www.engenmuseum.org
Open: Daily 9–6; closed on selected holidays.
Admission: Free
Handicapped Accessible: Partially

Located in the Utah Olympic Park at the site of the 2002 Olympic Nordic Ski Jumps, the Alf Engen Ski Museum was built to commemorate the ski history of Park City and its Olympic experience. Interactive ski simulations and a photographic diary of the 2002 Olympics make the trip up the hill well worth it. These simulations help you get an inkling of what it might be like to go 90 miles per hour on an Olympic downhill course with nothing between you and the ground but a helmet and spandex suit. Perhaps the most visceral aspect of the whole experience is standing beneath the Nordic ski jumps and realizing just exactly what their scale is. Also at the museum is the Intermountain Ski Hall of Fame, a registry of the skiers considered to have had a significant impact on the skiing of the Intermountain West region.

PARK CITY OLD TOWN MUSEUM AND TERRITORIAL JAIL
528 Main Street
435-615-9559
www.parkcityhistory.org
Open: 11–5 Mon. through Sat.; 12–6 Sun.
Admission: $10 adults, $5 children 7-17, free 6 and under.
Handicapped Accessible: Yes

This is a great one-stop, town-center trip that will efficiently guide you through Park City's mining, skiing, and even the punitive history of the Old West. Exhibits include recreated mine shafts, stagecoaches, and the original 1885 Park City Territorial Jail. With its front door right on Main Street, this is a convenient history lesson that can be taken in between visiting galleries or after a morning of skiing. A recent renovation has modernized the facility and brightened its interior, making it a more inviting space for visitors.

Gardens and Parks

Park City has two main city parks, and no more. The lack of parks is perhaps due to the fact that the population of Park City spends most of their outdoor time out of the city limits. In case you would like to throw an outdoor barbecue, these small parks have picnic and barbecue facilities available for group reservations. Call Park City for more information (435-615-5401; www.parkcity.org). South Park (1354 Park Avenue) is located just south of the Old Miner's Hospital. Rotary Park (Payday Drive) is tucked just behind the Park City Golf Course, which surrounds you with even more greenery.

Although not a typical city park with swing sets and manicured grass, the **Historic Union Pacific Trail** (435-649-6839; www.stateparks.utah.gov) is a great opportunity for joggers, walkers, and bikers to stretch their legs without gearing up for a serious hike. This 28-mile section of former railroad track follows part of the path of the first transcontinental railroad. The trail is paved in places, but much of this asphalt is flanked by wide gravel shoulders that give your knees reprieve from pounding. Though few joggers reach the end, a long day of biking could get you to the mouth of Echo Canyon. Access to the trailhead and parking is in Prospector Park, in Park City at the junction of UT 224 and UT 248 (also called Park Avenue and Kearns Boulevard).

Amusement Parks

What Park City lacks in roller coasters and other traditional amusement park rides, it makes up for with other one-of-a-kind gravity-powered mountain adventures. Winter or summer, you can find some sort of fast-moving seat that will send you screaming down a track or slope of sorts.

The **Alpine Slide** (Park City Mountain Resort; 1-800-222-7275; www.parkcitymountain .com) at Park City Mountain Resort was not part of the Olympics, but was certainly inspired by the events. A descent of 550 vertical feet over nearly 0.5 mile will thrill you and your children. Because of built-in passenger speed control, this is a safer venture than it sounds. While at Park City Mountain Resort in the summer, check to see if their outdoor **Climbing Wall** will be in service. Not a proper training facility, this recreational wall is fun for novices and children. Another treat for kids is the **Little Miners Park** (Park City Mountain Resort; 1-800-222-7275; www.parkcitymountain.com). A miniature train, carousel, and carnival-style airplane make this a safe day of outdoor adventure for younger children.

The Alpine Slide was fun, but you want to take it up a notch. You have only to sit back and "relax" as the-passenger-with-an-experienced-driver at the **Bobsled Rides** of the Utah Olympic Park (3419 Olympic Parkway; 435-658-4200; www.olyparks.com). With speeds of up to 70 mph, a minimum age of 14 and some serious guts are required. Cost is $65 per person and you should call ahead to schedule a ride.

If you've always wanted to go 50 mph down an Olympic ski hill but just don't have the knees, the **Zip Lines** at the Utah Olympic Park (3419 Olympic Parkway; 435-658-4200; www .olyparks.com) are a perfect summer opportunity for such a thing. With two separate lines, "Ultra Zip" and "Extreme Zip," you can travel the lengths of both the K120 Ski Jump Hill and the freestyle bumps course. Passengers ride in seats.

Historic Buildings and Sites

Many historic buildings and homes dating back to the 1880s exist on and around Main

Street. Although you can begin investigating these with a virtual tour online (www.parkcity history.org), you may be able to guess fairly accurately which of the homes are original; the modest size and simple, charming architecture of these homes suggest their era.

Park City's Main Street, although repeatedly devoured by pandemic fires before 1900, has retained essentially the same configuration and flavor. The steep streets are packed with compact buildings. Many of the buildings have undergone serious face-lifts, replacing flammable wood with reliable brick. The façades have changed as well. The onetime suppliers of a working town have now been replaced by the trappings of a wealthy mountain town. Awnings of lighting and electrical companies have been replaced by bronzed signs of galleries, restaurants, and saloons. The historic buildings of Main Street are still functional homes or businesses. For example, Kampai, a Japanese restaurant (586 Main Street), is found in the old Park City Mortuary. Also on Main Street is the 1881 Miners Union Hall and Egyptian Theatre. The old Utah Coal and Lumber Building on the corner of Main and Heber Streets is now the Easy Street Brasserie & Bar.

Olympic statue, north of Park City Jonathan Echlin

If you are curious about Park City's history, a convenient duck into the **Park City Historical Society & Museum's** doors (528 Main Street; 435-649-7457; $7 admission to the museum, as listed above) will kick off an informational tour. Inside this museum, originally built in 1885 as the City Hall, you will have a chance to check out Park City's old Territorial Jail and see exhibits of restored stagecoaches, mining equipment, and other artifacts that illustrate what Utah pioneer and mining life was like more than 100 years ago. The museum offers a walking guide that will point out some of the more than 100 historical buildings and homes in Park City. Along your way, you may notice than few of the old town's buildings are older than 1898, the year a fire consumed more than 200 buildings in the town.

St. Mary's Catholic Church Old Town Chapel (121 Park Avenue; 435-649-9676; www.st marysparkcity.com), on the southern end of town, is the oldest continuously operational church in Utah. Looking at the purposeful brick architecture of the church, you might not guess that it was built during the time all of the other buildings in Park City flew into construction. In fact, the original wooden church of 1881 burned to the ground. Not to be deterred, the congregation commissioned a second church. This time it was constructed with deliberate masonry, and the church was opened for service in 1884.

Washington School Inn (543 Park Avenue), previously the George Washington School, was opened in 1889. It retained its original function until 1931 when a declining student population forced its abandonment as a school. It was purchased for use as a social hall by the Veterans of Foreign Wars in 1936 and was used for a few decades as such.

Egyptian Theatre, downtown Park City
Jonathan Echlin

Egyptian Theatre (328 Main Street; 435-649-9371; www.egyptiantheatrecompany.org) was built in the 1880s with $30,000 worth of funds raised from the community (compared with the $13,000 used to build the George Washington School). This lavish opera house, like almost every other building in Park City, was consumed in the fire of 1898. The Dewey Theater was built on the current site of the Egyptian Theatre. Though the theater has undergone many face-lifts and name changes, it has remained a constant thread throughout Park City's patchy history.

Old Miners Hospital (1354 Park Avenue) was built on land donated by the Nelson Family at the base of present-day Park City Mountain Resort. Opened in 1904, it served as a hospital until the 1950s when its facilities became obsolete, and it was abandoned. It later became a boardinghouse, and soon after, a youth hostel. When it was threatened with demolition because of its loca-

Old Miners Hospital |Jonathan Echlin

tion, Parkites went into a flurry of fund-raising to save this historical building, which was moved to its current location and became home to the Park City Public Library in 1982. The volunteers that spearheaded this effort performed much of the reconstruction labor to save on costs. In 1993 the library outgrew its walls, and the Old Miners Hospital became a community center.

Additionally, some of the old mining history of the town is preserved at the ski areas. **Park City Mountain Resort** is located in the hills of some of these old mines, including the dominant Silver King Mine. Skiers and mountain bikers today can see some of the old infrastructure from the chairlifts. Some of this includes buildings and water pumps. Additionally, the functional Mid-Mountain Lodge at Park City, adjacent to the Pioneer Lift, is a preserved old social hall and boardinghouse for the Silver King Mine. In its century of use, it fed a thousand or more miners daily, and was where many miners took their nightly slumber. It became home to the U.S. Ski Team in 1970, and was relocated 400 feet to avoid demolition in 1987. Now it serves mountain guests with restrooms and a restaurant.

Echo Canyon (20 miles northeast of Park City), although now bustling with the traffic of I-80, has a distinct place in U.S. history as the passageway for most east-west migrations. Animals and pursuing indigenous hunters of prehistory migrated seasonally through this portal. Fur trappers and traders accessed the region through this canyon too, and it proved to be one of the only passable routes through the Rocky Mountains for pioneers and prospectors headed to California. Accordingly, the Overland Express, Pony Express, first transcontinental railroad, and Lincoln Highway all ran through here to connect the eastern plains to the Utah desert and beyond.

A jog or mountain bike ride can help you take advantage of the **Historic Union Pacific Rail Trail**. This state park is a 28-mile section along the path of the first transcontinental railroad. Closed to motorized traffic, the gently graded trail connects Park City to Wanship, Coalville, and eventually the Echo Reservoir. The Echo Canyon Dam was completed in 1930 after three years of work by the Bureau of Reclamation.

Sports Teams

Again, Park City offers anything you could ever want, but in a flavor all its own. You won't find a professional football team within 400 miles of Park City, but you will find the headquarters for the **U.S. Ski and Snowboard Team** (www.usskiteam.com). Under the umbrella of this organization are all kinds of World Cup–level ski teams, from alpine racing to Nordic jumping, disabled alpine racing, Nordic racing, and freestyle competition. The natural surroundings and accompanying presence of these world-class organizations begets virtual farm teams, inspiring kids as young as two years old to get out and make "pizzas" on the snow. Half-pipes teem with professional and aspiring park rats, and race gates are slapped by the shins and forearms of skiers in training and World Cup racers.

Chairs at Silver Lake Village, Deer Valley
Jonathan Echlin

Many of the World Cup events are easy to attend as a spectator. For alpine racing, go to **Park City Mountain Resort**. The events take place both in the daytime and evenings. If you are not fortunate enough to catch a World Cup event, plenty of local races take place, in which the youth and young adults of the region compete. **Deer Valley Resort** hosts many World Cup Freestyle events. Their regulation moguls course and aerial jumps are lit up at night for competitions and adjoining free concerts.

Nightlife

Although Park City's original function as a mining town has diminished, along with the shoot-'em-up saloons and women of ill repute, the boisterous flavor remains. Park City has a history of having the most concentrated, consistently vibrant nightlife of any city in Utah. During Prohibition, Park City had 21 bars open for business, and all but one continued to serve drinks throughout these dry times. This attitude continues today, and you will notice only very minor restrictions imposed by state law.

Because of serving restrictions in bars, a mixed drink can contain only 1.5 ounces of liquor by law; your bartender is not trying to insult you with a weak drink. Ordering "side cars" (extra shots that you could formerly mix into your own drink) is no longer an option, after the 2009 increase in shot size. Luckily, though, the idea of "Private Clubs" also vanished in 2009, and now a bar is just a bar—no membership of any kind required—just a valid ID and 21 years of age. A state liquor store is the only place where wine, liquor, and "real beer" can be purchased outside a bar or restaurant. There are three state liquor stores within the Park City area, two in town: the largest in the area (1901 Sidewinder Drive, Prospector Square; 435-649-7254; open 10 AM–8 PM) and a smaller, yet closer one (524 Main Street; 435-649-3293; open 11 AM–10 PM). Another can be found in Kimball Junction (Kimball Plaza at Kimball Junction; 435-658-0860; open 11 AM–7 PM). All are closed on holidays and Sundays.

Park City has many different areas of activity, each like a small town within the same community. These are Main Street, Kimball Junction, and the ski resorts. Each area is rich with activities, restaurants, and nightlife, so many people begin and end the day in the same place. Park City's **Main Street** and environs has the highest concentration of bars and nightclubs. A Park City institution for more than 20 years, **Cicero's Nightclub** (306 Main Street; 435-649-6800; www.ciseros.com) tends to draw young crowds with big-name artists and large sound systems. This is a place where stars unite during the Sundance Film Festival, and parties continue into the early morning. **Club 412** (412 Main Street above Bistro 412; 435-649-8230) offers quiet live music in an intimate atmosphere with aromas of the French kitchen below. **Harry O's** (427 Main Street; 435-655-7579; www.harryos-pc .com) is another nightclub in the vein of Cicero's. With a four-sided bar downstairs, go-go dancers, and a spacious dance floor, this establishment has a perfect setup for catching a major music group. For a surprisingly low cost, you can gain VIP seating in the horseshoe balcony above with service from a private cocktail waitress. The **Hungry Moose Sports Pub** (438 Main Street; 435-649-8600) is a place where families are welcome and sports fans congregate. Pitchers of beer, finger food, and big-screen televisions are the game here. **J. B. Mulligan's Club & Pub** (804 Main Street; 435-658-0717) is another establishment where you can relax in a less glitzy atmosphere among sportscasts and very inexpensive beers on Mondays. **The No Name Saloon** (447 Main Street; 435-649-6667; www.noname saloon.net), formerly the Alamo Saloon, is a small space with an impressive collection of liquor and antiques. The buffalo burger is popular, and the copper bar sets a good old-fashioned mining town aesthetic. **The Spur** (352 Main, behind 350 Main Restaurant; 435-615-1618; www.thespurbarandgrill.com) is a fun, darkened bar with live music and a cozy, wooden dance floor. A pub menu is available for casual diners. For late-night eats, **Butcher's** (751 Main Street; 435-647-0040; www.butcherschophouse.com) is the one of the only establishments serving food into the early morning. **O'Shucks Bar & Grill** (427 Main Street; 435-645-3999) serves mighty large draft beers, has in-the-shell peanuts for munching, and keeps its grill open until 1am.

Kimball Junction has an installment of Park City's **Red Rock Brew Pub** (1640 West Redstone Center Drive; 435-575-0275; www.redrockbrewing.com). Though this functions primarily as a restaurant—as opposed to a pub—this is a great place to enjoy an extended dinner without sitting on your neighbor.

Finally, the mountain resorts function year-round as social venues. These would not be complete without sufficient après ski opportunities (see Chapter 4, Ski Country). During

The famous Utah snow blankets a neighborhood   Jonathan Echlin

winter, après ski cocktails dominate the scene, but the summer months bring a completely different experience with live outdoor concerts (see the "Music" section of this chapter).

Finally, you would not want to miss the **Friday Night Gallery Strolls**, which begin at 6 PM at the Kimball Art Center (638 Park Avenue; 435-649-8882; www.kimballartcenter.org) on the last Friday of each month (except January, when the Sundance Film Festival consumes Park City). These evenings are filled with hors d'oeuvres and jazz.

Salt Lake City 2002 Winter Olympic Facilities

The Utah Winter Sports Park and Olympic Sports Park (2990 Bear Hollow Drive; 435-658-4541; www.olyparks.com) immediately south of I-80 in Kimball Junction can be reached by following signs to the Park City Visitor's Center. The Center has the most user-friendly and awe-inspiring collection of Salt Lake City 2002 Winter Olympic information. For your pleasure, the park now has the Alf Engen Museum with Intermountain West Ski Hall of Fame and a Bobsled Ride. This was an actual competition site of the 2002 Olympics and today hosts some of the U.S. training facilities for the bobsled, Nordic ski jumps, luge, and skeleton. Freestyle ski jumpers put on quite a show for spectators during summer months while training over the splash pool. As a passenger, you can ride in a bobsled (driven by an experienced athlete) or fiddle with the simulation machines in the Alf Engen Ski Museum between inspecting historic ski memorabilia.

Soldier Hollow (Wasatch Mountain State Park, Midway; 435-654-2002; www.soldierhollow .com), about 20 minutes south of Park City in Midway and now open to the public for aerobic recreation and competition, was Park City's second major site for Olympic competition. A challenging, hilly course for Nordic skiers, today it offers less strenuous activities, such as tubing, snowshoeing, and summer hiking. For all information relating to these Park City Olympic facilities, call 801-581-5445.

Libraries

Park City has but one library, the Park City Public Library (1255 Park Avenue; 435-615-5600; www.parkcitylibrary.org). A small library, it does offer Internet access and a collection of media. The library opened in 1917 and has undergone several relocations that required full community assistance, from fund-raising to a book brigade and actual volunteer construction efforts.

ARTS AND ENTERTAINMENT

Park City is one of Utah's hotbeds for arts and entertainment. Naturally, the winter months are heavily affected by the Sundance Film Festival. During January, every theater is booked back-to-back with screenings. An arts and entertainment entourage, comprised of nationally popular musicians and artists, follows the festival. When the festival is over, the ski industry keeps entertainers coming to Park City. Summer is packed with outdoor arts and music festivals that draw Salt Lake citizens up from the valley.

Venues

Although many restaurants and bars in Park City are vibrant with live music, only a few venues in this petite mining town are large enough for major events. The Canyons (www .thecanyons.com) and Deer Valley (www.deervalley.com) come alive in the summer with the erection of stages in their amphitheaters. Surprisingly, they also host outdoor concerts in the winter. For further information on particular festivals, see the "Music" section of this chapter.

For Park City comedy and drama, the **Egyptian Theatre** (328 Main Street; 435-649-9371; www.egyptiantheatrecompany.org) has been the go-to venue since 1889. Comedy nights can be taken in at the **Side Car** (333 Main Street; 435-645-7468; www.sidecarbar .com). The **Eccles Center for the Performing Arts** (1750 Kearns Boulevard; 435-655-3114; www.ecclescenter.org) is the town's staple performing arts center with capacity for dance troupes and rock groups alike. Clubs **Suede**, **Harry O's**, and **Cicero's** (as listed in the "Nightlife" section of this chapter) are classic venues for loud and large groups whose audiences appreciate glitter, good drinks, and indoor warmth. The Kimball Art Center (638 Park Avenue; 435-649-8882; www.kimball-art.org), a working studio, community center, and triple gallery, is the gathering place for many gallery strolls and festivals.

Film

Park City is virtually synonymous with the Sundance Film Festival. Although Park City actually has more film events than just the intense January of Sundance, the festival must be thanked for its impact on Park City's heightened film awareness and venues. One year-round resource for independent films is the Park City Film Series (1255 Park Avenue, Santy Auditorium; 435-615-8291; www.parkcityfilmseries.com). Screenings include Sundance hits as well as other less mainstream pieces.

Obviously this discussion would not be complete without a synopsis of the **Sundance Film Festival** (http://festival.sundance.org). Each year this festival changes and grows, and so what exactly will happen at a particular festival is difficult to pinpoint. However, you can be sure that the third week of January will turn Park City into a bizarre dream town with private house concerts by bands like Metallica and appearances by a wide range of celebrities. Other surprises always pepper this Hollywood red carpet affair. Although it is rooted firmly in independent films, the festival now attracts the same glamour and fame that any major music or film festival would.

During that one week, the walls of every building in this town practically burst (and some probably literally have) with all of the attendees. Every venue in town adopts a strict, maximally efficient schedule of back-to-back screenings, and entire parking lots are covered in tents with lines of waiting viewers snaking out. With literally hundreds of films selected from applicant pools several factors larger, any screening that you can catch will be worthy. All are accompanied by brief panel discussions with directors, producers, or any representative of the film.

When night falls, Park City becomes a fervent party. Though tickets can be hard to get for film screenings, all but the most popular or exclusive parties can be accessed with a valid ID and cover charge. Main Street is one continuous chain of parties, formal or impromptu. Many would-be exclusive parties are poached by scalpers, and tickets can become suddenly available via a "friend of a friend." Regardless, during the festival you should expect changes and remain as flexible as possible. The spontaneity of the people and the entropy of the event are what make it all possible.

For those coming to Park City during the festival, beware that hotel rates more than triple, and restaurants are booked out to private parties. Some residents rent their homes for the week and catch the quickest flight to Baja. If you are in Park City during this week, make sure you are here to revel in the festival; otherwise you will have trouble just trying to get lunch.

Music

An indispensable part of Park City's vitality is its music scene. Summer is when the scene really flourishes, with more outdoor series and festivals than you could possibly attend. These concerts range from Utah Symphony and Opera performances to rock, bluegrass, and country. All year, live music can be heard in Main Street bars and clubs, such as the No Name Saloon and Harry O's. You can stomp your boots on the wooden floor or wear glitter under neon lights.

Mountain Town Stages (435-901-7664; www.mountaintownstages.com) strives to bring national and international musicians to play in the beautiful mountain setting of Park City. It would be worth perusing their schedule to see what they have programmed in various venues during your visit. **Park City Jazz Foundation** (435-940-1362; www.parkcity jazz.org) is a community organization whose activities include professional workshops and various concerts, such as the **Park City Jazz Festival**, which is held at the end of August every year. **The Park City Singers** (435-649-9589; www.parkcitysingers.com) offer a casual way to add some music to your trip. A local group of singers, the emphasis of this

Kimball Art Center |Jonathan Echlin

group is on the joy of music rather than strict adherence to tradition. If you are seeking a more honed group, **Sonolumina** (435-649-5309; www.sonolumina.com) is a fully professional chamber group, with a rigorous annual schedule packed with studio time and public concerts, usually given in the St. Mary of Assumption Catholic Church (www.stmaryspark city.com).

With regard to festivals, the overwhelming majority take place during the pleasant summer nights. The exception is the **Park City & SLC Music Festival** (435-649-5309; www.pc musicfestival.com), which incorporates chamber renditions of celebrated pieces in conjunction with renowned solo artists from around the world. Venues alternate between various places in Park City and Salt Lake City, so be sure to check ahead. This new festival is a combination of the former Autumn Classics and Park City International music festivals. During the summer, **The Canyons Resort Spring Concert Series and Saturday Summer Concert Series** (The Canyons Resort; 435-649-5400; www.thecanyons.com/events) takes place every Saturday night from 6–8:30 PM in The Canyons Resort Village in July and August. The genre of music changes from concert to concert, but is usually rock or blues. Also look for the **Sunday Locals Concert Series** at The Canyons, taking place all summer long, and free to the public. Just to the south, Deer Valley Resort (435-645-6510; www.deer valleymusicfestival.org) hosts a recurring series called the **Twilight Concert Series** from the end of June through August in its Snow Park Lodge Outdoor Amphitheatre. Enjoy the music of the Utah Symphony and Utah Opera in Deer Valley's mountain setting. Although professional troupes, they lighten up a bit for the summer series and give a variety of performances from pops to the classics. Throughout the summer, the Park City Performing

Arts Foundation presents **Concerts in the Park** (435-655-3114; www.ecclescenter.org). These free concerts feature local musicians as well as big stars at Deer Valley Resort. Although of interest mainly to film lovers, the **Park City Film Music Festival** (435-649-5309; www.parkcityfilmmusicfestival.com) may be an interesting way for you to get a peak into local film culture and gain awareness of the impact music has on films. This includes seminars for composers and live public performances. Put on by the Park City Jazz Foundation (435-940-1362; www.parkcityjazz.org), the **Park City Jazz Festival** takes place at the end of August each year, showcasing renowned and local performers.

Theater

Although based out of its historic location on Main Street, the Egyptian Theatre (328 Main Street; 435-649-9371; www.egyptiantheatrecompany.org) gives outdoor shows from the beginning of July through the middle of August, in addition to their year-round indoor schedule. Off the Top Comedy Troupe (435-647-5678) is Park City's only improvisational comedy group, performing weekly at the Side Car (333 Main Street; 435-645-7468; www.sidecarbar.com). Shows begin at 8:30 PM every Tues.

Performance and Dance

Based out of the Eccles Center, the Park City Performing Arts Foundation (1750 Kearns Boulevard; 435-655-8252; www.ecclescenter.org) prides itself on giving the widest possible variety of performances to visitors and locals. One of their specialty programs is the Pillow Theater, a series dedicated specifically to children. Also be sure to watch out for their ballet and opera performances throughout the year, as well as other eclectic international performances and performing arts series.

Looking down Main Street Jonathan Echlin

RECREATION AND RENTAL INFORMATION

Although skiing is foremost on many travelers' minds when arriving in Park City, there is much more to do during any season. Even if you were never to put your feet in ski boots, there would still be a lifetime of territory to discover, and different means by which to explore it. During the summer months, days can be filled with mountain biking, trail running, shopping, and fly-fishing. Winter brings snowshoeing, cross-country skiing, ice skating, and more.

If you are traveling with kids, they will probably be less interested in cross-country skiing and shopping than you are. Winter **inner-tubing** is a science at **Gorgoza Park** (Exit 141/Jeremy Ranch on I-80, 3863 West Kilby/Frontage Road; 435-658-2648; www.parkcity mountain.com), with safe tubing, lattes for cold (and tired) parents, and a towrope that takes you to the halfway point or all the way to the top. Rates are paid according to time increments, so you can leave without feeling obligated to get your money's worth despite frozen appendages. Like a bowling alley, the park has been groomed with sunken lanes, so you won't shoot off at unexpected angles. If your kids grow tired of controlled-gravity sliding, the park rents miniature snowmobiles.

Events and Races

Park City is the events host. Summer or winter, nearly as many sporting events occur as music shows. Although there are far too many to list here, certain categories of interest are worth noting. During the winter, the mountain resorts host many events like World Cup Skiing races and World Cup Snowboarding races and half-pipe competitions. The Huntsman Cup, a preeminent disabled alpine ski race, takes place at Park City Mountain Resort each year. Soldier Hollow (Wasatch Mountain State Park, Midway; 435-654-2002; www .soldierhollow.com), just 20 minutes south of Park City in Midway, hosts many **Nordic skiing** and **biathlon** events. Additionally, this former Olympic facility puts on **dogsled races**. Though participants in these premier events are granted entry by invitation only, spectators are welcome and add to the excitement of the events.

During the summer, the **Utah Olympic Park** (2990 Bear Hollow Drive; 866-659-7275; www.olyparks.com) invites many Olympic hopefuls to its summer camps. You can watch as they fine-tune their ski jumping, skeleton, luge, and bobsled skills. Each Saturday at noon the skiers demonstrate their nerve in **Big Air Shows**. Summer brings the **National Mountain Bike Races** (http://www.usacycling.org/nmbs/) to Deer Valley for three days. Though Park City has changed immensely in the last 50 years, it has not strayed from its love of rodeo. The **Summit County Fair & Rodeo** (www.summitcounty.org/fair) brings some electricity to the air.

Nearby Areas

Park City is absolutely surrounded by forest and mountains. Immediately nearby are The Canyons, Deer Valley, and Park City Mountain Resorts, where people play outdoors year-round. The Canyons' specialty for recreation, aside from an enormous amount of lift-served skiing terrain, is the access it provides to backcountry skiers in the winter. Deer Valley is known for its outstanding mountain biking and hiking trails. During the summer, a short and steep road-bike ride to the top of Guardsman's Pass, accessed by Marsac Avenue (and many of Deer Valley's neighborhood lanes), gives you an unbelievable view of the mountain territory surrounding Park City. A dirt road continues beyond where the pave-

A snowcat parked on Guardsman Pass Jonathan Echlin

ment ends and connects to other small Wasatch towns. **Park City Mountain Resort** has a network of hiking trails that lead from the base area up through Jupiter Bowl, among other destinations. Also close to downtown is the **Swaner Nature Preserve** (1258 New Main Street, Kimball Junction; 435-649-1767; www.swanernaturepreserve.com). Tucked into Kimball Junction by way of meandering roads, it would be worth a call ahead or glance at their Web site for specific directions.

To the south of Park City is Midway and Heber. West and adjacent to Midway is **Wasatch Mountain State Park** (www.utah.com/stateparks). With camping, golf, and horseback riding, among other things, it has an abundance of recreational activities. Also in Midway is **Soldier Hollow** (Wasatch Mountain State Park, Midway; 435-654-2002; www.soldierhollow .com), a Nordic ski, snowshoe, and inner-tubing haven. Farther south is **Deer Creek**, **Deer Creek Reservoir**, and the **Provo River**, known for boating and fly-fishing. To the east of Park City is the **Jordanelle Reservoir**.

Farther away is **East Canyon**, accessed by Jeremy Ranch (Exit 143 on I-80) or Mountain Dell (Exit 134 on I-80). This offers a steep out-and-back road-bike ride, as well as mountain biking trails. It also connects to Salt Lake City via Emigration Canyon. The small towns of **Francis** and **Kamas** are excellent places to park your car and take traffic-free, gentle canyon road-bike rides. The **Uinta Range** is cherished by locals for its utter lack of crowding and nearness to Park City. Rock climbers and backpackers especially love the wilderness of the Uintas. Also keep an eye out for the extensive **Wasatch-Cache National Forest**.

Local Running and Inline Skating

Most local running is done on trails. Due to the congestion in town and extreme relief of the hills, rollerblading would be adventurous at best, but more likely hazardous. The Historic Union Pacific Rail Trail State Park (435-649-6839) is a 28-mile trail that originates in Park City. Access to the trailhead is in Prospector Park, at the junction of UT 224 and UT 248 (also called Park Avenue and Kearns Boulevard). This trail is predominantly gently graded gravel or dirt. Joggers can find a lot of fun getting lost in the picturesquely sculpted neighborhoods in Park City and Deer Valley's hills. Interval workouts are easy do on these sloped roads. The higher you go, the more extravagant the homes. Recommended starting points are at Prospector Park and Deer Valley. Also consider any of the hiking trails listed in this chapter for a trail run.

Golf

Though Park City lacks the sheer number of golf courses that Salt Lake City has, their closeness and picturesque setting are ample compensation. Each course strongly encourages reservations.

Jeremy Country Golf & Country Club (8770 North Jeremy Road, Jeremy Ranch; 801-531-9000; www.thejeremy.com) is a private, 7,123-yard, par-72, 18-hole mountain course designed by Arnold Palmer. It is always ranked among the best in Utah. You can access this course by the Jeremy Ranch exit (Exit 143) on I-80, just a few miles west of Park City. Follow signs to the course, which sits just north of the interstate.

Although **Mountain Dell Golf Course** (Exit 134 on I-80; 801-582-3812) is a slight drive down the hill from Park City; its two separate 18-hole courses in a mountain setting make this challenging public course worth the short trip. This is a par-72 course in a canyon setting.

Park City Golf Course (12 Thaynes Canyon Drive; 801-521-2135), an 18-hole; par-72, 6,400-yard course, is located very near the bottom of Park City Mountain Resort. Originally designed by William Neff, the course was redesigned and reopened in 2003. William Neff, Jr. brought this from a 9- to an 18-hole course. The pro shop is tucked in the Hotel Park City on Thaynes Canyon Drive.

Biking and Bike Rentals

Unless you've brought your bike, your first stop will have to be a rental store. Cole Sport (1615 Park Avenue; 435-649-4806; www.colesport.com) is a renter of all trades and large volumes. They rent both road and mountain bikes, with a variety to choose from. If rentals are definitely in your plans log on to their Web site, where you can enter your sizing information and reserve a bike for yourself. Jans Mountain Outfitters (1600 Park Avenue; 435-649-4949 or 1-800-745-1020; www.jans.com), just down the street from Cole Sport, rents bikes too. Also a winter sports and fly-fishing rental shop, they give classes in all of their sports. Both road and mountain bikes are available here. Stein Eriksen (7700 Stein Way, Stein Eriksen Lodge, Deer Valley; 435-901-9056; www.steineriksen.com), at the base of Deer Valley, specializes in mountain and downhill bikes in conjunction with the summer chairlift service of Deer Valley. White Pine Touring (1790 Bonanza Drive; 435-649-8710; www.whitepinetouring.com) takes mountain biking as seriously as it does hiking, rock climbing, skiing, and snowshoeing. Offering both rentals and guiding services, this is a good choice for people seeking expert advice.

Road Biking

Because of Park City's compact geography and convoluted neighborhood streets, good long rides within the city are hard to come by. However, a good, very short ride can be had by making your way to Marsac Avenue (also UT 244) on the southern end of town, near Deer Valley. Main Street, Park Avenue, and Swede Alley all zigzag their way here, so look at a map. Continue on this road and you will quickly gain elevation and a great view of the town at Guardsman's Pass. At this ridge, you will have to turn back unless you are on a cross bike; UT 224 turns to dirt before it loops southwest and connects to the top of Big Cottonwood Canyon. On your return trip, you can loop this with Royal Street, which essentially switchbacks up the same hillside, although through more neighborhoods and intersections.

For a longer, more gradual ride, a quick eastward car trip is recommended. Departing on bike from Kamas (just east of Park City on UT 248), you can ride south into the town of Francis, and take UT 35 as it heads southwest up through gradual high mountain canyons and farm country. Utah 35 continues through several rural towns. In Coalville, you can park your car appropriately and ride east on UT 133 to the southwest corner of Wyoming in about 20 miles. This road traverses beautiful western ranch countryside, and although it seems to roll gently, you will be surprised by the amount of downhill on the return trip. For these rural rides, you should be fully self-sustained with bicycle repair equipment, food, and plenty of water.

Mountain Biking

The mountain biking in Summit County is almost endless, and the terrain a complex garden of mountains and canyons. Because of this, you may consider taking a guided trip, or picking up a trail map and some insider knowledge from a bike shop. **All Seasons Adventures** (435-649-9619; www.allseasonsadventures.com) guides scores of outdoor sports, making their staff fully knowledgeable about the area. **Beyond Limits** (435-640-6435; www.byndlimits.com) leads custom adventure and travel tours. **Cole Sport** (435-649-4806; www.colesport.com) and **Jans Mountain Outfitters** (435-649-4949; www.jans.com) specialize in rentals and sales, although tours can be booked in advance. **The Mountain Bike School** (435-658-3556) specializes in all levels of technical riding. **Sport Touring Ventures** (435-649-1551; www.mtnbiketours.com) specializes in mountain biking, and has many different options available from business to student trips, easy to expert. **White Pine Touring** (435-649-8710; www.whitepinetouring.com) is a versatile guide service with extensive regional knowledge. **Young Riders** (435-655-2621; www.youngriders.com) focuses on developing kids into proficient athletes. Limited drop-in classes are available.

For downhill thrills, **The Canyons** (435-649-5400; www.thecanyons.com), **Deer Valley** (435-645-6625; www.deervalley.com), and **Park City Mountain Resort** (1-800-222-7275; www.parkcitymountain.com) all offer lift-served downhill adrenaline fests. At The Canyons you can rent bikes at Canyon Mountain Sports (The Canyons Resort Village; 435-615-3440) and ride the Flight of the Canyons Gondola to mid-station. Check out The Canyons' Web site for a summer trail map. At Deer Valley you can catch the Silver Lake Express from the Snow Park Lodge. You can also take the Wasatch Express Lift from Silver Lake Lodge. Bike rentals are available at both of these lodges. Call 1-888-754-8477 for reservations and more information. At Park City Mountain Resort, you can rent bikes in the Mountain Village. Either ride the Town Lift or Payday Lift to access their trail system. You should protect yourself with a helmet and be a proficient biker, as hazards are what define this sport. Call ahead for specific hours and rates. For a longer cross-country trip, you can do a traverse between The Canyons and Park City Mountain resorts; see **www.utah mountainbiking.com** for a highly informative list of route descriptions on this route, and dozens of others immediately in the area.

If you've located a bike shop and trails map, you may consider inquiring about some of the following trails. The **King Road to Silver Lake Trail** takes you from city center, past the ruins of the old Silver King Mine, and up switchbacks in the Jupiter Bowl of Park City Mountain Resort. For an easier ride, consider the **Historic Union Pacific Trail** or the **Lost Prospector Loop**. The **Mormon Trail** is a historic ride. Because of the inherent danger of wrecks, dehydration, and becoming lost, you should always ride with a friend, repair kit, sustenance supply, compass, and map. Many of these trails are purely single track, and unmarked trail junctions will almost certainly arise. **The Mountain Trails Foundation** (www.mountaintrails.org) publishes a "Park City Trails Map" that is distributed in retail and rental stores. Utah's premium source of free, up-to-date information is **www.utah mountainbiking.com**. The product of mountain biking zealots, this free online resource has directions and illustrated information for dozens of rides in the Park City area alone.

Hiking and Snowshoeing

The hiking opportunities in Park City are infinite, with loops, flats, steeps, and pavement. The trails listed below don't even begin to scratch the surface, but offer a representative variety. For history buffs, the Mormon Trail, just above the Jeremy Ranch Golf Course, should be considered a must. Because this path was originally chosen for its relative ease in crossing the Wasatch, this isn't a very strenuous hike. You should try to imagine, though, that this was the final stretch of a 1,300-mile journey for the Mormons coming west—and only two-thirds of the way for pioneers going all the way to California. Traversing creek bottoms and ponds, this is a relatively cool, canine-friendly summer route. This section of trail continues about 4.5 miles, at which point you must turn around and return by way of the same path.

The **Moose Hollow Trail**, with its more strenuous pitch and frequent switchbacks, gives you reprieve from sudden mountain bike encounters. The trailhead is in Jeremy Ranch, and departs from the Moose Hollow neighborhood. Beware of moose encounters; these animals are inherently much more aggressive than many people would suspect. If you do see a moose, respectfully back away, leaving it to its territory. To completely avoid mountain bikers, go to Deer Valley's **Silver Lake Trail**. The trailhead for this hikers-only trail is in the Silver Lake Village, and the destination is the top of Bald Mountain.

Although all of the ski resorts offer summer hiking, snowshoeing is neither advised, nor allowed on the ski runs during the winter. However, it is available at **Soldier Hollow** (Wasatch Mountain State Park, Midway; 435-654-2002; www.soldierhollow.com). Any of the non-resort hiking trails listed in this section will serve well as snowshoeing trails, but you should be cautious that heavy snowfall can create hazardous avalanche conditions. For current information on avalanche danger with regard to location, slope aspect, and recent snowpack, visit the **National Avalanche Center's** Web site: **www.avalanche.org**. This is the world's foremost avalanche awareness Web site.

Rock Climbing

The most local crags to Park City can be found in Echo Canyon, northeast of Park City along I-80. The Uinta Mountains, some of Utah's most concentrated and best summer sport (and traditional) climbing, is just about 45 minutes' drive east of Park City on the Mirror Lake Highway. Although a drive from Park City to the more famous Big Cottonwood, Little Cottonwood, or even American Fork Canyons is not out of the question, you should absolutely take advantage of Park City's proximity to the Uinta Mountains. Approaches to the crags are short, and the number of climbs at each crag is high. These high, glaciated wilderness crags give supreme climbing opportunities in relative isolation. Just as for Salt Lake City visitors, Maple Canyon, Joe's Valley, Ibex, St. George, and Indian Creek all are strongly recommended for serious climbers with as little as one free day and a rental car. The people you meet may have traveled from as far away as Europe or Russia to climb there.

For an afternoon in a rock gym, a guidebook, or local advice, go to the **Double Diamond Climbing Wall** (in the Black Diamond Gymnastics Center, 6400 North Highway 224; 435-615-1833; www.blackdiamondgym.com). This small wall can provide a short afternoon of exercise.

Air Adventures

If you wish to push the adventure aspect of your trip, consider taking a hot-air balloon ride. It will be a unique tour of the spectacular Utah backcountry, and double as a once-in-a-lifetime experience. Most companies offer sunrise trips because of the inherent stillness of the morning air. Many of these rides include a sunrise toast with champagne.

Park City's thriving regional ballooning companies are **ABC Ballooning** (435-649-2224), **All Seasons Adventures** (435-649-9619; www.allseasonsadventures.com), **Morning Star Balloons** (435-645-7433; www.morningstarballoons.com), **Park City Balloon Adventures** (435-645-8787; www.pcballoonadventures.com), **Skywalker Balloon Company** (801-557-5322; www.skywalker.at), and **Wasatch Ballooning** (435-657-2233 or 1-866-759-7787).

Fishing

The best fly-fishing near Park City is found on the Provo River, which is as close as a 15-minute drive from town. The Provo, with its bounty of blue-ribbon brown and rainbow trout, originates in the Uinta Range and flows through Jordanelle and Deer Creek Reservoirs before reaching Provo, and eventually the fresh waters of Utah Lake. Much of the land through which the river flows is private property, with exclusive access granted to guiding companies. Currant Creek and mountain lakes in the Uinta Mountains are also suitable destinations. Farther from Park City you will find Strawberry Reservoir, Pelican Lake, Starvation Reservoir, and the Green River flowing through the famous **Flaming Gorge National Recreation Area**.

If you lack familiarity with the sport or area, you may consider one of many guide options. **All Seasons Adventures** (435-649-9619; www.allseasonsadventures.com) offers fishing on the Weber and Provo Rivers, starting with trips as short as a half-day. **Four Seasons Fly Fishers** of Heber (435-657-2010 or 1-800-498-5440; www.utahflyfish.com) has a broad jurisdiction that includes the Green River, Provo River, and Uinta Basin. If you are thrilled with their service, you can book trips with them as far away as Argentina. **Jan's Mountain Outfitters** (1-800-745-1020; www.jans.com) gives summer fly-fishing lessons as well as guided trips to exclusive mountain ranch destinations. **Park City Fly Shop** (435-645-8382; www.pcflyshop.com), a catch-and-release company, fishes the Provo River and is the only company with exclusive rights to certain "trophy sections" of the Green River. They encourage multiple-day outings. **Trout Bum 2** (435-658-1166; www.troutbum2.com)

A ski railing downtown Jonathan Echlin

tours Utah for trout, also making trips to remote destinations for salmon, steelhead, and saltwater fish.

Boating, Kayaking, Canoeing, Rafting, and Sailing

If you're a seasoned boater, all you'll need is a conversation with a kayak bum at a boat shop, enough cars for a shuttle, and equipment. Locations to bookmark are the Green River, Provo River, and small creeks. Most guided whitewater trips happen on sections of the big rivers of eastern and southern Utah such as the Green, Yampa, and Colorado. Trips on these rivers often run several days, although a few last only one day. Government permits are difficult to attain during peak season, and applicants must demonstrate high levels of competence. Because of this, you may choose to consult with guide services like Adrift Adventures of Jensen (1-800-758-5161; www.adrift.com), Dinosaur River Expeditions of Park City (1-800-345-7238; www.dinoadv.com), or Sherri Griffith Expeditions of Moab (435-259-8229 or 800-332-2439; www.griffithexp.com). These guides have access to sections of river blocked to many by permit restrictions and basic access logistics.

River sports within closer proximity to Park City may be your only option. Though the trips will not be on the legendary big rivers of the Southwest, they can be a great way to explore Park City's natural environs. **High Country Rafting** (801-224-2500; highcountryrafting.com) guides day trips down the gentle rapids of the Provo River. They also offer fly-fishing and inner-tubing. **All Seasons Adventures** (435-649-9619; www.allseasons adventures.com) gives more placid tours of nearby state parks and bodies of water via inflatable, tandem, and sea kayaks.

For flat-water adventures, **Invert Sports** (801-413-9602; www.utahboatrental.com) offers rental packages, from motorboats with trailers to towing vehicles with drivers if you'd like. They also have water-ski and wakeboard gear, a fleet of Jet Skis, and safety equipment. Although they will be able to offer you recommendations, you might try Smith and Morehouse Reservoirs, Trial and Washington Lakes, and Rockport State Park.

Horseback Riding

Considering Park City's utterly mountainous surroundings, it is not at all surprising that horseback riding is a popular sport. If you didn't pack your horse and trailer, contact Park City and Deer Valley Stables (1-800-303-7256; www.rockymtnrec.com/PCStab.htm). They lead short trail rides and "meal rides," and have two High Uinta guest ranches for genuine retreats. Red Pine Adventures (435-649-9445 or 1-800-417-7669; www.redpinetours .com) gives near-town rides on private lands. Wind in Your Hair Riding (435-336-4795; www.windinyourhair.com) offers preparatory lessons for novices, and Paso Fino rides near Park City. Booking in advance is suggested, as horseback riding is in high demand among locals and visitors.

Tennis and Swimming

Park City Racquet Club (1200 Little Kate Road; 435-615-5401; www.parkcityrecreation.org) has seven tennis courts as well as many other fitness gym–type classes and equipment. This facility is the official training center of the U.S. Ski and Snowboard Team. Park City Aquatic Center (2465 West Kilby Road; 435-645-5617) is an indoor facility that offers specified time slots for lap swimmers.

Scuba Diving

Yet again, Utah has something to offer where you would least expect it. The Homestead Resort (700 North Homestead Drive, Midway; 1-888-327-7220; www.homesteadresort .com) in Midway is the site of the wildly unique "Crater." This is a 90-foot-deep, beehive-shaped limestone cave, whose natural entrance was the skylight above. Accessible now by a manmade hole in a side wall, the waters of this cave maintain a temperature of around 95 degrees F (35 degrees C) and can be explored with scuba apparatus. Others just choose to swim here and lounge on the dock.

SHOPPING

Park City has as much discretionary income as it has leisure time. Shops of all varieties flourish, making shopping in Park City fun and unrestricted. Most of the stores are found in six major areas. Within these areas, most traffic is pedestrian, which makes perusing simple and leisurely. **Main Street**, **Summit Watch Plaza**, and **Park Avenue** are nestled in the narrow, historic downtown district. Because of the compact geography, these shops tend to be smaller boutique and fine arts shops. **Kimball Junction** sits 6 miles north of Park City where UT 224 meets I-80. Its spacious layout allows for larger stores and shopping centers. This is where the coveted Tanger Outlet Stores are located. The villages at **The Canyons**, **Deer Valley**, and **Park City Mountain Resort** are where you can find many high-end specialty and outdoors shops.

Boutiques and Fine Arts

Park City's mining and skiing history, Rocky Mountain location, wealthy population, and thriving tourism have given rise to a saturation of boutique galleries. Many galleries appeal to visitors (and locals) with art related to Rocky Mountain culture. Others import worldly fine arts to Utah by collecting works from national and international artists. For boutique clothing and specialty shops, head directly to Main Street. Here you will find many clothing shops, including those that specialize in children's apparel.

On the last Friday of every month (except January during the Sundance Film Festival),

Sculpture at a downtown shop |Jonathan Echlin

the **Kimball Art Center** (638 Park Avenue; 435-649-8882; www.kimball-art.org) organizes the **Park City Gallery Association's Gallery Stroll & Live Jazz Nights**. The strolls last from 6–9 PM and begin at the Kimball Art Center. Five dollars covers all admission and hors d'oeuvres for this Main Street event. The **Park City Kimball Arts Festival** takes place on the first weekend of August every year, drawing 200 artists and 40,000 spectators. During this festival, the entirety of Main Street is packed with artist tents, food vendors, colorful balloons, and summer attire. Another Kimball Art Center production is the popular **Annual Kimball Art Auction & Gala**, which takes place in conjunction with the Arts Festival.

With so much art in such a concentrated area, Park City makes afternoon strolls fruitful and convenient. Each gallery has unique appeal, and most are very near each other. It is amazing with all of these galleries on Main Street that there is room available for the restaurants, hotels, and shops in this compact mining town.

Artworks Gallery (461 Main Street; 435-649-4462; www.artworksparkcity.com) showcases variable contemporary media and fine crafts ranging from pottery to fiber, jewelry, glass, and wood works.

Coda Gallery (804 Main Street; 435-655-3803; www.codagallery.com) is filled with warmth, colors, and reflection of the Coda movement.

Crosby Collection (419 and 513 Main Street; 435-658-1813 and1-800-960-8839; www.crosbycollection.com) has Native American art and collectibles, including blankets, jewelry, and pottery from Hopi, Navajo, Pueblo, and Zuni artists.

David Whitten Gallery (523 Main Street; 435-649-3860; www.davidwhittenphoto.com) features the Utah and North American landscape photography of David Whitten.

Images of Nature (364 Main Street; 435-649-7598; www.mangelsen.com) is a collection of Thomas D. Mangelsen's nature photography available in prints, as well as in books, calendars, and posters.

District Gallery (formerly Iron Horse Gallery) (1205 Iron Horse Drive; 435-649-3445; www.ironhorseartgallery.com) features a Lyman Whitaker sculpture garden as well as many other items, including blown glass, bronze sculptures, fountains, oil paintings, and photographs.

Julie Nester Gallery (1280 Iron Horse Drive; 435-649-7855; www.julienestergallery.com) displays primarily the mixed-media, painting, and sculpture of new and familiar living artists.

Kimball Art Center (638 Park Avenue; 435-649-8882; www.kimballartcenter.org) is Park City's art hub and the organizer of the year-round gallery strolls. A nonprofit organization, this community center hosts classes and auctions. The Art Center has three on-site galleries.

Meyer Gallery (305 Main Street; 435-649-8160; www.meyergallery.com) has carved out a more serious niche among Park City's discerning art collectors and appreciators. Here the modern works of prolific national artists are exhibited.

The Mountain Trails Gallery (301 Main Street; 435-615-8748; www.mountaintrails galleries.com) is where you will find the affecting regional paintings of Rocky Mountain landscapes of tonalist influence. Bronze sculptures here are inspired by the region and range from miniature to colossal.

Phoenix Gallery (508 Main Street; 435-649-1006; www.phoenixparkcity.com) is a three-level space hosting the contemporary creations of local and national painters, glassblowers, and sculptors.

Christine Balaz

The Redstone Gallery (1678 West Redstone Center Drive, Kimball Junction; 435-575-1000; www.theredstonegallery.com) has a slightly less serious approach to art, and although its pieces include a variety of legitimate multimedia works, it claims its fanciful copper frogs as its trademark.

Scanlan Windows to the World (545 B Main Street; 435-658-3696 or 1-800-254-1875; www.scanlan.com) brings images from around the world to Park City with photographs by international travelers Debora and John Scanlan.

Stanfield Fine Art (751 Main Street; 435-658-1800; www.stanfieldfineart.com) appeals to

Park City downtown in summer   Christine Balaz

a spread of tastes by spanning many genres and styles of lithographs, etchings, paintings, and works in bronze and glass.

Stone Art Gallery (333 Main Street; 435-647-0227; www.fineartonstone.com) includes watercolor, ceramics, and handmade juniper furniture and lamps. An on-site working studio produces a collection of unique paintings and sculpture on stone by Nick and Felix Saez.

Taminah Gallery/Montgomery Lee Fine Art (608 Main Street, 2nd Floor; 435-655-3264; www.taminah.com) is a fine art gallery featuring realistic and impressionistic paintings and sculptures. Works on display include landscape and still-life paintings and wildlife sculpture, although the gallery also specializes in large bronze commissions.

Terzian Galleries (309 Main Street; 435-649-4927 or 1-866-949-4927; www.terzian galleries.com) has contemporary multimedia works from around the nation, including those of local artists.

The Thomas Kearns McCarthey Gallery (449 Main Street; 435-658-1691; www.mccarthey gallery.net) has a surprising niche in Russian impressionist paintings and is one of the leading dealers in the United States.

Wild Spirits Nature Photography (614 Main Street; 435-200-0071 or 1-800-570-8962; www.wildspiritsparkcity.com) displays the photographic works of Tom Till and Gary Crandall, both Utah residents. Their subjects include wildlife, Park City, and the Wasatch Mountains.

Farmers' Markets

If you feel like a scenic drive on a sunny afternoon, take a trip to the Heber Valley Farmers Market (Heber City Municipal Park, Heber City; 801-654-4555). Held a short trip south of Park City, this market lasts from the middle of June through the end of August, Thurs. from 4–7 PM. Here you can find flowers, artisan breads, and a great dinner of Asian cuisine on or off the grill.

The **Park City Farmer's Market** (Cabriolet Parking Lot, The Canyons Resort; 435-649-5400; www.parkcityfarmersmarket.com) takes place each Wednesday afternoon from 12–6 PM, barring weather catastrophes. It begins in late May and continues through October. The market offers fresh produce, as well as local handicrafts and arts including pottery, jewelry, and paintings. Visit the Web site for information about Monday and Friday markets at other locations.

Malls and Squares

Park City lacks traditional malls, and does not have room for squares. Rather, Main Street acts as a cultural center, historical tour, and high-end gallery mall. There is actually a small Main Street Mall (333 Main Street) that houses a few restaurants and western shops, like Cowboy Culture and Southwestern Expressions. Kimball Junction is Utah's home to a branch of The Tanger Outlets (6699 North Landmark Drive; www.tangeroutlet.com /parkcity), a one-stop shopping trip for beloved national brand stores at lowered prices. Here you'll find Banana Republic, Coach, Fossil, and Van Heusen, among more than 60 others. Also in Kimball Junction is the Redstone Center with Red Rock Brewery, Casa Bella Furniture & Design, Backcountry.com, and more.

3

Provo

Provo, a city of just over 110,000 people, is located on the incline between the fresh water of Utah Lake and the 11,000-foot peaks of the Wasatch Mountains. Similar in appearance and location to Salt Lake City, Provo is Salt Lake's chaste younger sister. Salt Lake City is clean; Provo is cleaner. Provo prides itself on its family values and community strength. In fact, Provo's violent crime rate is 80 percent lower than the national average. "Garden City" Provo and Brigham Young University are must-see destinations for Mormons seeking solidarity in their faith, or for the curious hoping to get a glimpse into a stronghold of Mormon life. The bottom line is that Provo has retained the original purpose of Salt Lake City: to be the cradle of Mormon religion and culture.

Provo, like Salt Lake City, began as an outpost and has grown into its neighbors. The urban conglomerate of Provo and Utah Valley actually consists of many cities that share each others' cultural resources. The original economy of Utah Valley was based on farms and orchards. As mining and other high-tech industries became more prevalent, the population became denser. As with any other modernizing city, farm after farm was turned into subdivisions. Today, if you start at the Center Street and University Avenue district of Provo, drive through the Brigham Young University campus, and take Canyon Road to Orem, you will see all the temporal layers of the valley. Old paint and engravings on downtown buildings tell of meat and packing companies. Modern dorms are adjacent to historic campus buildings. Farther away, mid-1900s ranch houses are interspersed with modern cul-de-sacs. Once in a while, you can still see the tree rows of an orchard. As many cars are parked outside modern grocers and strip malls as can be found in the lots of historic creameries and fabric stores.

The communities of Salt Lake City and Provo were established as Mormon strongholds and each has grown fervently ever since. Salt Lake City, since its first decades of existence, has attracted people of other creeds. Provo has never strayed from its roots, and has remained deeply devout. Everything in Provo is observant of the Church of Jesus Christ of Latter-day Saints, from the "modest fashions" shops to the higher education. Of the city's 110,000 people, roughly 35,000 are students at Brigham Young University (BYU). Large enough to be a city of its own, its level of cultural activity is much more concentrated than the rest of Provo, and much different than most other universities across the nation. BYU is one of the showpieces of this richly Mormon city; the first-tier university, sponsored by the Church of Jesus Christ of Latter-day Saints, is the largest private university in the nation.

Brigham Young University prides itself on educating its students to be at once worldly and observant of the church's ideals. Although the university attracts students from around the world, ecclesiastical recommendations and a solid understanding for the Mormon religion are required for admission. It should not surprise anyone that the student body is

Mouth of Rock Canyon, east of Provo Christine Balaz

nearly 98 percent Mormon, nor that the international experience of the student body is strongly correlated to the international missions required of young Latter-day Saint (LDS) men. Indeed, roughly 2,000 international students attend the university annually, coming from more than 120 countries around the world. These students represent the global Mormon community.

To the north of Provo is Orem, established in 1919 as a community of Utah Valley farmers. Today, the homes of 85,000 residents have all but replaced its orchards and fields of less than 100 years past. Like the rest of Utah, Orem is growing at a rapid rate, and attracting more cultural resources to its residents. Utah Valley University (Utah Valley State College until 2008), with a combined student population of 25,000, receives recognition from the *U.S. News & World Report* as one of the top four Western Region public universities. Naturally, the campus has cultural outpourings such as the Woodbury Art Museum. Orem is known as the "Family City." More than 80 percent of its residents live in family households, with nearly 70 percent of the homes lived in by owners.

Melded together in northern Utah Valley are the interconnected towns of Alpine, American Fork, Cedar Hills, Eagle Mountain, Fairfield, Highland, Lehi, Lindon, and Pleasant Grove. These towns have filled in like patchwork, quickly replacing their farmland predecessors. Although mostly residential, these towns will likely be on your tour, as you pass through them en route to Timpanogos Cave in American Fork Canyon and the hiking trails in Rock Canyon. Fairfield and Saratoga Springs lie to the west of Utah Lake's northern tip. You may visit these on a rural bike ride. The grand total is an amalgamation of museums, restaurants, neighborhoods, and shops. There is Thanksgiving Point in Lehi, Orem's University Mall, Provo's downtown Musical Theater, and the country roads around Utah Lake.

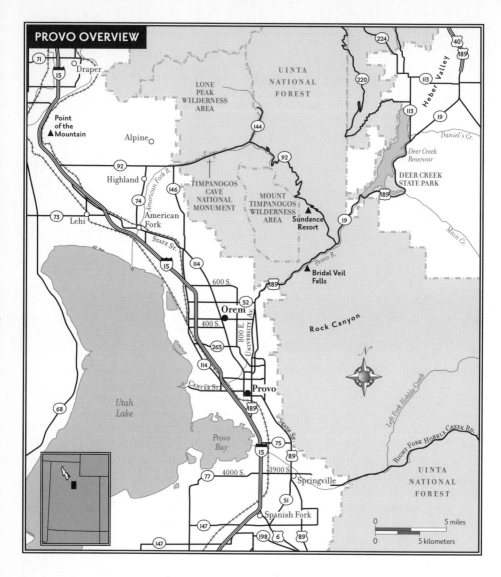

The Sundance Resort, a playground for Hollywood celebrities and local families, is just 20 minutes east in Provo Canyon. Provo now seems just a neighborhood in this collective.

LOCAL HISTORY

Timpanogotzis Indians were comfortably at home in Utah Valley when it was first breached by Europeans on September 23, 1776. Franciscan explorer-priests Dominguez and Escalante encountered this tribe, self-named for its fish-eating practices, on an exploratory mission. Dominguez and Escalante thought favorably of the landscape and climate of Utah Valley but never returned. Because Utah Valley was sufficiently isolated from California's cities, the Timpanogotzis were left to their own devices for decades to come. Later called Utes, they comfortably subsisted on the fish from Utah Lake's fresh waters.

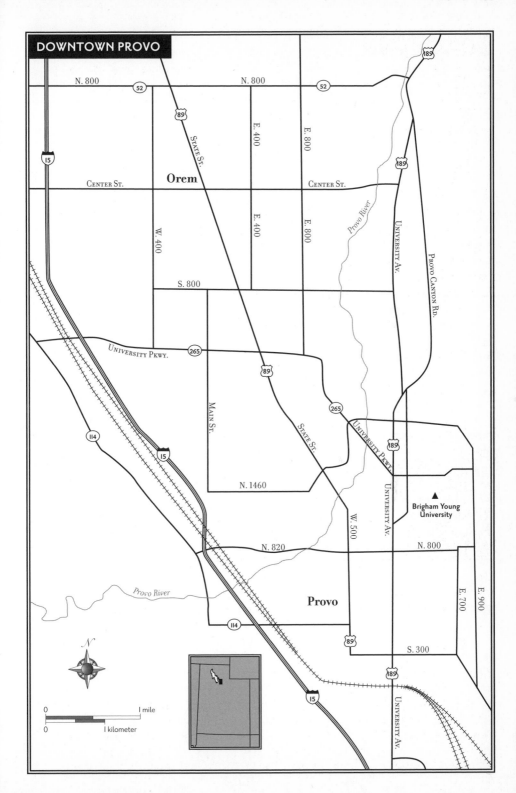

DOWNTOWN PROVO

Orem

Provo

Brigham Young University

Provo River

N

0 _____ I mile
0 _____ I kilometer

They were occasionally visited by a lone trapper or trader. Even in the heyday of trapping, trappers traveled alone or in small groups, leaving little impact on the land and rarely presenting a threat to the indigenous peoples. One such 19th-century fur trapper who passed through the area often was Etienne Provost. Though Provost never made a permanent home in Utah, he managed some heroic feats in the region. Evidently, he was able to escape from a hostile party of Snake Indians, which claimed the lives of eight of his party. This is the man from whom Provo would later take its name.

Provo's first intensive settlement efforts came shortly after the arrival of the Mormons to Salt Lake City in July 1847. The extreme length and difficulty of the westward trek and the harsh climate in Utah killed many and left the remainder struggling to survive. It took nearly two years for the Mormons of Salt Lake City to establish themselves and refortify for another outward colonization effort. Established in March 1849, Provo was the first Mormon colony founded in Utah after Salt Lake City. It immediately became another center of Mormon faith. Generally, the Utes and Mormons coexisted peacefully. However, a few battles between settlers and displaced Utes occurred. Some lasted for several months, resulting in deaths in each party.

When President James Buchanan sent federal troops to Salt Lake City in 1858, a substantial Mormon migration to Provo ensued. It was sensed by the Latter-day Saints that "The Place" was slowly being infiltrated—and even governed—by the very "gentiles" they had hoped to escape. With this movement, Provo was unofficially baptized by the Mormons as their orthodox stronghold. Salt Lake City's Mormonism would become increasingly diluted and more casual. Even Brigham Young moved south. Provo temporarily grew to be the largest city in Utah. This marked the formative beginning of the divergence between Salt Lake City and Provo.

The first transcontinental railroad was completed in 1869 at Promontory Point, just north of Salt Lake City. The sudden connection to the outside world, as well as the masses of laid-off railroad workers, brought an insurgence of new residents to Salt Lake City. Because Provo failed at acquiring a stop on the Transcontinental Railroad, it did not grow in the same fashion that Salt Lake City did, allowing Provo to retain its religious integrity.

Provo developed by its own means, and with its growth came municipal development. The Territorial Insane Asylum (now called the Utah State Hospital) was founded in 1885. Orchards sprang up throughout the valley. Agriculture begot the massive Lehi Sugar Factory and Provo Woolen Mills. Mining and proximity to railways gave rise to steel plants, including Ironton, and the Mormon Cooperative Movement. This was the church's attempt to resolve the competition that local laborers and producers were facing with increasing globalization. Because of the inevitable entwinement of non-Mormons in the economy, and the movement's requirement that laborers accept lower wages, the Mormon Cooperative Movement did not endure.

In 1875 Brigham Young Academy (seedling of Brigham Young University) was founded. This LDS-sponsored university has since grown into the largest private university in the nation, as well as the largest that is religiously affiliated. With national-caliber sports and academic programs, BYU has historically had a hand in creating and fostering Provo's private industry. With its Missionary Training Center, it has always served as one of the major educational centers for the Church of Jesus Christ of Latter-day Saints.

Provo, like Salt Lake City, saw strain and prosperity with industrial growth and integration into the United States. Passing decades saw the rise and fall of various independent unions and conflicts among political groups. Non-Mormons inevitably integrated into

University Avenue in front of old Brigham Young Academy Christine Balaz

Provo's society and economy, although never to the same degree as in Salt Lake City. Never-theless, resentment, conflict, and sometimes violence resulted. At the height of this dissi-dence and scandal, a union leader was murdered in 1915. It was generally assumed that the Church had a hand in the death.

Since these times, Provo has grown economically as well as socially. Higher education flourishes at BYU and nearby Utah Valley University, with nearly 65,000 students between the two. The high-tech industry brought many businesses to Provo. Provo has forged ahead as the stronghold for Mormon faith and community. Its nearness to Salt Lake City and its attractions give Provo access to worldliness, but its slight distance allows it to be a haven for the LDS Church that is only lightly touched by the outside world.

NEIGHBORHOODS

Provo and its surrounding towns have grown into each other such that each now functions practically as a neighborhood. **Lehi**, to the northwest, is home to Thanksgiving Point and all of its attractions, including a golf course, restaurants, and gardens. **Alpine**, **Highland**, and **Cedar Hills** form the gateway to American Fork Canyon. **Orem**, with the Utah Valley University Campus, is stacked immediately to the north of Provo. The dominant and thriv-ing sector of Provo is its **BYU Campus** and adjoining historic **Downtown**, with its old brick buildings. Located at Center Street and University Avenue, this is where you will find bou-tique shops and restaurants. The suburbs of Provo continue south through **Springville** and

Angel Moroni, Provo Temple Christine Balaz

Spanish Fork, from which you depart south on I-15 or southeast on US 6 to Utah's desert lands.

DRIVING IN PROVO

Driving in Provo is as simple as driving in Salt Lake City, but much less congested. Provo has a few major north-south roads. University Avenue runs through the heart of town, connecting historic downtown to the BYU campus, and beyond. State Street is the jugular of Orem, bringing traffic south to Provo. Canyon Road runs parallel to University Avenue, but traverses the foothills, orchards, and neighborhoods above the business district below. Provo and Orem have many substantial cross-streets, but the most notable is University Parkway. You should be aware of the difference between University Parkway and University Avenue. University Parkway is a mostly east-west-running, major boulevard that eventually dips southeast into town; University Avenue is a north-south-running street that is also called UT 189, and is the dividing line between "west" and "east" streets.

LODGING

Provo's lodging is very different than that of Salt Lake City and Park City, with far fewer bed & breakfasts and highbrow accommodations. Most Provo-area accommodations are national chains. Naturally, these are of reliable quality but modest ambience. These lodging establishments, like most of the valley's homes and buildings, are relatively new. Also, like many of the area's attractions, the unique or preferred lodging options are often found outside Provo's city limits. Because the tourism industry of Provo is much more modest than those of Park City and even Salt Lake City, you will save a bundle of cash with your lodging. Regarding handicapped access, the options listed as "accessible" have elevators and ramps where necessary, but are not necessarily fully equipped for all needs. Inquire for specific information.

Hotels and Motels

BEST WESTERN COTTON TREE INN

2230 North University Parkway
Provo, UT 84601
801-373-7044; 1-800-662-6886
www.cottontreeinns.com
Price: Inexpensive
Credit Cards: AE, MC, V
Handicapped Accessible: Yes
Pets: No
Special Packages: Flight and lodging packages available upon booking

On the banks of the Provo River, this hotel is simple, yet has enough amenities to make you feel welcome. Perhaps the biggest perks of the hotel are related to its location. Five blocks from BYU center and three blocks from its football headquarters, LaVell Edwards Stadium, you can enjoy the attractions of campus without worrying about the stress of competitive parking. Free local and national papers are available each morning, as well as a continental breakfast.

Wireless Internet and meeting spaces make this a good option for business travelers.

COURTYARD BY MARRIOTT

1600 North Freedom Boulevard (200 West Street)
801-373-2222
www.marriott.com
Price: Moderate
Credit Cards: AE, Disc, MC, V
Handicapped Accessible: Yes
Pets: No
Special Packages: Special promotions, as available

A modest, yet thoroughly appointed establishment, this Courtyard is a step up from many other chain hotels. One of the nicer hotels in Provo, it has 100 guest rooms available for visitors with a liking for the downtown area. Two blocks west of BYU, two blocks north of the Utah Valley Regional Medical Center, and just south of the Riverside Country Club, this hotel places you right in the heart of town. The simple decor is handsome and colorful, moving away from the staid schemes of budget hotels. Breakfast buffet is available each morning, as well as standard amenities such as wireless Internet and personal voice mail.

DAYS INN PROVO

1675 North Freedom Boulevard (200 West Street)
Provo, UT 84604
801-375-8600; 1-877-308-3356
www.daysinn.com
Price: Inexpensive to Moderate
Credit Cards: AE, DC, Disc, MC, V
Handicapped Accessible: Yes
Pets: Yes
Special Packages: Discounts for Missionary Training Center families, summer recreation packages

Yet another option in Provo with affordable rates and standard hotel amenities, the Days Inn is a good home base for adven-

Temple Hill neighborhood overlooking Utah Valley and Utah Lake   Christine Balaz

tures in the Wasatch Mountains or on Utah Lake. During the summer, the hotel offers special packages for golf courses and amusement parks. An added bonus to this hotel is its easy walking distance to restaurants and the Cougar Stadium at BYU. For business travelers working remotely, fax and copy services are available. Although not a deluxe establishment, this hotel receives praise from past customers for reliably high service.

HAMPTON INN
1511 South 40 East
Provo, UT 84601
801-377-6396
www.hamptoninn.com
Price: Moderate
Credit Cards: AE, Disc, MC, V
Handicapped Accessible: Yes
Pets: Yes
Special Packages: Romantic and family packages

Hampton Inn brings you the comfort and cleanliness necessary for any trip at an affordable price. The furniture and bedding are basic, yet the service is thorough. Hot breakfast is available in-house, or even in sacks to go. Basic hotel amenities, such as pool, lounge, meeting areas, and round-the-clock coffee and tea are available. Pets are allowed by discretion. This is slightly farther from the BYU campus, but near Main Street and the University Mall.

LA QUINTA INN PROVO TOWN CENTER
1460 South University Avenue
Provo, UT 84601
801-374-9750
www.lq.com
Price: Inexpensive to Moderate
Credit Cards: AE, Disc, MC, V
Handicapped Accessible: Yes
Pets: Yes
Special Packages: No

Another simple, modern hotel, the La Quinta of Provo offers the standard comforts a hotel should, all within walking distance of Provo Town Center. Here you will find the business, dining, and shopping districts all rolled into one. Guests enjoy a hot complimentary breakfast buffet and modern facilities. If you stay here, you are also very near I-15 and Provo Bay of Utah Lake. This hotel has 78 guest rooms, and pets are welcome.

LA QUINTA INN & SUITES OREM UNIVERSITY PARKWAY

521 West University Parkway
Orem, UT 84058
801-226-0440
www.lq.com
Price: Moderate
Credit Cards: AE, Disc, MC, V
Handicapped Accessible: Yes
Pets: Yes
Special Packages: No

In close proximity to BYU and even closer proximity to Utah Valley University, this hotel is near most of the attractions in Provo and Orem. For the business traveler, meeting spaces are available, as well as a fitness center and 24-hour heated indoor pool and Jacuzzi. With 130 guest rooms, but only four suites, be sure to book ahead if a suite is high on your priority list. Pets are welcome. Breakfasts include fresh waffles, fruit, cereal, and bagels.

PROVO MARRIOTT HOTEL & CONFERENCE CENTER

101 West 100 North
Provo, UT 84601
801-377-4700; 1-800-777-7144
www.marriott.com
Price: Moderate to Expensive
Credit Cards: AE, DC, Disc, MC, V
Handicapped Accessible: Yes
Pets: No
Special Packages: Special promotions, as available

One of the area's finer hotels, the Provo Marriott will be a familiar stop on your visit. The spacious lobby with modern furniture, bold color patterns, and high ceilings leads you into the moderately upscale 330 guest rooms. Varying room sizes are available, according to group size and luxury wants. A major conference center, it has over 28,000 square feet of meeting space divided among 21 rooms. For meals, two on-site restaurants are available. Allie's American Grill serves breakfast, lunch, and dinner. Season's Bar serves dinner to members.

TRAVELODGE

124 South University Avenue
Provo, UT 84601
801-373-1974
www.travelodge.com
Price: Inexpensive
Credit Cards: AE, DC, Disc, MC, V
Handicapped Accessible: Yes
Pets: No
Special Packages: Flight and car rental packages

Considering the unmatched downtown location and extremely inexpensive rates, this is one of Provo's best deals. The interior is simple, yet cozy. Guests have access to free breakfast, high-speed Internet, and a fitness center. This Travelodge has a spacious outdoor pool for the warm summer months. Nonsmoking rooms and daily newspapers are available. Although not fancy, this is a remarkable bargain in the heart of downtown Provo. Free parking is available.

Bed & Breakfasts and Inns

HINES MANSION BED & BREAKFAST

383 West 100 South
Provo, UT 84601
801-374-8400; 1-800-428-5636
www.hinesmansion.com
Price: Expensive
Credit Cards: AE, DC, Disc, MC, V
Handicapped Accessible: No

Pets: No
Special Packages: Various packages including fly-fishing

The only luxury bed & breakfast in Provo, the Hines is your opportunity to experience intimate service in the heart of the city. Originally built in 1895, the rooms were remodeled in 1995, incorporating handsome new woodwork into the varying angles of the historic brick structure. Each of the 10 rooms has its own private bath with jetted tub. Because this is the only B&B of its kind in Provo, book well in advance if you really desire a stay here. A bottle of sparkling cider (the driest champagne of all) is laid in a basket on your bed upon your arrival. If you would really like to up the romance, the innkeeper will design floral arrangements, make up a strawberries-and-cream dessert, or even arrange a horse-drawn-carriage ride upon request.

SOMEWHERE INN TIME

175 North State Street
Lindon, UT 84042
801-785-9777
www.somewhereinntime.com
Price: Moderate to Expensive
Credit Cards: AE, Disc, MC, V
Handicapped Accessible: Yes
Pets: No
Special Packages: Weekday discounts, wedding packages

Located on five green and landscaped acres just north of Provo, the Somewhere Inn Time exudes romance and coziness. Each room has a different theme, although these are more subdued than in other bed & breakfasts. Most of the beds are overstuffed four-poster beds. Breakfast is served to each room every morning. A large, modern home opened as a B&B in 1998, this has a full wrap-around balcony overlooking the property and large windows to catch the sun. Be aware that this is an extremely popular wedding destination, so if you would

like more solitude, call ahead to be sure your stay does not coincide with any undesired commotion. No children or liquor are allowed.

VICTORIAN INN BED & BREAKFAST

94 West 200 South
Springville, UT 84663
801-489-0737; 1-888-489-0737
Price: Inexpensive to Expensive
Credit Cards: AE, DC, Disc, MC, V
Handicapped Accessible: No
Pets: No
Special Packages: No

This 1892 mansion, originally built as a family home, was sold and became the Kearns Hotel in 1909. Purchased again and remodeled to include modern comforts such as Jacuzzi tubs, plumbing, and electricity, the Victorian Inn Bed & Breakfast is an excellent place to stay if you seek historic charm and are willing to drive a short distance to gain it. The Victorian Inn has an air of formality. Each of the themed rooms is decorated according to the Victorian period.

Vacation Rentals

The nearest vacation rentals to Provo are in the picturesque mountains of the Sundance Resort (801-225-4107 or 1-800-892-1600; www.sundanceresort.com). More information on these Sundance cottages is included in Chapter 4, Ski Country.

RESTAURANTS

Provo's restaurant scene is overtly one of casual local eateries, chain restaurants, and hole-in-the-wall ethnic cuisine. The ethnic cuisine, most of which is found around the intersection of Center Street and University Avenue, is usually marked by outstanding food with informal, quirky settings, and very understated signage and atmosphere. Although their presence is not as blatant,

Provo does have a handful of formal dining establishments dispersed throughout town; the demographic here simply does not demand the upper-echelon dining that is required of Salt Lake City and Park City. For the best restaurant selection, park anywhere near the Center Street and University Avenue intersection and begin walking. Here you will find Japanese, Italian, Vietnamese, and Indian cuisine of varying formalities.

For a guaranteed fine-dining experience in a beautiful setting, consider taking a drive to the Sundance Resort (801-225-4107 or 1-800-892-1600; www.sundance resort.com). Here you will find superb creations made from local ingredients, as well as wine and liquor on the menu. Restaurants at Sundance are the **Tree Room** and **Foundry Grill** (as listed below). **The Owl Bar** is a historic bar from the actual Butch Cassidy days.

BOMBAY HOUSE
473 North University Avenue
Provo Downtown

801-373-6677
www.bombayhouse.com
Cuisine: Indian
Serving: D
Open: Mon. through Sat.
Price: Moderate to Expensive
Credit Cards: MC, V
Reservations: Yes
Handicapped Accessible: No

This is a prime example of superb, other-worldly cuisine in a very unassuming atmosphere. Located conveniently near the BYU campus, the Bombay House brings its native heritage to diners through music, artwork, incense, and cuisine. The recipes were brought to Utah from Chennai, India, by the owner who emigrated to practice the Mormon religion, and later graduated from BYU. Sometimes the ingredients are very literally imported from India, when local substitutes would yield a substandard result. Open since 1993, this was the pioneering Indian cuisine establishment in the area and has been warmly accepted by locals. Vegetarian meals are available.

Provo is known for its wide streets Christine Balaz

BRICK OVEN

111 East 800 North
Provo
801-374-8800
www.brickovenprovo.net
Cuisine: Pizza
Serving: L, D
Open: Mon. through Sat.
Price: Inexpensive
Credit Cards: AE, MC, V
Reservations: Large parties only
Handicapped Accessible: Yes

The Brick Oven serves exactly what you would expect from the name. With fresh ingredients and substantial pizzas, this restaurant is slightly more upscale than others of its kind. In business for more than 50 years, this establishment has neared perfection in its trade, aging their marinara sauce for two days, grating fresh cheese daily, and making their own draft root beer and apple beer. It is known locally to have one of the best salad bars in town. This is a perfect opportunity for a casual dinner or family-style lunch. The original brick oven, now out of service, as well as BYU photographs and memorabilia, create the homey ambience.

BUONA VITA

98 West Center Street
Provo
801-377-4522
Cuisine: Italian
Serving: L (Mon. through Fri.), D (Mon. through Sat.)
Open: Mon. through Sat.
Price: Moderate to Expensive
Credit Cards: AE, MC, V
Reservations: Yes
Handicapped Accessible: Yes

A clean, modern atmosphere with deeply hued accent walls, wooden floors, and brushed steel, this restaurant has more of an Italian American ambience than a Mediterranean one. Your meal will be one from the list of Italian classics, and can be accompanied by wine. A branch in Orem is part of **Chefplex** (1755 State Street, Orem; 801-765-0822), a group of four restaurants in a twisted fast-food concept. Here you can get burgers as well as Italian, Thai, and Mexican food that you order by using touch screens. The ambience here, with colorful walls and murals and modern stamped-steel counters, does not have the feeling of a fast-food restaurant at all. This is an inexpensive, efficient way to satisfy a group of kids or adults in disagreement about where to eat.

CHEF'S TABLE

2005 South State Street
Orem
801-235-9111
www.chefstable.net
Cuisine: Contemporary American
Serving: L, D
Open: Mon. through Sat.
Price: Moderate to Expensive
Credit Cards: AE, Disc, MC, V
Reservations: Yes
Handicapped Accessible: Yes

This is considered one of Utah Valley's fine restaurants, a preferred choice for those seeking longer meals and delicately prepared foods. The ambience adds significantly to the experience with European antiques furnishing the building, stained-glass windows, and a vaulted ceiling. The finest preparations of tenderloin, duck, fish, and the like are accented with fresh, tender vegetables prepared equally as deliberately. To avoid crowds, try dining before or after the seven o'clock hour. As one of Utah Valley's premier eating establishments, this comes under high demand.

THE FOUNDRY GRILL

Sundance Resort
7 miles east on UT 189, 2 miles north on UT 92
1-866-932-2295

Downtown Provo dining Christine Balaz

www.sundanceresort.com
Cuisine: Contemporary American, regional
Serving: B (Sun. only), L, D (closed 4–5)
Open: Daily
Price: Expensive to Very Expensive
Credit Cards: AE, Disc, MC, V
Reservations: Yes
Handicapped Accessible: Yes

Timbered walls, stone fireplaces, and angled ceilings give this elegant restaurant a touch of rustic charm. The food here matches. Simple, yet inexplicably elegant, the whole is substantially more than the sum of the parts. The concept of fundamental minimalism is even built into the name. Each dish is made from the freshest available ingredients and prepared in an apple wood oven.

HARVEST

3003 North Thanksgiving Way
Thanksgiving Point
Lehi
www.thanksgivingpoint.com
801-768-4990
Cuisine: Regional, Mediterranean
Serving: L, D
Open: Mon. through Sat.
Price: Moderate
Credit Cards: AE, Disc, MC, V
Reservations: Yes
Handicapped Accessible: Yes

Harvest is another choice for post-shopping dinners away from the bustling campuses of Orem and Provo—a 20-minute drive north, if you're willing. Dishes served are based on regional fare, but carry Mediterranean overtones. Flatbreads, seafood, pastas, poultry, and other braised items are served along with herbs, mustards, and chutneys. If you enjoyed the fresh air and beauty of the Thanksgiving Point Gardens or wagon rides, this will be a good way to extend your experience.

LA CARRETTA PERUVIAN RESTAURANT

340 East 1200 South
Orem
801-229-2696
www.lacarretaperuvianrestaurant.com
Cuisine: Peruvian
Serving: L, D
Open: Mon. through Sat.
Price: Inexpensive
Credit Cards: MC, V
Reservations: Yes
Handicapped Accessible: Yes

Though you wouldn't guess by its strip-mall-esque exterior, this restaurant has been serving Utah Valley for nearly 15 years. Peruvian culinary tradition is delivered to beef, chicken, seafood, and vegetable entrées. Though lesser known to Americans than French or Chinese menus, Peruvian is considered to be among the most gastronomically colorful cuisines in the world. Here grill items are popular; they are plated with fresh corn, potatoes, leafy greens, tomatoes, and many, many delicious sauces and dressings. A kid's menu of "safer" items makes this a possibility for families with children who have bland palates. If you are farther north, try the American Fork installment (852 East State Street; 801-763-9920).

LA CASITA UNO

333 North Main Street
Springville
801-489-9543
Cuisine: Mexican
Serving: L, D
Open: Mon. through Sat.
Price: Inexpensive
Credit Cards: AE, Disc, MC, V
Reservations: Yes
Handicapped Accessible: Yes (with assistance)

Open for nearly three decades, La Casito Uno has perfected its family recipes. Located south of Provo, in Springville, this restaurant is a favorite stop for cyclists returning from a ride around Utah Lake. Ingredients are fresh and portions are large.

MAGLEBY'S GRILL & OYSTER BAR

4801 North University Avenue
Provo
801-374-6249
www.maglebys.com
Cuisine: Surf and turf
Open: Mon. through Sat.
Price: Moderate to Expensive
Credit Cards: AE, Disc, MC, V
Reservations: Yes
Handicapped Accessible: Yes

Magleby's is a local favorite, open since 1980. An odd—yet delicious—juxtaposition of seafood and meats makes up the fare here. With a variety of seafood extending from shrimp to mahimahi and poached salmon, this restaurant has one of Utah Valley's most extensive fish selections. For those not keen on seafood, a wide variety of gourmet meat preparations are available, like kebabs, prime rib, filet medallions, and carvings.

OSAKA JAPANESE RESTAURANT

46 West Center Street
Provo Downtown
801-373-1060
Cuisine: Japanese
Serving: L, D

Fabric Mill Fabrics in front of the Wasatch Range   Christine Balaz

Open: Mon. through Sat.
Price: Inexpensive
Credit Cards: AE, MC, V
Reservations: No
Handicapped Accessible: Yes

Much cozier than many brightly lit, squared-corner Japanese restaurants, Osaka has small couples benches and traditional sculptures. Their classic fare, such as sushi, miso soup, and salads is rendered well, and is the favorite of locals. The comfortable atmosphere, reasonable pricing, and gracious service make this a relaxing dinner location. Oddly, this downtown restaurant does not tend to draw large crowds; you can dine on excellent food in peace, without shouting over dozens of college students. All dishes are listed at less than $10.

OTTAVIO'S RISTORANTE ITALIANO
77 East Center Street
Provo
801-377-9555
www.ottavios.com
Cuisine: Italian
Serving: L, D
Open: Mon. through Sat.
Price: Moderate to Expensive
Credit Cards: AE, Disc, MC, V
Reservations: Yes
Handicapped Accessible: Yes

One of Provo's romantic dinner spots, Ottavio's classic Italian cuisine is a downtown favorite. Gourmet plating with fresh herb garnishes adds to the effect. During dinner the lights are turned low. Wooden floors and potted plants seem to integrate into the murals depicting a Mediterranean scene. An accordion player makes tasteful appearances here, serenading guests. Year-round, many celebrities associated with the Sundance Resort frequent the restaurant. Patio dining is available during the warm months. For great food with less of a show, visit their lunch buffet. The food makes the transition well. A wine selection is available.

PORTER'S PLACE
24 West Main Street
Lehi
801-768-8348
Cuisine: American
Serving: L, D
Open: Mon. through Sat.
Price: Inexpensive to Moderate
Credit Cards: AE, Disc, MC, V
Reservations: No
Handicapped Accessible: Yes (restrooms are not)

This restaurant commemorates one of the LDS Church's favorite characters of the pioneer days, Porter Rockwell. Rockwell is catalogued in history along with the likes of Butch Cassidy and Jesse James. His infamy among frontiersmen was paired with a fervent faith in the LDS Church; he was at once extremely gracious with innocents and fear-inspiring toward enemies. With a thuggish build and a quick hand for martial law, he served as the bodyguard of early church leaders Brigham Young and Joseph Smith. Rockwell also had an unfortunate streak of being accused of many crimes, including the failed assassination of Missouri's then governor Boggs. Now furnished with Wild West furniture salvaged from an old Montana tavern, this restaurant keeps

with the pioneer tradition, with different meat cuts as the centerpiece of each plate. Other offerings include seafood, hamburgers, and a soda fountain. This restaurant is family friendly.

TOUCH OF SEOUL/SPICY COREA
43 North University Avenue
Provo Downtown
801-377-7330
Cuisine: Korean
Serving: L, D
Open: Tues. through Sat.
Price: Inexpensive
Credit Cards: MC, V
Reservations: No
Handicapped Accessible: Yes

Touch of Seoul (also called Spicy Corea) is the perfect midday stop. Located in historic downtown Provo, this restaurant serves dishes brimming with fresh carrots, lettuce, sprouts, and other vegetables. Dishes are accompanied by authentic pickled cabbage, water chestnut, teriyaki potatoes, and seaweed. Most dishes are rice and noodle bowls that come with the choice of chicken, beef, or tofu. Some entrées feature squid. Touch of Seoul offers excellent, stimulating cuisine in an utterly uncrowded restaurant.

THE TREE ROOM
Sundance Resort
7 miles east on UT 189, 2 miles north on UT 92
801-223-4200
www.sundanceresort.com
Cuisine: Contemporary American, regional
Serving: L, D
Open: Daily
Price: Moderate to Expensive
Credit Cards: AE, Disc, MC, V
Reservations: Yes
Handicapped Accessible: Yes (inquire)

For a truly high-end, secluded dinner retreat, you should think about the Tree Room at Sundance. This lodge-style restaurant has rough-cut pine, stonework, and southwestern woven blankets to remind you where you are. The atmosphere is softened to a high-end romantic level by open-hand service and the careful placement of linens and elegant lamps. All around the dining room you see beautiful indigenous handiwork and windows peering out into the surrounding evergreens. The food fits right into this forested setting, with regional game and fish, as well as select cuts of beef and seafood. Each plate is served with vegetables, and sauces are crafted with herbs from a local source when possible. The Sundance Resort is a year-round celebration center of the arts, and so you should check the Web site calendar if you want your dinner to coincide with special events.

ATTRACTIONS

Museums and Galleries

Brigham Young University has two main fine arts gallery spaces, the B. F. Larson Gallery and Gallery 303. Both are open 9–5, Mon. through Fri., and are located in the third level of the Harris Fine Arts Center (north of the Wilkinson Student Center, accessed by East Campus Drive, Brigham Young University; 801-422-2881; www.byu.edu). Additional displays can be found on the third and fourth floors of the building. The works here are displayed for the education of students as well as visitors, and include traveling exhibitions in addition to competition student work.

Other galleries spread throughout campus and Utah Valley have individualized subject matter. Many focus on the history and religious art of Mormonism, juxtaposed against other worldly themes. Some museums charge no admission, but all appreciate donations.

ALPINE ART CENTER

450 South Alpine Highway
Alpine
801-763-7173
www.alpineartcenter.com
Open: 9–5 Mon. through Fri.; 3–6 Sat.; closed Sun.
Admission: Free
Handicapped Accessible: Yes

The Alpine Art Center is a modern facility framed by the Wasatch Mountains. Surrounded by lush green lawn, natural streams, wildflowers, shaded pathways, and 10 acres of sculpture gardens, this 33,000-square-foot building is home to galleries, community functions, classes, and the **Adonis Bronze Fine Art Casting Facility**. Dinners, dances, and grand piano concerts regularly take place here. Because of its expansive beauty and dining facilities, this is a popular place for weddings. Keep an eye on their events listings.

CONSERVATION MOUNTAIN MUSEUM AT CABELA'S

2502 West Grand Terrace
Lehi
801-766-2500
www.cabelas.com
Open: 10–5 Tues. through Sat.; 3–6 Sun.; closed Mon.

Admission: Free
Handicapped Accessible: Yes

A 30-foot-tall exhibit of three-dimensional habitat simulations, this museum is filled with wild game taxidermy from around the globe, actual fishponds, running streams, and waterfalls. A surprising chance to peak into hunting and sporting history, their retail store also has a gun library, archery and shooting ranges, an aquarium with 55,000 gallons worth of re-created habitat for Utah's native fish, and a restaurant where you can sample wild game and other cuisine.

CRANDALL HISTORICAL PRINTING MUSEUM
275 East Center Street
Provo
801-377-7777
www.crandallmuseum.org
Open: 9–12 Mon. through Fri.; recommended demonstrations by appointment (minimum of 15 required)
Admission: Call to inquire; $45 minimum charge and reservations required
Handicapped Accessible: Yes

The Crandall Historic Printing Museum is a necessary stop for those planning to visit the **L. Tom Perry Special Collections** at BYU (listed below). The founder of the museum, inspired by the significance of the religious printed word, has archived printing techniques dating back more than 550 years to Johannes Gutenberg. An authentic replica of the Gutenberg Press, similar to the one developed in Mainz, Germany, stands for viewing. During a guided tour, you can see how this press would have actually been used in the 15th century. Simulations of historical techniques illustrate the labor-intensive molten-lead castings of yore, with demonstrators in full character. Wild-

A downtown statue Christine Balaz

looking old-fashioned tools and heavy workbench replicas more often are suggestive of medieval torture devices than benevolent printing tackle. Tribute is also given to other historic figures of influence, including Benjamin Franklin and E. B. Gradin. This museum is the fruit of founder Louis Crandall's collection, started in 1954.

EARTH SCIENCE MUSEUM
1683 North Canyon Road
Provo
801-422-3680
www.byu.edu
Open: 9–5 Mon. through Fri.; closed on university holidays

Admission: Free; donations accepted
Handicapped Accessible: Yes

An exciting offering of the paleontological work of BYU, this museum draws from the richness of regional digs, with fossils gathered from Utah, Montana, Idaho, and Wyoming. These states are among the most fruitful known dinosaur "graveyards" in the world. The museum was built in 1976 and its galleries are laid out in a pleasing fashion. These skeletons, ranging from 380 million to 15,000 years of age, are housed in stately display cases. The purpose of the gallery is to educate through information and stimulation of the imagination, rather than through loud displays and lighted button panels. An integral and influential part of modern paleontology, the researchers at BYU have contributed many breakthrough discoveries to the world of fossils.

JOHN HUTCHINGS MUSEUM OF NATURAL HISTORY
55 North Center Street
Lehi
801-678-7180
www.hutchingsmuseum.org
Open: Tues. through Sat. 11–5; closed Sun. and Mon.
Admission: $4 adults, $3 children 3-12, seniors, and students (with ID) 13–18, special family and group discounts
Handicapped Accessible: Yes

Each room in this museum is dedicated to a certain branch of natural history. Mammals, fossils, shells, and bird eggs are featured along with Native American, Wild West, and pioneer rooms. ("Pioneer" is Utahan for "Mormon.") Much of the museum is dedicated to Utah's natural history, but some exotic displays exist as well. The museum is located in the old Veterans Memorial Building, and commemorative plaques are available for viewing.

L. TOM PERRY SPECIAL COLLECTIONS
Room 1130, Harold B. Lee Library
Campus Center, west of Wilkinson Student Center
Provo
http://sc.lib.byu.edu
801-422-2927
Open: 8–9 Mon. through Thurs.; 8–6 Fri.; 10–6 Sat.; closed Sun.
Admission: Free
Handicapped Accessible: Yes

In conjunction with a visit to the **Crandall Historic Printing Museum** (listed above), a trip to the L. Tom Perry Special Collections in BYU library will round out a day of printing history and give you a chance to see some of the original Mormon texts. In these collections you will see old and rare books and, if you visit the printing museum, learn how they were created. This is the site of World War II volumes, other historic printed material, and even book conferences. You will get a sense of seriousness about this topic, as the Perry Special Collections are integral to many education departments at BYU. The collections include historic Mormon and Americana texts, as well as many other unrelated genres, such as the sciences, Renaissance and Reformation, Victorian and Edwardian, fine prints, and a collection of Larson Yellowstone's art from Yellowstone National Park.

MONTE L. BEAN LIFE SCIENCE MUSEUM

645 East 1430 North
Brigham Young University
Provo
801-422-5051
http://mlbean.byu.edu/home
Open: 10–9 Mon. through Fri.; 10–5 Sat.; closed Sun.
Admission: Free
Handicapped Accessible: Yes

The Monte L. Bean Life Science Museum incorporates professional work and community contributions into its galleries. Every year it holds a local photography competition that showcases some of the best community work in the area, with subject matter that includes regional wildlife and helps you gain more insight into Provo's natural surroundings. This museum showcases the diverse living world of snakes, spiders, reptiles, mammals, fish, and other fauna from around the world. Plenty of facts are available for the digestion of adults, while stimulating hands-on displays prod kids' interests. Visiting lecturers frequent the museum. Also, there are live animal "shows" almost daily; check the Web site for details. Open since 1978, this museum has long sought to educate the community about the diversity and frailty of the natural world, and so helps oversee the **Lytle Ranch Preserve**, 36 miles west of St. George. This 462-acre working preserve is a Mojave oasis that is home to hundreds of plant and animal species, 20 of which are found nowhere else in the state.

MUSEUM OF ART

492 East Campus Drive
Brigham Young University
Provo
801-422-8287
http://moa.byu.edu
Open: 10–6 Mon. through Fri. (open until 9 Thurs.); 12–5 Sat.; closed Sun.
Admission: Free, fee for special exhibits
Handicapped Accessible: Yes (via north entrance)

In the heart of Mormonism's spiritual and cultural center, the Museum of Art has a permanent collection rich in religious interpretive and historical art. Annexed to BYU, it also attracts a variety of traveling exhibitions and keeps its own collection spanning modern and ancient times, and places near and far. A four-story modern facility with more than 100,000 square feet of floor space, the triangular building itself was designed to enhance the art installations through play with light and space. A café overlooks an outdoor sculpture garden. With nearly 350,000 visitors annually, the museum is able to attract the work of acclaimed artists and attain art loans from prestigious institutions.

MUSEUM OF PEOPLES AND CULTURE

700 North 100 East
Brigham Young University
Provo
801-422-0020
http://mpc.byu.edu

Old BYU Women's Gymnasium   Christine Balaz

Open: 9–6 Mon. through Fri.; closed Sat. and Sun.
Admission: Free; fee for guided tours
Handicapped Accessible: Yes

A teaching facility, the Museum of Peoples and Culture's exhibits are the products of BYU ethnology and archaeology students. The research, creation, design, and installation of all exhibits is headed by these advanced students, although the professionalism that results would lead you to believe otherwise. Common themes of faith, birth, death, and history spread over a global scope help students and visitors examine these topics as they pertain to cultures from around the world. Obtain a free parking permit at the museum.

NORTH AMERICAN MUSEUM OF ANCIENT LIFE
2929 North Thanksgiving Way
Thanksgiving Point
Lehi
801-766-5000
www.thanksgivingpoint.com/museum
Open: 10–9 Mon. through Sat.; closed Sun.
Admission: $9 adults, $7 seniors, $7 age 12 and under
Handicapped Accessible: Yes

Located within the entertainment center of Thanksgiving Point, the North American Museum of Ancient Life is a favorite for kids of all ages. Of the 122,000 square feet of exhibits, most visitors will remember the massive assembled dinosaur skeletons and myriad associated visuals. With more than 60 skeletons, this collection has more than any

Thanksgiving Point Christine Balaz

other in the world. The museum also has many other exhibits including a Night Skies Tunnel and exhibits that adults might find more interesting, like working paleontology exhibits and life-sized dioramas depicting pioneers and indigenous tribes. For more intense entertainment, check out the **Mammoth Screen Theater**, with a 50- by 70-foot seamless screen and enthralling sound system.

OREM HERITAGE MUSEUM

SCERA Center
745 South State Street
Orem
801-225-2569
www.scera.org
Open: June through Aug., 12:30–4:30 Mon. through Sat.; Sept.–May, 3–7 Mon. through Sat.
Admission: Free
Handicapped Accessible: Yes

This museum attempts to convey a complete story of Orem's history. It begins with the stories and artifacts of indigenous peoples as long ago as 10,000 B.C. Pioneer stories are told, along with those of the local economy. An exhibit is dedicated to local World War I and Korean War soldiers and World War II POWs. Features of the museum are a blacksmith shop and 1940s railroad diorama, as well as displays depicting the major formative industries of the region.

SPRINGVILLE MUSEUM OF ART
126 East 400 South
Springville
801-489-2727
www.sma.nebo.edu
Open: 10–5 Tues. through Sat.; 3–6 Sun.; closed Mon.
Admission: Free, donations accepted
Handicapped Accessible: Yes

The Springville Museum of Art, founded in 1937, is Utah's oldest museum of the visual arts. Housed in a Spanish Revival building and surrounded by curvaceous European-style landscaping, the museum houses many global exhibitions, as well as the thematically typical— but nonetheless fascinating—Mormon spiritual collections of Utah. Many special events, including concerts, traveling exhibitions, and seminars, are offered at the museum, so be sure to check their Web site around the time of your visit.

WOODBURY ART MUSEUM
575 East University Parkway
Second Level, University Mall
Orem
801-426-6199
www.uvu.edu/museum
Open: 12–8 Tues. through Sat.; closed Sun., Mon.
Admission: Free, donations accepted
Handicapped Accessible: Yes

Pieces displayed in the exhibits include paintings, sculptures, and photographic work of artists from Utah, the United States, and around the world. The Woodbury also hosts special events and lectures in conjunction with Utah Valley University. Annexed to Utah Valley University, with an enrollment of nearly 30,000 students, the Woodbury is able to attract the work of excellent artists.

Gardens

THANKSGIVING POINT GARDENS
3003 North Thanksgiving Way
Thanksgiving Point
Lehi
801-768-4999; 1-888-672-6040
www.thanksgivingpoint.com
Open: 10–8 Mon. through Sat. (last Sat. in Mar. through last Sat. in Oct.)
Admission: $10 adults, $6 age 12 and under, $9 seniors (65+)
Handicapped Accessible: Yes

The Gardens at Thanksgiving Point cover 55 acres and are navigated by curving brick walkways, with vine-supporting promenades and evergreen and deciduous trees. Various themed pockets include the Waterfall Gardens, Monet Garden, Fragrance Garden, and Parterre Garden. Imaginative kids enjoy the Secret Garden. Summer concerts take place in an outdoor amphitheater whose backdrop is a cliff bank with waterfalls cascading down its face. A nonprofit community center, the gardens also offer instructional home gardening classes, children's workshops, and a Noah's Ark splash pool and fountain for hot days.

Amusement Parks

SEVEN PEAKS RESORT WATER PARK

1330 East 300 North
Provo
801-373-8777
www.sevenpeaks.com
Open: Seasonally (June through early Sept.), 11–8 Mon. through Sat.
Admission: Variable, available in full and half-day rates
Handicapped Accessible: Partially

Few things can cure a hot Utah summer afternoon faster than a true water park. Seven Peaks has every imaginable form of water-park recreation. A wave pool, circulating "Lazy River," waterslides, tubing falls, and children's pool can take the ya-ya's right out of the kids and give them an appetite for dinner. Additionally, there is a volleyball court, burger stand, and picnic areas. Acres of pool space and green grass allow you to spread out your beach towel without fear of being trampled by someone else's children.

THANKSGIVING POINT

3003 North Thanksgiving Way
Lehi
801-768-2300; 1-888-672-6040
www.thanksgivingpoint.com
Open: 10:30–7:30 Mon. through Sat.; 12–7:30 Sun. (summer only)
Price: Variable
Handicapped Accessible: Partially

Although not a traditional amusement park by any means, Thanksgiving Point has many different educational and entertainment features that make it a fulfilling stop for parents and children. The **Thanksgiving Point Gardens** cover 55 acres with flowers and greenery. **Farm Country** is a chance for kids to feed and pet docile farm animals. Here they can learn how the animals are raised and kept. Children adore the "baby" animals, and lucky visitors can even witness hatching chicks and pet young foals. Wagon rides are available. **The Barn** and **Electric Park** are venues for concerts and group gatherings. Another family pleaser is the **North American Museum of Ancient Life** (listed in the "Museums" section of this chapter) with the largest collection of assembled dinosaur skeletons in the world. If you have half a day to spend, head over to the 7,728-yard **Golf Club at Thanksgiving Point**. With 18 holes and a 22,000-square-foot clubhouse, this Johnny Miller course is worth a visit.

TRAFALGA FAMILY FUN CENTER

168 South 1200 West
Orem
801-224-6000
www.trafalga.com

Open: 10 AM–midnight Mon. through Thurs.; 10 AM–1 AM Fri. and Sat.; Closed Sun.
Price: Variable
Handicapped Accessible: Partially

This is a clean, sunny atmosphere where your kids can burn off some extra energy and get colorful stimulation. Here you can experience safe adventure in a fun atmosphere that will entertain both kids and adults. For children with trusting parents, go-cart rides are available. Indoorsy children can head to the arcade games or billiard tables while their athletic siblings swing in the batting cages. A fun, yet challenging miniature golf course has giant obstacles that dwarf the players. This is a colorful, entertainment-saturated environment that will amuse anyone for hours.

Historic Buildings and Sites

To guide you on your way, cruise by the Utah Valley Convention and Visitors Bureau center (111 South University Avenue, Provo; 801-851-2100 or 1-800-222-8824; www.utahvalley .org) and pick up a Provo Historic Buildings Tour Booklet. This will take you on a quick tour of Provo, and can tell you of buildings and sites that you can recognize as you go about your normal business and recreation. Many of the buildings are located just north of the Visitors Center, around the University Avenue and Center Street intersection. Another guide option available at the Visitors Center is the Utah County Historic Sites Brochure. This takes you a bit farther than the streets of Provo to historically significant sites, like the American Fork Presbyterian Church, Lehi Roller Mills, Peteetneet Academy, Provo Town Square, and Provo Tabernacle. If you'd prefer a guided tour, contact the Historic Lehi Bus Tour (394 West Main Street, Lehi; 801-768-0307). This is a perfect way for enthusiasts to see old massacre sites and historic structures without trying to drive at the same time. In the bus, you will travel along the former route of the Overland Coach and Pony Express to the remains of Camp Floyd. Now an inn, this was once the predominant western military camp of the U.S. government in the 1850s. Come prepared for a six-hour tour.

Provo City Library Christine Balaz

Historic Academy Square (550 North University Avenue; 801-852-6650; www .provo.lib.ut.us), now called Provo Academy Square Library, was opened as Brigham Young Academy (later Brigham Young University) in 1892. Built by a son of Brigham Young, Don Carlos Young, it was used by the university and Brigham Young High School until 1968, when it was vacated for 20 years. Demolition threats served as the ultimatum that ended this abandonment, and the building was rescued by a flurry of fund-raising and community backing. Today it houses the Provo City Library.

Though a 20-minute drive southwest of Lehi, the **Camp Floyd–Stagecoach Inn State Park** in Fairfield is certainly worth visiting. A major U.S. government outpost during the late 1850s and 1860s, this was home to a 3,500-person army sent to monitor and, if necessary, regulate Mormon activities. This initiated the founding of Fairfield. Hundreds of buildings went up to house the military personnel and accompanying civilians. At that time, Fairfield was nearly half the size of Salt Lake City. When the anticipated Mormon Rebellion never actually came to fruition, the camp slid into more routine functions like surveying, Indian relations, and aiding the Overland Coach and Pony Express. Accessible by UT 73, this state park is closed from mid-Oct. through Mar. Open daily 9–5.

The **Provo Tabernacle** (100 South University Avenue, Provo; 801-377-5700) was opened in 1898 after 15 years of construction, and has been in use ever since. An original tower, too heavy for the roof to support, was removed in the 1950s after multiple closures and partial condemnations due to roof sag. The four original corner towers still exist. Every year during the holiday season Handel's Messiah is performed here.

Provo Mormon Temple (2200 Temple Hill Drive; 801-375-5775) was built from 1969 to 1972. Although its history is short, this building is significant in the Mormon Church. It is the busiest temple in the world. The **Missionary Training Center** and BYU, both major crucial educational centers for Mormon youth and adults, are just down the hill, adding to the importance of the facility.

The **Utah County Courthouse** (51 South University Avenue, Provo) is actually Provo's third courthouse since the 1860s. The first was built in 1866 at a cost of just over $5,000. Five years later it became a jail, where a public execution for a double murder was held. This building was eventually sold to the Provo Woolen Mills, and a second courthouse was commissioned and dedicated on October 14, 1873. The men who built it were paid partly with cash, partly in grain and stock in Provo Woolen Mills. Again, the growing city needed to expand into a larger courthouse, and the present neoclassic courthouse was opened in 1925 after six years of construction.

Sports Teams

Sports fans in Provo are Brigham Young University Cougars fans. With almost 35,000 students, this NCAA school has typical big sports like basketball, football, baseball, and soccer, as well as less common sports like gymnastics and volleyball. If you are a die-hard BYU, Steve Young, or Ty Detmer fan and want to check out some of the Cougars' 110-year sporting history, visit Legacy Hall in the Student Athletic Center (south of 1230 North and east of University Avenue; 801-422-2118; www.byucougars.com). Admission is free, and the museum is open from 7 AM–9 PM. Because nothing is better than rival state universities, BYU's 64,000-seat LaVell Edwards Stadium sells out for BYU Cougars/University of Utah Utes games. The 23,000-seat BYU Marriot Center holds basketball games, and the state-of-the-art Miller Park is where baseball and softball are played. The George Albert Smith Fieldhouse seats 5,000 people and hosts many volleyball game and gymnastics competitions.

Nightlife

Nightlife in Provo? The answer depends on your idea of an evening out. If your goal is a romantic dinner and a trip to the theater, you will be completely satisfied in Provo. If you would prefer a night of cocktails and socializing, you might want to make the 20-minute drive to the Sundance Resort. The Owl Bar (801-225-4107), in its beautiful wooded sur-

The Utah County Courthouse Christine Balaz

roundings, has a rustic ambience. The actual bar here is a relocated, antique rosewood bar visited habitually by Butch Cassidy in his prime. If hungry, you can order from the Foundry Grill menu.

If you are staying in town, check out the **BYU Theater Ballet**, **Chamber Singers**, **Wind Symphony**, or **Chamber Orchestra** (801-422-3575; http://pam.byu.edu). BYU Theater Ballet is part of America's largest university dance program. These companies usually each have only one show running at a time. The **Utah Valley Symphony** (www.utahvalley symphony.org) performs at the Provo Tabernacle (100 South University Avenue) and is another source of refined entertainment. Check online for performance schedules.

For a step down in formality, you might try the **Center Street Musical Theater** (177 West Center Street, Provo; 801-373-4485; www.csmtc.com). A favorite of Provo locals is the comedy scene. **Comedy Sportz** (35 West Center Street, Provo; 801-377-9700) is a lively improvisational comedy center, attracting performers from around the country who allow the audience to choose the performance topics and themes. **Johnny B's Comedy Club** (177 West 300 South, Provo; 801-377-6910) is a more toned-down, family-friendly establishment.

Not subtly named, **A. Beuford Gifford's Libation Emporium** (190 West Center Street, Provo; 801-373-1200; www.abgsbar.com) has a full bar that is often accompanied by live music. You can line up your quarters and join a game of pool. **Club Omni** (153 West Center Street, Provo; 801-375-0011) is an alcohol-free establishment that attempts to appeal to all ages with an extensive variety of music spread over three dance floors.

Many popular events are held at the **Alpine Art Center** (450 South Alpine Highway, Alpine; 801-763-7173; www.alpineartcenter.com). In conjunction with the **Alpine Community Art Council**, four concerts are held here annually. Master pianists from around the world come to play the concert grand Fazioli piano. This has been acclaimed as one of the best recording pianos in the world. The Main Gallery can seat 250 for concerts and dances and 180 for dinners, and is wonderful for dances and events.

Colleges and Universities

Brigham Young University (www.byu.edu) of Provo has almost 35,000 students. It is the country's largest private university and is sponsored by the Church of Jesus Christ of Latter-day Saints. Both a prestigious academic institution and a center of Mormon faith, the university holds its students and applicants accountable in both categories. Ecclesiastical recommendations are just as necessary as good SAT scores. Likewise, having neatly kept hair, modest clothing, and gracious behavior will keep you enrolled. It was established in 1875 and has a 110-year athletic history. Orem's Utah Valley University (www.uvu.edu) is a community college–type institution with a total enrollment of nearly 25,000. Many of the students here have families of their own and day jobs, so it somewhat lacks the stereotypical college scene of dorms, fraternities, and coffee shops. Other smaller or specialty-type trade schools in the area are the American Institute of Medical-Dental Technology in Provo, Provo College, and the Stevens-Henager College of Business.

ARTS AND ENTERTAINMENT

Music

Provo is the hub of Utah Valley's music scene. It draws talent and audiences from its Wasatch Front neighbors. Because the bar scene in Provo is much less important than family values, most of the musical emphasis here is on established orchestral and vocal groups. Many of these are associated with Brigham Young University. Provo's most popular annual music festival is the Blue Sky Concert Series taking place during June and July in Pioneer Park on West Center Street. The free concerts last just over an hour and happen each Monday night.

Brigham Young University student housing, Provo Christine Balaz

The **Utah Valley Symphony** (801-852-7007; www.utahvalleysymphony.org) was established in 1957. This full-sized, nonprofit assembly of 75 musicians can be seen performing at the Provo Tabernacle (100 South University Avenue). They perform five concerts spread over 10 shows every year. **Brigham Young University** has more musical groups of varying style than you could possibly see on your visit. For performance schedules particular to each group, see their Web site, **http://pam.byu.edu**. **The BYU Singers**, an ensemble of a few dozen men and women, perform pieces from the classics to Broadway and folk. The **Chamber Orchestra** is a mostly string ensemble that performs in intimate settings. The **Concert Band** (also called Wind Symphony) is a 47-piece set of wind, percussion, and brass instruments that plays marches and classical arrangements as well as contemporary pieces. The **Folk Music Ensemble** is a five-musician group that employs vocals, a banjo, guitar, mandolin, and fiddle to perform bluegrass and country music. **Jazz Legacy**, a group of brass, piano, banjo, and other instruments, dresses the part to play Dixieland Jazz. The **Jazz Singers** is a group of 14 vocalists that performs a cappella or with instrumental accompaniment. **Living Legends** is a group of Native Americans, Polynesians, and Latin Americans that performs the music of their peoples with choreographed dances. The 230-vocalist **Men's Chorus** is the largest college choir of its kind in the United States, performing a variety of music from spiritual to contemporary. The **Philharmonic Orchestra** is a string and wind group of 80 musicians playing music from all periods. The all-brass **Synthesis** blends jazz, Latin, blues, and swing. **Vocal Point** is the college's a cappella group/glee club.

Theater
Because Utah Valley is historically and continuingly very Mormon, some aspects of the town have remained disproportionately underdeveloped, like the bar scene, while other aspects,

especially those pertaining to family-related fun, have flourished. The theater scene falls right into the second category. There are many, many theater venues and just as many troupes. Many of these troupes are very community-oriented and community-grown, and so the productions here tend to be amateur and lighthearted.

Just south of Provo in Springville is the **Art City Playhouse Theater** (254 South Main Street, Springville; 801-735-4543), a nonprofit theater that spans the range of comedy, drama, and musical performances. The emphasis is on enjoyment rather than perfection. If you wish to combine dinner and theater, get tickets to a show at the **Center Street Musical Theater** (177 West Center Street, Provo; 801-373-4485; www.csmtc.com), where you can choose between western and Italian cuisine in a family-oriented environment. Lindon's contribution to the theater scene is the **Valley Center Playhouse** (780 North 200 East, Lindon; 801-785-1186; www.valleycenterplayhouse.com), which has been giving Monday and Friday performances for decades. Many plays have LDS themes, which you might appreciate if you are a member of the church or if you are just curious about the lives and values of Mormons.

The **Hale Center Theater** (225 West 400 North, Orem; 801-226-8600; www.haletheater.com) performs anything from westerns to classics. Some of their repertoire comes from the more than 80 plays written by Ruth and Nathan Hale, founders of the theater and prominent figures in LDS theater. The **Provo Theatre Company** (105 East 100 North, Provo; 801-379-0600) is a fully professional troupe whose season lasts September to June and consists of six different productions.

Provo's theater scene is of course enhanced by the **BYU Performing Arts Department** (http://pam.byu.edu/pam). Along with its many musical groups, the Arts Department has two theater troupes. The **Young Ambassadors**, a musical theater and dance group, combine dances and modern music to create American drama all their own. The **Young Company** dresses the part, wearing exaggerated costumes of bold colors to perform in front of children and their families.

Recreation and Rental Information

Nearby Areas

Provo sits just off the eastern edge of Utah Lake, near the shores of Provo Bay. Unlike the Great Salt Lake, the long and narrow Utah Lake contains fresh water. This instantly increases the number of potential activities to be had at Utah Lake State Park (801-375-0731). If you fish here, you have a chance of catching bass, catfish, panfish, and walleye. Motorboats are allowed here, and waterskiing and Jet Skiing are popular. The lake is large enough, with nearly 100,000 acres of surface area, that paddlers can find solitude as well.

Most of the natural gems of Utah County are in the Wasatch Range. Perfect for recreation in the summer months, these canyons stay a dozen or more degrees cooler than the nearby valleys. **American Fork Canyon**, just east of Alpine on UT 92/144, is the unmistakably gaping chasm that swallows the Alpine Highway. This is where you can begin the "Alpine Loop" road bike or spend summer afternoons rock climbing on the limestone cliffs. Here you can visit the **Timpanogos Cave National Monument** or relax at any of the numerous picnic areas.

Provo Canyon and its scenic byway take you northeast out of Provo via UT 189, and up to Heber Valley. If you are doing the Alpine Loop (by road bike or by car), turn left at UT 92 and head north toward American Fork Canyon. Along the way, you should make a stop at the

Bridal Veil Falls, a 600-foot ribbon of water pouring into the Provo River. If you have more time, hike (via paved or dirt trails) to the **Cascade Springs**, an area of clear trout pools and limestone terraces, or visit the famous **Sundance Resort**.

The **Sundance Resort** (www.sundanceresort.com) with its General Store, Foundry Grill, Tree Room, Owl Bar, Sundance Summer Theater, Sundance Institute Screening Room, and of course, Ski Resort, should be visited by anyone, day or night.

Rock Canyon is dead east of Provo, just above the Missionary Training Center and Provo Temple. It is not paved, and so is a favorite place for hikers of leisure. Although the floor of the canyon stays relatively flat, this is another dramatic Utah canyon with steep limestone walls, and it is a common destination for rock climbers. Just a bit farther south is **Spanish Fork Canyon**, accessed by UT 6. This highway is heavily trafficked by travelers en route to Price, the San Rafael Swell, or Moab, making the canyon less popular for recreation.

Local Running and Inline Skating

Provo River Parkway is a scenic, paved, 14-mile trail that spans the distance between Utah Lake and Provo Canyon's Vivian Park. Because of its gentle grade, green surroundings, and pavement, the parkway is a popular and convenient trail for joggers and inline skaters. Beware that this is a multiuse trail and bikers, although they are supposed to travel at a reasonable speed, may appear sud-

Downtown Provo Christine Balaz

denly. The northeastern end of the trail passes by Bridal Veil Falls, where hot bodies can cool off in the chilly natural pool. Although the trail extends all the way down to Utah Lake, a good place to park is at the mouth of Provo Canyon, on 800 North Street in Orem.

Opportunities are nearly endless for in-town running and inline skating. Provo and Orem's streets are generally wide, quiet, and safe. The major exceptions are University Avenue of Provo, State Street in Orem, and University Parkway. A scenic tour of ranch homes and occasional orchards can be had via **Canyon Road**. If you wish to stay closer, jog around either large campus. You will be impressed with the active student body.

Golf

Utah's golfing opportunities extend far beyond Salt Lake City and Park City. Utah Valley has a fair number of its own courses to add to Utah's millions of acres of greenery. Most golf courses require reservations, and some enforce dress codes, so it is prudent to call ahead. As with Salt Lake City, golf in Utah Valley is popular enough to bring its many courses into high demand, so you may want to book a few days in advance to get your ideal tee time on your course of choice.

Cascade Golf Center (1313 East 800 North, Orem; 801-225-6677; www.cascadegolfcenter
.com) is a 6,055-yard, par-71, 18-hole course. Minigolf is also available on the premises.

The **Golf Course at Thanksgiving Point** (3000 North Thanksgiving Way, Lehi; 801-768-
7401; www.thanksgivingpoint.com) is another one of Utah's gems, once ranked among
the 10 best courses in the country by Golf Digest. Utah's largest golf course, with 7,728
yards spread over 200 acres, this Johnny Miller course has a 22,000-square-foot clubhouse for entertaining.

Hobble Creek Golf Course (Hobble Creek Canyon Road, Springville; 801-489-6297) is an
18-hole, par-71 canyon course that many consider to be among Utah's best public courses.

Mathew Dye created the **Links at Sleepy Ridge** (700 South Sleepy Ridge, Orem; 801-434-
4653; www.sleepyridgegolf.com), with 7,017 yards of mildly hilly fairways and holes that
challenge any skill level.

The Reserve at East Bay (1860 South 380 East, Provo; 801-373-6262; www.eastbaygolf
.com) has two separate courses, an 18-hole champion course and a 9-hole executive
course. Designer William H. Neff, inspired by Utah Lake to the south, created many
man-made lakes and wetlands along the fairways that now serve as habitat for waterfowl.

Seven Peaks Resort (1450 East 500 North, Provo; 801-375-5155) is an 18-hole, 3,328-yard
course whose trademark hilliness makes for a challenging game and scenic views.

The **Spanish Oaks Golf Course** (2300 Power House Road, Spanish Fork; 801-798-9816)
begins flat and leisurely and finishes with a challenging back nine made difficult by
dog-legged fairways. The 18-hole course is par-72.

Tri-City Golf Course (1400 North 200 East, American Fork; 801-756-3594) is an 18-hole
course, open since 1971. The trees hugging many of the fairways act as hazards, yet frame
the Wasatch Mountain backdrop very well.

Biking and Bike Rentals

Perhaps you need to get excited about the ride you are about to do, rent a bike, buy some
spare inner tubes, or join a group ride. The only shop in the area that rents bicycles is Outdoors Unlimited (1151 Wilkinson Student Center, on the northeast corner of 1060 North
and East Campus Drive; 801-422-2708; http://outdoors.byu.edu) on the BYU campus. They
rent road and mountain bikes, as well as practically anything you could need for a ride,
including child trailers, helmets, and two-way radios. Because they are the only rental
facility in town, you should call well ahead. (If they are out of your size, or you are coming
into the area via Salt Lake City, you should consider renting your bicycle there. Information
regarding Salt Lake City bicycle rentals is listed in the same section of that chapter.) Bing-
ham Cyclery (187 West Center Street, Provo; 801-374-9890; www.binghamcyclery.com)
does not rent, but is staffed by a bunch of bikers that probably have an aggregate of a million miles in their legs. Racer's Cycle Service (159 West 500 North, Provo; 801-375-5873;
www.racerscycle.net) also does not rent bicycles, but it is a place to discuss your road or
mountain bike ride and get a supply of spare tubes. They have a weekly group road ride,
leaving every Saturday at 10 AM from the shop. It is a no-drop ride, but you are expected to
keep an 18–20 mph pace. Pedersen Ski & Sports (1300 South State Street, University Mall,
Orem; 801-225-3000) offers bicycle retail to the Orem area.

Road Biking

Provo has a nearly ideal climate for road biking. The only season when cycling is limited is
winter, although clear, sunny days make winter riding frequently possible. During spring

and fall, when most of your warmth is gleaned from the sun, you can stay in the valley and wear a light jacket. Perfect for these seasons is the **Utah Lake Loop**. This loop totals around 100 miles of mostly flat terrain. The west side of the lake is a long stretch of unpopulated road without services. It is imperative that you come doubly prepared for this ride; if you encounter problems, you are on your own. Prevailing winds can make for a surprisingly difficult flat ride. If you do not wish to do the entire loop, you can go out as long as you wish, and then double back. For wind conditions and other information, call Utah Lake State Park at 801-375-0731.

If you've brought your legs, lungs, and energy drinks, consider the incredibly scenic **Alpine Loop**. This rugged mountain loop leaves Orem and heads up Provo Canyon, past the Sundance Resort, into American Fork Canyon, eventually returning to Utah Valley in Alpine. This can be ridden through the spring, summer, and fall, although it is best done in the summer when the canyon air is comfortably warm. Along the way, you'll pass Bridal Veil Falls and Mt. Timpanogos as you traverse the rugged alpine Wasatch and the lush depths of its canyons. This ride should be treated as a completely unsupported mountain ride. If you do not wish to do the whole Alpine Loop, you may consider heading toward the mouth of Provo Canyon and picking up the **Provo River Parkway** at 800 North Street in Orem. From here, Bridal Veil Falls is only 8 miles up the canyon.

Mountain Biking

The Utah Valley vicinity has hundreds of mountain bike trails in seemingly infinite variations and combinations. Because each has its own challenges arising from technical riding, elevation change, length, and accessibility by car, you may want to select your ride by discussing your desires with any of the people at the bike shops listed above. Most rides here, because they are along the slopes of the dramatically steep Wasatch Mountains, have significant elevation gains, and most have at least a few spots of technical riding. One loop that many like is the **Bennie Creek Cutoff Trail**. This loop covers 8.1 miles, but more than 90 percent of the elevation gain takes place on 4.5 miles of pavement. The ride originates along the **Nebo Scenic Loop**, south of Payson. For more explicit directions, visit **www.utah mountainbiking.com**, which describes the ride with photographs, detailed trail descriptions, maps, and GPS coordinates.

An easily accessible, easily ridden trail is the Utah Valley portion of the **Bonneville Shoreline Trail**. This trail system is similar to its Salt Lake Valley sister and traverses the foothills of the Wasatch Mountains along the old shoreline of ancient Lake Bonneville. The Provo portion of the trail overlooks the cities below and is accessible at the Rock Canyon parking area. The Provo Canyon portion of the trail is accessible by US 189 at the Bridal Veil Falls exit. The trail is on the south side of the road. You can loop this with the **Provo Canyon Parkway**. Another portion of the Bonneville Shoreline Trail connects Orem to Pleasant Grove. Several hundred feet above the valley floor, you will be able to get a bird's-eye view of the towns below, as well as Utah Lake. There is very little elevation gain, and most riders do the trail as a 9-mile, out-and-back trip. It is also possible to loop back on city streets. To reach the trail in Orem, take 800 North Street east, making a left on 800 East Street and heading north, turning right on Cascade Drive. This road jogs back and forth up the hillside to the parking area. These trails (except the one in Provo Canyon) have plenty of sun exposure and should be ridden in the cool hours of the early morning or late afternoon during the summer.

Many, many more trails exist, and you should certainly seek further information, depending on your riding and navigation skills. A list of classic, must-do rides for each area is listed on **www.utahmountainbiking.com**, but many of the rides listed require at least intermediate technical skills, above-average fitness, and vehicular shuttles. If you fall into these categories, look these rides up.

Hiking and Snowshoeing

Because hikers are more versatile than all but the most skilled mountain bikers, there are even more options for hiking in the Utah Valley. The Big Baldy/Battle Creek Trail, although dangerously technical for mountain bikers, is a spectacular, high-alpine delight for hikers. You will traverse limestone ridges, stroll across grassy mountain parks, and receive shrubby shade. Great mountain views, as well as valley views below are some of the many perks of this 15-mile loop. To make this a more reasonable distance, do an out-and-back, avoiding the Bonneville Shoreline segment of the trail. Accessed through Pleasant Grove's 100 East Street (Canyon Highway) heading toward the mountains, turn right on 500 North (Grove Creek Drive) and into the paved parking area.

    Mount Timpanogos is the biggest hiking destination in Utah for a reason. With a dramatically high peak, wildflower parks, an alpine lake, herds of resident mountain goats, and even a small glacier, it has everything you could want in a hike. The trail is not strenuous, but it is fairly long, so you may want to consider a partial trek. Two popular access

BYU's "Y" and Provo City Library Christine Balaz

points to Mount Timpanogos are the Timpooneke Trailhead in American Fork Canyon (7.5 miles and 4,600 vertical feet of elevation gain to summit) and the Emerald Lake Trailhead (6.5 miles and 3,200 vertical feet to summit). Along the Timpooneke Trail, you can see the wreckage of a B-52, although you must take a 0.5-mile detour to a signed toilet upon entering the Timpanogos Basin. More information and a printable map for this hike can be found on the **Climb Utah** Web site (www.climb-utah.com/WM/timp.htm).

For a less adventurous nature stroll, visit the **Provo River Parkway**, listed above in the "Running and Inline Skating" section of this chapter.

Rock Climbing

The Utah Valley abuts some the Wasatch Range's best rock climbing. Most of the routes here are single-pitch sport-climbing routes, although one notable exception is the Lone Peak Cirque. The difficulty and length of the approach prevents any casual parties from even reaching the base of the climbs. Rock Canyon, the mouth of which is very near the Provo Mormon Temple, and American Fork Canyon, east of Alpine on the Alpine Highway, are the two main sport-climbing destinations in the area. Most climbs in these canyons are on limestone. Loose rock in these canyons is not unheard of, so a helmet in the pack is advised. Little Cottonwood Canyon, Big Cottonwood Canyon, Uinta Mountains, Maple Canyon, Ibex, St. George, Indian Creek, and Moab are nearby destination climbing areas for bouldering, traditional climbing, and sport climbing. Hansen Mountaineering (1799 North State Street, Orem; 801-226-7498; www.hookedonclimbing.com) and Out-N-Back (1797 South State Street, Orem; 801-224-0454) are two shops where you can purchase guidebooks or any equipment you may have forgotten to bring.

If you don't have the time or know-how to climb outside, you should consider visiting a climbing gym. Indoor climbing can be a great introduction to the safety techniques and athletic movement of the sport or a convenient way to stay in shape. **The Quarry** (2494 North University Parkway, Provo; 801-418-0266; www.quarryclimbing.com) in Provo has nearly 100 routes for beginners and experts alike. With something for everyone, it has wall space divided among a top-rope and lead-climbing wall, a multifeatured bouldering area, and a crack-climbing area. The wall has varying steepness, from overhanging to vertical and slabby. If you go to The Quarry in Provo, you will be able to rent shoes and a harness. Drive a bit north to **Momentum Climbing** (220 West 10600 South, Sandy; 801-990-6890; www.momentumclimbing.com), a new and very well-done indoor rock climbing gym. This gym is most known for its excellent roped climbing (lead climbing and top rope), but its bouldering cave and other fitness facilities and classes are great assets.

Fishing

Because most fishing expeditions require some amount of driving, Provo anglers share many streams and lakes with Salt Lake City and Park City fishers. Hobble Creek Canyon and Provo Canyon, each with scenic byway highways, have fishable sections of their own and lead anglers to high mountain lakes and reservoirs. Because Provo's fishing destinations are exactly the same as those of Park City and Salt Lake City, refer to the "Fishing" sections of those chapters for more information.

Boating, Kayaking, Canoeing, Rafting, and Sailing

If you are an experienced whitewater enthusiast and have your equipment on hand, all you need to do is go to a local shop and buy a guidebook or have a conversation with a sales clerk. Unfortunately, many of the reliable, relatively safe whitewater locations are on the big waters of the more distant **Green River**. The **Provo River** and small nearby creeks also have offerings, but have flows much more susceptible to spring runoff and summer droughts. Needless to say, small-creek paddling can be many times more dangerous than large river expeditions.

If you would like to join a guided raft trip, you will likely drive east or southeast to the **Green, Yampa, or Colorado rivers**. Accessibility and regulatory issues make these rivers difficult to run on your own without thorough advanced planning. **Adrift Adventures** of Jensen (1-800-824-0150; www.adrift.com), **Dinosaur River Expeditions** of Park City (1-800-345-7238; www.dinoadv.com), and **Sherri Griffith Expeditions** of Moab (435-259-8229 or 1-800-332-2439; www.griffithexp.com) have permits on these rivers and the know-how to access some of the more remote spots.

Most visitors have time restrictions, and cannot afford to spend whole days or weeks on a river trip. A short trip on the Provo River can raise your heart rate substantially. **High Country Rafting** (6 miles east of Provo along UT 189; 801-224-2500; www.highcountry rafting.com) offers perfectly fun, yet overwhelmingly safe raft, kayak, and even tubing trips down the Provo River. (If you enjoy your experience with them, consider making a fly-fishing expedition with them next time you are in town.) **All Seasons Adventures** of Park City (435-649-9619; www.allseasonsadventures.com) is a good choice if you prefer flat water to whitewater. You can relax on lakes and reservoirs in inflatable, tandem, and sea kayaks.

For flat-water, motorized adventures, **Invert Sports** (801-413-9602; www.utahboat rental.com) offers the whole package, from motorboats to Jet Skis with towing vehicles and trailers, water-ski and wakeboard gear. **Daytrips Outfitters** (1-800-649-8294; www.day trips.com) rents boats for waterskiing and fishing, wave runners, pontoon boats, and even canoes and kayaks. Of course, Provo is practically waterfront property on the Provo Bay of Utah Lake. With nearly 100,000 acres of surface area, you can fish, kayak, canoe, or zip along by motor or wind power. The fish you can expect to catch in Utah Lake include white and black bass, channel catfish, panfish, and walleye. Other nearby lakes are Morehouse Reservoir, Smith Reservoir, Washington Lake, and Trial Lake.

Horseback Riding

Though horseback riding is not as popular in Provo as in the more rural mountains of Park City, you can go to the Sundance Stables (435-654-1655; www.rockymtnoutfitters.com), a division of Rocky Mountain Outfitters near the Sundance Resort. They offer private rides to groups of six or less in order to bring you the most personal, serene experience with nature.

For more options, Park City has a plethora of horseback riding options, including **Park City/Deer Valley Stables** (1-800-303-7256; www.rockymtnrec.com/PCStab.htm), **Red Pine Adventures** (435-649-9445 or 1-800-417-7669; www.redpinetours.com), and **Wind in Your Hair Riding** (435-336-4795; www.windinyourhair.com), as listed in this section of Chapter 2, Park City.

Tennis

The best, most accessible tennis courts in Provo are on the Brigham Young University campus. You can choose among the 14 newly renovated, lighted outdoor courts or the four regulation-sized indoor courts. Both sets of courts are found near the Smith Fieldhouse, which is just south of 1060 North Street and a block east of University Avenue. The outdoor courts are just south of this building; the indoor tennis building is directly east of the fieldhouse. Another option is the Gold's Gym and Tennis Club (44 East 800 North; 801-765-4653) in Orem.

Swimming

Brigham Young University (www.byucougars.com) has three Olympic-sized, heated swimming pools with lanes demarcated for serious lap swimmers, as well as lanes for casual dog paddlers. Family groups are allowed, but the function of the pool is athletic rather than purely recreational. Housed in the Stephen L. Richards Building on the western side of the BYU campus, the pools are accessed by West Campus Drive, just south of 1230 North Street. The Provo Recreation Center and Swimming Pool (1155 North University Avenue; 801-852-6610) also has a pool that services lap swimmers and offers swimming lessons, water aerobics, and many other forms of exercise and rehabilitation. For casual, kid-friendly swimming and waterslides, go to the Seven Peaks Resort Water Park (1330 East 300 North, Provo; 801-373-8777), as listed in the "Amusement Parks" section of this chapter.

SHOPPING

Much of Provo's shopping is grouped into malls and centers, where you can shop boutique and department stores. Historic **Downtown Provo** (www.downtownprovo.org) is a collection of city blocks surrounding the intersection of University Avenue and Center Street. This district offers unique shops, many restaurants, and close proximity to BYU, the City Library, and Mormon Tabernacle.

Boutiques and Fine Arts

The Downtown Provo Gallery Stroll takes place on the first Friday of each month. Every stroll is free and includes live music and various refreshments, depending on the evening. The stroll usually lasts from 6–9 PM and visits the Anderson Gallery at the Provo City Library (550 North University Avenue; 801-852-6657; www.provo.lib.ut.us; various historic and modern paintings), Coleman Studios (117 North University Avenue; 801-225-5766; www.colemanart.com; southwestern paintings), the Freedom Gallery (230 West Center Street; 801-375-1150; various modern sculpture and paintings), Gallery OneTen (110 South 300 West; 801-623-0615; www.galleryoneten.blogspot.com; various modern sculpture and paintings), Terra Nova Gallery (41 West 300 North; 801-374-0016; www.terra novagallery.com; various modern paintings and sculpture, religious themes), and the Utah County Gallery (151 South University Avenue; 801-785-2059; various paintings).

Other fine art galleries in the area include the **Alpine Art Center** (450 South Alpine Highway, Alpine; 801-763-7173; www.alpineartcenter.com; various modern and historic sculpture and paintings), **B. F. Larson Gallery & Gallery 303** (1679 North Campus Drive, Provo; 801-378-2881; various modern and historic sculpture and paintings), the **Springville Museum of Art** (26 East 400 South, Springville; 801-489-2727; www.sma .nebo.edu; various modern paintings), and the **Woodbury Museum of Art** at Utah Valley University (800 West University Parkway, Orem; 801-426-6199; www.uvu.edu/museum; various modern photography, sculpture, paintings).

If at Sundance, make a trip to the **Art Shack** (Sundance Resort; 801-223-4535; www
.sundanceresort.com). A continuation of Sundance's celebration of life and the arts, this is
a haven for artists, aspiring and established. Single-day workshops are available in a variety of mediums, and resident artists are often happy to discuss their work with you.

Specialty Shops and Farmers' Markets

As specialty shops go, **Cabela's** (2502 West Grand Terrace, Lehi; 801-766-2500; www
.cabelas.com) is tops for outdoorsmen. With 150,000 square feet of floor space for fly-
fishing, hunting, and camouflage gear, this is a true paradise for some. To help you really
get into the spirit, this store even has a 30-foot-tall natural game habitat display, a
55,000-gallon aquarium of Utah's native fish, a gun library, archery and shooting
ranges, and a restaurant where you can sample wild game.

The **Provo Downtown Business Alliance Farmers Market** takes place each Saturday from
8 AM–1 PM at the northwest corner of Pioneer Park (500 West and 100 South), weather
permitting. In addition to fresh vegetables and fruits, the market often has live music
and other special events.

Lehi Roller Mills (833 East Main, Lehi; 1-877-311-3566; www.lehirollermill.com) is a specialty food shop that has grown from its 1906 origins in flour production. Still rooted in
the production of fundamentally excellent flours, this establishment shares the art of
baking and food preparation through simple, yet exquisite recipes. They also sell gift
baskets including house-made baked goods with accompanying gourmet sauces and
spreads.

Sundance Resort (northeast of Provo via UT 189 and 92; 801-225-4107 or 1-800-842-
1600; www.sundanceresort.com) has its own handful of unique shops in its Resort Village. **The Deli** (801-223-4211) has fresh pastries and sandwiches made to order, as well
as shelves and barrels full of the local cheeses, spreads, and other high-end gourmet
products, some of which are made at Sundance. Do not be fooled by the name of the
General Store (801-223-4250). A fine casual clothing store, among other things, the
General Store became so popular that the Sundance mail-order catalog arose to bring
these goods to people around the nation. The General Store has special events year-
round, such as jewelry shows. Inventive toys are available as well. Do not miss the **Art
Shack Gallery** (801-223-4535), which sells the creations of local artists and on-site
glassblowers.

Malls and Squares

Provo Towne Centre (1200 Towne Centre Boulevard; 801-852-2401; www.shopprovotowne
centre.com) has more than 100 stores, mostly of the department and national chain
variety. Victoria's Secret, Hollister, the Gap, and others make this a one-stop trip for
clothing and other accessories. A major mall, this also has a movie theater and the Red
Robin Restaurant.

As if its golf course, expansive gardens, and museums weren't enough, **Thanksgiving Point**
(3003 North Thanksgiving Way, Lehi; 801-768-2300 or 1-888-672-6040; www.thanks
givingpoint.com) also has a small selection of shopping. Its major store is the Emporium
of furniture, but it also has a country shop at Farm Country and a shop at the gardens.

Shops at Riverwoods (4801 North University Avenue, Provo; 801-802-8430; www.shop
satriverwoods.com) is an open-air collection of higher-end shops, salons, and restau-

rants. Clothing stores, children's shops, and specialty stores can all be found here. The outdoor gardens and movie theater add to the offerings.

University Mall (575 East University Parkway; 801-224-0694; www.shopuniversitymall .com) has many of the country's favorite big stores, including Costco, Macy's, and Nordstrom, as well as smaller specialty and ethnic boutiques. Casual and slightly upscale dining is available on the premises.

4

SKI COUNTRY

Right up there with Utah's reputation for Mormons is its fame for having "The Best Snow on Earth." This claim could easily be the truth. Every winter, weather systems move east across the great southwestern deserts of California and Nevada. These fronts pass smoothly across this open terrain until they slam against Utah's Wasatch Range, which rises suddenly 7,000 feet from the valley floor. These craggy mountains that wring the snow out of the clouds have terrain that complements their precipitation.

Naturally, ski resorts have sprung up all over the Wasatch Range. Because of the demand coming from the metropolitan area of Salt Lake City, four major ski areas operate within 30 to 40 minutes of downtown. Brighton and Solitude are perched at the top of Big Cottonwood Canyon, and the more famous Alta and Snowbird are in the sister Little Cottonwood Canyon.

Park City has three destination resorts literally in town. The Canyons, Deer Valley, and Park City Mountain Resort could each be enough to turn a village into a ski town. The Canyons covers more than a half-dozen distinct mountains and is a favorite jumping-off point for backcountry skiers. Deer Valley is practically a town within itself, with three separate villages and many luxury homes lining the slopes. It is renowned for its unsurpassed customer service, dining, and grooming. Park City Mountain Resort has many facets. It is at once a favorite for hikers accessing challenging backcountry terrain, as well as a terrain park haven and the training center for the U.S. Ski Team.

To the north, near Ogden, are Powder Mountain, Snowbasin, and Wolf Creek Utah. Powder Mountain has the most skiable acres of any North American ski resort. If you ski here a week after the last fresh snowfall, you will still be able to get fresh tracks somewhere. Snowbasin is owned by the same company as Sun Valley Resort and is saturated with luxury. Wolf Creek Utah is a tiny family mountain perfect for beginners. All of these resorts are beloved for their excellent terrain, snow cover, and utter lack of crowds.

Just east of Provo is the Sundance Resort. This beautiful mountain is only a small part of the goings-on here. Fine dining, working artist studios, and cultural festivals also make this resort an all-around celebration of life. Just as with the Ogden area resorts, Sundance is remarkably uncrowded.

Each mountain has its own flavor. Some, like Deer Valley, are the ultimate in lavish ski lodges and vacation rentals. Others, like Alta, have everything you need regarding lodging, nightlife, and rentals, but prefer to avoid the "resort" category. Although all of these resorts have on-site rentals, some people prefer to rent in town. The benefit of renting at the ski area is the convenience of repairing or exchanging damaged or malfunctioning equipment. However, renting in town can feel less rushed and crowded than trying to rent at the mountain. These in-town rentals are listed at the end of this chapter.

Backcountry ski tracks in wet snow Christine Balaz

For as many lift-served acres as Utah has, there is several times as much backcountry terrain. Virtually anywhere there is a mountain, there is skiing. Entire series resembling encyclopedia sets have been published to describe this resource. Many ski tours in and around Salt Lake City and Park City connect the tops of Millcreek, Little Cottonwood, and Big Cottonwood Canyons to the Park City side of the Wasatch and The Canyons Resort. Though the driving distance between Salt Lake City and Park City would lead you to believe otherwise, the two towns are divided by but a quick backcountry ski tour.

For Nordic skiing, Utah has about as many flavors as you could want. Soldier Hollow in Midway is a serious training facility and was a host to the races of the 2002 Winter Olympics. Millcreek Canyon, near Salt Lake City, offers random trails as well as groomed skiing on the winter-closure roads. Many other Nordic skiing facilities exist, including those at Sundance Resort, Solitude, Alta, and Mountain Dell Golf Course.

Whatever your skiing preferences, Utah has something for you. Even if you are traveling as a family and each member wants something different, you will still be able to find a way to please everyone.

Luckily, 2009 saw the passing of the famous Utah "private club," meaning that bars are now open to all customers over the age of 21—no membership fee required. Regardless of the lowered alcohol content of much of Utah's beer, the après ski in Utah should not be taken lightly, especially with regards to post-après driving. Utah's ski areas are usually 7,000 to 11,000 feet above sea level, each with abundant sun exposure and dry desert air. While this makes the snow like champagne, it also makes the beer like champagne. The effects will catch you off guard. Keep this in mind, and pace yourself with water and food intake.

Hiking into a summer ski tour Edward Lyman

Salt Lake City: Cottonwood Canyons

Salt Lake City's four ski resorts are located in Big and Little Cottonwood Canyons, southeast of downtown. Big Cottonwood Canyon is the northernmost canyon of the two, and this is where Brighton and Solitude Resort are located. Little Cottonwood is the next major canyon to the south of Big Cottonwood. This is where Alta and Snowbird are. Because of the nearness of each canyon's ski areas, skiers can expect that these neighboring resorts share some resources. If you wish to ski at Alta, but the lodging is completely booked, you could reasonably stay at Snowbird, just a mile lower in the canyon. If on-site resort lodging is completely booked, or you do not mind commuting to save some cash, you may consider lodging in the valley below. These accommodations options are listed at the end of this section.

Transportation

Because Alta, Brighton, Solitude, and Snowbird are self-contained resorts located high above the city, the only relevant public transportation is that which will get you to and from the airport and city below. The canyons are serviced by Utah Transit Authority's public buses and many private airport shuttle services. Utah Transit Authority operates a fleet of shuttle buses that take passengers from the canyon base park-and-ride-lots and various Salt Lake Valley locations directly to the ski area of your choice. Pickup frequencies and locations vary. Inquire with your hotel or visit www.rideuta.com for specific route information and potential delays. Private shuttles are listed below.

Advanced Transportation (1-866-647-3999; www.advtransportation.com), private and group direct shuttle service between Salt Lake Airport and ski areas

All Resort Express (1-877-658-3999; www.allresort.com), individual and group direct shuttle service between Salt Lake Airport and ski areas

Canyon Transportation (1-800-255-1841; www.canyontransport.com), private and group shuttle service between restaurants, resorts, and airport; errands

Le Bus (1-800-366-0288; www.lebus.com), group shuttle service; charter buses and large charter vans available

Lewis Stages (1-800-862-5844; www.lewisstages.com), charter buses, as well as private and small group shuttle service (see All Resort Express above)

Utah Transit Authority or UTA (801-743-3882; www.rideuta.com), public transportation in Salt Lake Valley, shuttles to canyons,

XPress Salt Lake City (1-800-397-0773; www.xpressshuttle.com), individual and group direct shuttle service between Salt Lake Airport and ski areas.

If you decide to drive yourself, you should be warned about Little Cottonwood Canyon. A deeply glaciated chasm, it is home to some of Utah's best, most famous skiing. The resorts here are among the largest and have the most vertical feet. The steepness of the slopes makes it difficult for vegetation to grow in many places. With few trees to hold the snow and block the sun, this canyon is susceptible to catastrophic, road-burying avalanches. Thus, the Utah Department of Transportation is exceedingly diligent about blasting avalanches to prevent accidental slides. During these blast sessions, they close the road to traffic. This means you will be stuck either in the valley or at the resorts for a number of hours. Also be

Little Cottonwood Canyon in autumn Christine Balaz

aware that snow tires and four-wheel drive or tire chains are required on all vehicles. Most rental agencies are familiar with this situation and will accommodate you effortlessly. To check the road conditions, call 801-933-2100.

Big Cottonwood Canyon

Brighton Resort

12601 East Big Cottonwood Canyon Road
Brighton, UT 84121
801-532-4731; 1-800-873-5512
www.brightonresort.com
Average Annual Snowfall: 500 inches (13 m.)
Area Elevation: 8,750–10,500 feet (2,670–3,200 m.)
Vertical Drop (without hiking): 1,750 feet (530 m.)
Lifts: 4 quad chairs, 1 triple
Trails: 66
Area: 1,050 acres
Difficulty: 20 percent beginner, 40 percent intermediate, 40 percent advanced
Lift Hours: 9–4; 4–9 Night Skiing Mon. through Sat. early Dec. through Mar.
Full Day: $58 adult, $30 senior (70 and over), free 10 and under, $30 children 11–12, $72 Brighton & Solitude combination
Half Day: $51 (9–12:30 and 12:30–4)
Special Features: Night skiing, extensive terrain parks, combination pass with Solitude

Brighton Village, like many early Utah settlements such as Alta and Park City, was originally a homestead that grew into a bustling mining town, and later a logging town. Named after the property's original homesteader of the 1850s, William Brighton, this has historically been a retreat for vacationers from Salt Lake City. Many of the original vacation cabins still stand, and a few are even used as guesthouses today.

Brighton's first lift went into operation in 1935 at the hands of Salt Lake City's Alpine Ski Club. This first lift system was a towrope devised of 0.5-inch rope and an elevator hoist. Throughout World Wars I and II the mountain underwent several ownership changes, and two T-bar lifts were added. After the wars, Brighton acquired a group of competition skiers, the Brighton Recreationalists, who erected the mountain's first proper single-chair lift on Mount Millicent in 1946. This was followed by the addition of two double-chair lifts in the mid-1950s. The concentration of chairlifts made Brighton popular among locals, even though passes for each lift had to be purchased individually. By 1963 skiers could ski all of the lifts with the purchase of one ticket.

Brighton now has seven lifts that occupy the upper cirque of Big Cottonwood Canyon. Because of this, the area has a distinct bowl shape. This yields very dramatic steeps on the upper pitches that gradually lessen into nearly flat slopes near the base. These lifts serve sweeping groomed trails and steep tree runs alike. Lifts bring you near the tops of Clayton Peak, Preston Peak, Pioneer Peak, and Mount Millicent. You can opt to drop into the regulated skiing beneath these peaks or hike above and beyond into the backcountry. All the lifts have an easy road to the base. This mountain is popular for snowboarders because of its extensive terrain parks and half-pipe.

Backcountry ski tracks in Big Cottonwood Canyon Christine Balaz

On-site Accommodations

Brighton's on-site accommodations are significantly fewer than Deer Valley, Park City Mountain Resort, or Snowbird. With no soaring hotels, the number of beds is cut dramatically. If on-site lodging is important to you, it is recommended that you call several months in advance.

BRIGHTON CHALETS

Office: 2750 East 9800 South
Sandy, UT 84092
801-942-8824
www.brightonchalets.com
Price: Moderate to Very Expensive
Credit Cards: AE, MC, V

Handicapped Accessible: No
Pets: No
Special Packages: First-time discounts

Brighton Chalets offers a variety of styles and sizes. Some modern and others invitingly rustic, all have the flavor of traditional Alpine ski cottages. These six homes offer resort-center location with the privacy of a single-family unit. With capacity ranging from 6 to 19 guests, this can be an option for couples or a family reunion.

BRIGHTON & SOLITUDE LODGING COMPANY

Brighton and Solitude Resorts, Salt Lake Valley

801-943-5050
www.solitudelodging.com
Price: Very Expensive
Credit Cards: AE, MC, V
Handicapped Accessible: No
Pets: No
Special Packages: Free ski packages at
Brighton and Solitude

The Brighton & Solitude Lodging Company
offers a variety of lodging options at the top
of Big Cottonwood Canyon. The accommodations at Brighton are condominium and
single home rentals. If you cannot get reservations for one of these ski-in, ski-out
options, they have more choices a few minutes from Brighton Center—some at Solitude
and some at the base of Big Cottonwood
Canyon. All homes are privately owned, so
decor and size varies. This company offers
lodging in the valley as well.

BRIGHTON LODGE
Brighton Resort Center
801-873-5512
www.brightonresort.com
Price: Moderate to Very Expensive
Credit Cards: AE, Disc, MC, V
Handicapped Accessible: Yes
Pets: No
Special Packages: Free ski packages at
Brighton

This modern mountain lodge-style, slope-
side hotel offers surprisingly reasonable
rates. Unfortunately, the lodge has only 20
guest rooms, so if you wish to stay here,
advanced booking is required. In keeping
with Brighton's family-friendly policy, children under six stay free with their parents.
If you cannot get a room but are determined
to stay here, you can check into a bunk or
twin bed in the hostel. All guests share
access to the outdoor Jacuzzi, fireplace,
continental breakfasts, and family-style
movies on the living room's big-screen television.

Prepping for the hike into a backcountry ski
Christine Balaz

HOME AWAY FROM HOME
Between Brighton and Solitude Resorts
801-205-9778
www.skiutahhomes.com
Price: Very Expensive
Credit Cards: AE, MC, V
Handicapped Accessible: No
Pets: No
Special Packages: No

Stay at one of Home Away from Home's
guesthouses, and you'll have the option of
skiing at Brighton or Solitude, according to
your preference for the day. Although the
properties are called cabins, their interiors
feature electricity, kitchens, beds, and
modern amenities. None of these cabins are
"fancy" or modern, but are comfortable,
cozy little winter homes. All of the homes

are located on one private, six-acre property. Guests have access to Jacuzzis, hot tubs, saunas, and games like Ping-Pong and billiards. Each unit has a private, full kitchen.

MOUNT MAJESTIC PROPERTIES

Brighton Resort
1-888-236-0667
www.mountmajestic.com
Price: Expensive to Very Expensive
Credit Cards: V, MC
Handicapped Accessible: No
Pets: No
Special Packages: No

Mount Majestic Properties is another option for on-site, single-family rentals at Brighton. Many of their rental homes have ski-in, ski-out access. Some have a good bit of history, having been built for Salt Lake City vacationers in the 1800s. These houses are spacious, well-lit, clean, and affordable. The management can assist you with babysitter location, grocery delivery, laundry, and massage service.

SILVER FORK LODGE AND RESTAURANT

11332 East Big Cottonwood Canyon
Between Brighton and Solitude
Brighton, UT 84121
1-888-649-9551
www.silverforklodge.com

Bench atop Big Mountain   Christine Balaz

Price: Moderate to Expensive
Credit Cards: AE, Disc, MC, V
Handicapped Accessible: No
Pets: No
Special Packages: No

This rustically cozy bed & breakfast has been hosting skiers and summer visitors since 1947. The wood-paneled rooms and pine furniture perfectly match the down comforters and flannel bedsheets. Guests are provided with a family-style breakfast and full bar for après ski cocktails and hors d'oeuvres. Dinners can be taken at the on-site restaurant. Here you will find American and regional cuisine in an equally charming pine- and stone-accented dining room.

On-site Dining

Alpine Rose (Base Area) is a cafeteria-style establishment that serves breakfast, lunch, and dinner. When graced by good weather, the deck becomes a grilling station. The **Brighton Chalet** (base of Mt. Millicent) has food that will quickly satisfy you without a trip to the bottom of the mountain. **Molly's Greens** (Base Area) is a popular lunch, après ski, and dinner spot for people 21 and over. On cold days, or when your thighs ache, lunch may roll into an après affair, or even into dinner.

On-site Après Ski and Nightlife

Molly's Greens (Base Area) is Brighton's on-site après ski locale. Guests at the **Silver Fork Lodge** are privy to a full bar. For nightlife at the Solitude Resort, see "On-site Après and Nightlife" in that section. No person under the age of 21 is allowed in a Utah bar, even if the person is a child accompanied by a parent.

Lessons

Brighton's lessons have been formatted for children, general adults, exclusive women's groups, and seniors. Both private and group lessons are available. Some lesson options include a day pass, so book ahead and save money. Group lessons for all categories span the full range of abilities. Telemark, alpine ski, and snowboard lessons are available. For meeting times and places, call **Brighton Ski and Snowboard School** (801-532-4731).

Child Care

Brighton has no on-site child care. However, if you would like to spend a day without your tricycle motor, consider calling **Guardian Angels** (801-598-1229; www.guardianangelbaby.com). Though not affiliated with Brighton Resort, they are a popular choice for locals and visitors. This dispatch service sends its own CPR- and first-aid-certified sitters to your room for a very reasonable rate. Based out of Salt Lake City, Park City, and Provo.

On-site Rentals

Brighton Mountain Rentals (Resort Center; 801-532-4731 or 1-800-873-5512; www.brightonresort.com), telemark and alpine ski and snowboard rentals, repairs, retail, tuning, Level 2, Brighton Center

Solitude Mountain Resort

12000 Big Cottonwood Canyon Road
Solitude, UT 84121
801-534-1400
www.skisolitude.com
Average Annual Snowfall: 500 inches (13 m.)
Snow Phone: 801-536-5777
Area Elevation: 7,988–10,035 feet (2,430–3,060 m.)
Vertical Drop (without hiking): 2,047 feet (620 m.)
Lifts: 1 high-speed quad chair, 4 double, 1 triple, 2 quad fixed
Trails: 64 over
Area: 1,200 acres
Difficulty: 20 percent beginner, 50 percent intermediate, 30 percent advanced
Lift Hours: 9–4
Full Day: $62 adult, $42 senior (70 and over), free 6 and under, $39 children 7–13, $72
Brighton & Solitude combination, multiple pass discounts, beginner lift discounts
Half Day: $52 (12:30–4)
Special Features: Nordic skiing, terrain park, combination pass with Brighton

Solitude's first real human impact was incurred with ore discoveries during the 1860s. Big Cottonwood Canyon's early economic activity was based on mining and later the harvest of timber. The area thrived during the next few decades, with literally hundreds of mines and voracious logging activity. The timber industry was so "successful" that it was able to harvest virtually every ancient tree in the canyon. The numerous old tailings piles from the mines were used to create Solitude's modern parking lots.

After struggling through the Great Depression, the last mine closed in 1950. Seven years later, skiing began at Solitude. Legend has it that founder Robert Barrett had been skiing at Alta and needed to use the lavatory. Not a member, he was turned away. Insulted, he was determined to create a ski area of his own. Solitude Resort began with the purchase of land and the construction of two lifts. Over time, more lifts filled in, and old technology was replaced with new.

Solitude has two different base areas for alpine skiers and a third for its Nordic Center. As you drive up Big Cottonwood Canyon Road, the first you encounter is the Moonbeam Base Area. This is the location of the Moonbeam Lodge as well as the ski school. Here you can park, buy a ticket, and ride the Moonbeam Lift up the mountain or the Link Lift up the canyon to arrive at the next base area, the Village at Solitude. This is the ideal parking area for guests staying at Solitude. Here is Eagle Springs East and Eagle Springs West, where you will find the resort lodging check-in and the Inn at Solitude. For lift tickets here, go to the Powderhorn Lodge, which also has a ski shop, restaurant, pub, and ski-school registration. Many other restaurants and pubs can be found in the Village at Solitude.

Solitude is cherished by locals for its nearly complete lack of crowding and less expensive lift tickets. Although the skiable acreage is significantly smaller than at other nearby resorts, the terrain is equally challenging and varied. On the back side of the resort is Honeycomb Canyon, a favorite of experts. Solitude's Nordic Center provides a challenging workout. Anyone visiting here will agree that Solitude is still an appropriate name for this resort.

On-site Accommodations

CREEKSIDE AT SOLITUDE

The Village at Solitude
Solitude, UT 84121
www.skisolitude.com
Solitude Resort Lodging
801-536-5765; 1-800-748-4754
Price: Moderate to Very Expensive
Credit Cards: AE, Disc, MC, V
Handicapped Accessible: Yes (made difficult by snow)
Pets: No
Special Packages: Ski and flight packages

This hotel has 17 condominiums with ski-in, ski-out access. The rooms range from studio apartments to three-bedroom condominiums. Each has a gourmet kitchen and fireplace, as well as access to ski and snowboard lockers and a rooftop hot tub. Additionally, guests here have free underground parking and on-site dining at the **Creekside Restaurant**. For the quality and ambience of the Creekside and its superb location, the prices are very reasonable.

THE CROSSINGS

The Village at Solitude
www.skisolitude.com
Solitude, UT 84121
Solitude Resort Lodging
801-536-5765; 1-800-748-4754
Price: Moderate to Very Expensive
Credit Cards: AE, Disc, MC, V
Handicapped Accessible: Yes (made difficult by snow)
Pets: No
Special Packages: Ski and flight packages

These town houses located in the Village at Solitude offer you on-site lodging with a little extra breathing room. All of the units have a full kitchen and private balcony, fireplace, and a two-car garage. Extra details, like stone countertops and jetted tubs, help make your stay here a touch more luxurious.

EAGLE SPRINGS LODGES

The Village at Solitude
Solitude, UT 84121
Solitude Resort Lodging
801-536-5765; 1-800-748-4754
www.skisolitude.com
Price: Moderate to Very Expensive
Credit Cards: AE, Disc, MC, V
Handicapped Accessible: Yes (made difficult by snow)
Pets: No
Special Packages: Ski and flight packages

The Eagle Springs Lodges offer another flavor of accommodations in the Village at Solitude. Built fittingly into its mountain surroundings in the style of Tuscan Italy, this accommodation offers the convenience of free underground parking and resort-center location and perks like private balconies, gas fireplaces, full kitchens, and access to **Club Solitude**. The newest of the Solitude accommodations, the units are immaculately clean and fully modern.

HOME AWAY FROM HOME

Between Brighton and Solitude Resorts
Solitude, UT 84121
801-205-9778
www.skiutahhomes.com
Price: Very Expensive
Credit Cards: AE, MC, V
Handicapped Accessible: No
Pets: No
Special Packages: No

See listing under Brighton Resort's "On-site Accommodations" earlier in this chapter.

THE INN AT SOLITUDE

Solitude Resort Center
Solitude, UT 84121
801-536-5765; 1-800-748-4754
Price: Very Expensive
Credit Cards: AE, Disc, MC, V
Handicapped Accessible: Yes (made difficult by snow)
Pets: No

Telemark skier in the Wasatch Jonathan Echlin

Special Packages: Ski and flight packages

This handsome, Bavarian lodge–style building has 46 guest rooms and is among the finer lodging options in Big Cottonwood Canyon. These units range in size and price from basic hotel rooms to more deluxe suites. The attractive lobby is paneled; wood and earth tones predominate. High ceilings and windows flood each room with light. To promote après ski relaxation, the hotel has a full spa, heated outdoor pool, and fine French dining at **St. Bernard's**, located within the Inn. Guests also have access to **Club Solitude**.

POWDERHORN LODGE
Solitude Resort Center
Solitude, UT 84121

Solitude Resort Lodging
801-536-5765; 1-800-748-4754
www.skisolitude.com
Price: Very Expensive
Credit Cards: AE, Disc, MC, V
Handicapped Accessible: Yes (made difficult by snow)
Pets: No
Special Packages: Ski and flight packages

Another option for one-, two-, and three-bedroom condominiums in the Village at Solitude Resort, the Powderhorn is yet one more variation on the mountain lodge theme. With private balconies and spacious living areas, this is a good option for family and group lodging. A tall structure with a highly visible clock tower, the Powderhorn offers its guests excellent views down Big

Cottonwood Canyon. Ski lockers are available to guests, and each room is equipped with a gas fireplace.

SILVER FORK LODGE AND RESTAURANT
11332 East Big Cottonwood Canyon
Between Brighton and Solitude
Brighton, UT 84121

1-888-649-9551
www.silverforklodge.com
Price: Moderate to Expensive
Credit Cards: AE, Disc, MC, V
Handicapped Accessible: No
Pets: No

See listing under Brighton Resort's "On-site Accommodations" earlier in this chapter.

On-site Dining

Last Chance Mining Camp Restaurant (near Village at Solitude) is a lunch establishment serving pizza, Mexican food, sandwiches, wraps, and the like. The **Stone Haus Pizzeria and Creamery** (Village at Solitude) serves three meals daily. Breakfasts consist of crepes, pastries, and smoothies. Lunch and dinner offer pizza. The on-site creamery makes great smoothies and desserts. The **Moonbeam Lodge** (Moonbeam Base Area) serves hot breakfast, skiers' lunches, and après ski snacks and beer. For bratwurst and other grilled treats, as well as beer and patio dining, the **Sunshine Grill** (between Moonbeam and Sunshine Lifts) is tops. Though not a restaurant, the **Village Store** (Village at Solitude) has enough basic snack food to get you through a day of skiing without stopping for a sit-down lunch. A sort of general store, this has other basics that might help you on your trip, like toothbrushes. Perhaps most important, this is the site of Solitude's **Utah Liquor Store**, the only place on the mountain where you can purchase a bottle of wine or liquor to bring back to your room.

Solitude also has more formal dining establishments. **Creekside Restaurant** (adjacent to the base of Apex, Powderhorn, and Sunrise Lifts, Village at Solitude; 801-536-5787) offers family-friendly fine dining with roots in Italian and American cuisine. Reservations during weekends and holidays are strongly recommended. **St. Bernard's** (Inn at Solitude, Village at Solitude; 801-535-4120) is another of Solitude's upper-echelon dinner establishments. French country cuisine and fireside dining make this restaurant romantic. A buffet breakfast is served daily. Reservations are encouraged. If you are up for a bit of night air and casual exercise, cross-country ski or snowshoe to **The Yurt** (0.75 mile from Village at Solitude; 801-536-5709). Dinners come in five courses. Seating is limited to 20, so advanced reservations are the only way to get a table. Because of the popularity of The Yurt, you should plan well ahead if your heart is set on dining here. The Stone Haus Pizzeria and Creamery is a great option for a quick meal with hungry children or a casual dinner with friends.

On-site Après Ski and Nightlife

The **Moonbeam Lodge** (Moonbeam Base Area) is a family-friendly restaurant that serves après ski snacks and beer. For a casual drink, go to **The Thirsty Squirrel** (Powderhorn Lodge, Village at Solitude). You can throw darts, play pool, chat with friends, or watch a game on the plasma-screen televisions. To help stave off your urgent appetite, munch on their selection of appetizers. **The Village Store** (Village at Solitude) has Solitude's only liquor store, the only place on the mountain where you can purchase a bottle of wine or liquor to bring back to your room. By law, prices in the store cannot be higher than the state standard. In Utah, no person under the age of 21 is allowed in a bar, even if the person is a child accompanied by a parent.

Lessons

Solitude's **Snow Sports Academy** (Moonbeam Base Area; 801-536-5730) has its roots firmly in the European ski instruction tradition. Developed by Leif Grevle, a former Norwegian World Cup skier, the academy emphasizes fundamental techniques as much as fun. Group and private lessons are available for adults and children. Durations of lessons vary. All skill levels are welcome. Some lesson packages include lift tickets. Reservations are recommended.

Child Care

Child care is available for children four and under. Children are to be dropped off at the **Snow Sports School** (Moonbeam Base Area; 801-536-5730). Daily activities include playtime outside. Parents must carry a cell phone during the day in case of emergencies, and reservations at least 24 hours in advance are recommended. For older children, or care at night, call **Guardian Angels** (801-598-1229; www.guardianangelbaby.com). They send CPR- and first-aid-certified sitters to your hotel room.

Off-piste skiing at Snowbird Jonathan Echlin

On-site Rentals

Moonbeam Lodge Rentals (Moonbeam Base Area; 801-517-7442; www.skisolitude.com), alpine ski and snowboard rental, repairs, tuning

Villager Rentals (Village at Solitude; 801-536-5734; www.skisolitude.com), alpine ski and snowboard rental, repairs, tuning

LITTLE COTTONWOOD CANYON

Alta Ski Area

P.O. Box 8007
Highway 210
Little Cottonwood Canyon
Alta, UT 84092
801-359-1078
www.alta.com
Average Annual Snowfall: 500 inches (13 m)
Snow Report: 801-572-3939
Area Elevation: 8,530–10,550 feet
(2,600–3,220 m.)
Vertical Drop (without hiking): 2,020 feet
(615 m.)
Lifts: 2 high-speed quad chairs, 1 high-speed triple chair, 3 double, 1 triple, 3 towropes, one tunnel conveyor
Trails: 116
Area: 2,200 acres
Difficulty: 25 percent beginner, 40 percent intermediate, 35 percent advanced
Lift Hours: 9:15–4:30
Full Day: $66 adult, $34 children 12 and under, $85 Alta & Snowbird combination, multiple day pass discounts, beginner lift discounts
Half Day: $56 (and 1–4:30)
Special Features: Skiing only, access to backcountry skiing, combination pass with Snowbird, Nordic skiing, snowcat skiing, free skiing after 3 p.m.

Shoes and gear after a Wasatch trail run
Christine Balaz

On your way into Little Cottonwood Canyon, you will feel as if you are being swallowed by the steep, glaciated granite walls. After traveling nearly a vertical mile to the base of Alta, you will be able to imagine the physical and sociological distance between the miners of historic Alta and the Mormons of Salt Lake City. Just before Alta, you'll notice a distinct cataract in the canyon formed by two cliff bands pinching the road from either side. The 16 breweries and dozens of saloons that occupied Alta as a 19th-century mining town earned this formation the name of "Hellgate," as dubbed by the pious Mormons below.

One of Utah's finest, yet quirkiest ski areas, Alta appeals to a very particular crowd. First, absolutely no snowboards are allowed on the property. Second, much of Alta's best terrain is accessed by traversing or hiking. People either love these aspects, or they hate them.

Whether the presence or absence of snowboarders affects a mountain is debatable. However, everyone will agree that mandatory hiking and traversing keeps the snow fresher longer—and makes for a better workout.

Alta's base area consists of two pullouts, where skiers are concerned. The first pullout you encounter when driving up Little Cottonwood Canyon Road (UT 120) serves the Wildcat Base Area. From here, you have access to bathrooms, the Wildcat Ticket Office, and the Alta Ski Shop & Demo Center. The parking lot here rarely fills. If you prefer to begin your day at the Albion Base Area, stay on Little Cottonwood Canyon Road a bit longer, until the second major turnoff. At the Albion Base Area are Albion Ticket Office and Albion Grill. From here, you can take the Albion or Sunnyside Lifts to the bottom of the Cecret, Supreme, and Sugarloaf Lifts. In case you end up at either base area wishing to be at the other, Alta has a Transfer Tow that drags skiers parallel to the road in either direction.

Alta's lodging has a footprint that extends beyond the Wildcat and Albion Base Areas. Accommodations begin lower in the canyon, along the Alta Bypass Road. Originating near the top of the Snowbird pullouts, the Bypass Road loops and meanders through the land between Snowbird and Alta and reconnects to the Little Cottonwood Canyon Road below the first Alta pullout (Wildcat Base Area). Along the upper curves of the Bypass Road are vacation rentals. In the Wildcat Base Area are the **Goldminer's Daughter** and **Alta Peruvian** lodges. Along the southeastern side of Little Cottonwood Canyon Road, between the Wildcat and Albion Base Areas, are the **Alta**, **Alta Rustler**, and **Snowpine** lodges. Conveniently, each of these lodges has access to the hill via its own tow lift that brings you to the Transfer Tow, and eventually either base area. The town office, police station, post office, and town library are also on this stretch of Little Cottonwood Canyon Road, on the western side. There is no lodging to speak of at the Albion Base Area, except for one hillside vacation rental, the Alta Alps Chalet, adjacent to the Cecret and Albion Lifts.

Because Little Cottonwood Canyon is a protected watershed, no pets are allowed in the canyon.

On-site Accommodations

Alta's guest beds are distributed among its many midsized lodges and several dozen condominiums. The lodges are described in detail below, and the names and contact information for condominium rental services are also listed. Alta and Snowbird both have elongated base layouts, with multiple exits and parking lots. For an excellent bird's-eye map of Alta's base area, visit the lodging section of the Alta Web site (www.alta.com). This map simplifies the base area to roads, lifts, and major landmarks. Although not completely comprehensive, it serves as a good starting point for orientation. As with any other resort lodging, prices fluctuate wildly across the seasons.

Alta has many condominiums and town houses, most of which are tucked into the base area with the rest of the lodges. For help with booking, you may consider contacting **Alta Chalets** (801-424-2426 or 1-866-754-2426; www.altachalets.com), **The Blackjack Condos** (1-800-742-8959), **Canyon Services** (1-888-546-5679; www.canyonservices.com), **Cliff Club Condominiums** (1-877-918-3332; www.snowbirdcondo.net), **Hellgate Condominiums** (801-742-2020), **Ironblossom Condominiums** (1-877-918-3332; www.snowbirdcondo.net), **The Miles Alta Vacation Home** (801-582-1371), **Tobin Powder Ridge Condos** (1-877-918-3332; www.altacondo.net), or the **Travis Home** (801-942-5219; www.thetravishome.com).

ALTA LODGE

P.O. Box 8040
Alta, UT 84092
801-742-3500; 1-800-707-2582
www.altalodge.com
Price: Expensive to Very Expensive
Credit Cards: Disc, MC, V
Handicapped Accessible: No
Pets: No
Special Packages: Many various ski packages

Open since 1939, this lodge was the first at the mountain, built by the Denver & Rio Grande Railroad for early Utah skiers. The hotel has only 46 rooms, and family-style dining is implemented at every meal. The lodge retains its welcoming atmosphere, though it has undergone much modernization. With a full-service restaurant on-site and slope-side location, convenience is paramount here. The Alta Lodge is located just east (up the canyon) from the Wildcat Lift. You can ski directly to the lodge, but you must take the very short Lodge Tow to the ski area. Full breakfasts and dinners are complimentary for guests.

ALTA PERUVIAN LODGE

P.O. Box 8017
Alta, UT 84092
801-742-3000; 1-800-453-8488
www.altaperuvian.com
Price: Moderate to Very Expensive
Credit Cards: AE, Disc, MC, V
Handicapped Accessible: No
Pets: No
Special Packages: No

Cozy guest rooms, thick timber beams, and low ceilings are the essence of this historic ski lodge. The Peruvian has a heated outdoor pool and hot tub, perfect for relaxing in the crisp, high mountain air and taking in the formidable peaks above you. Locals and visitors love the Peruvian for its bar. Every morning sees a continental breakfast, followed by lunch, and a savory family-style

dinner. The lodge plays nightly movies and also has a game room for guests.

ALTA'S RUSTLER LODGE

P.O. Box 8030
Alta, UT 84092
801-742-2200; 1-888-532-2582
www.rustlerlodge.com
Price: Expensive to Very Expensive
Credit Cards: AE, Disc, MC, V
Handicapped Accessible: Yes
Pets: No
Special Packages: Discounts for specified dates, as available

Open for six decades, the Rustler Lodge has every kind of room to fit your budget, from expansive rooms with fully glassed walls to dormitory-style bunkrooms. The common tie of these rooms is a classic ski lodge feel, created by timber-beam trimmings and earth-tone decor. The Rustler Lodge takes care of your caloric needs with heaping breakfasts and dinners for all guests. The heated pool, steam room, and Jacuzzi are pleasing bonuses.

GOLDMINER'S DAUGHTER LODGE

P.O. Box 8055
Alta, UT 84092
801-742-2300; 1-800-453-4573
www.skigmd.com
Price: Expensive to Very Expensive
Credit Cards: AE, Disc, MC, V
Handicapped Accessible: Yes
Pets: No
Special Packages: No

The Goldminer's Daughter is a community center at the ski hill with a day spa, medical center, restaurant, gallery, and ski shop. Amazing winter and summer activities are available at your doorstep if you stay here. Near the Collins and Wildcat Lifts, guests of this lodge have ideal ski-in, ski-out access. The **Goldminer's Saloon** and **Top of the Lodge Restaurant** are just icing on the cake. Simple, neat hotel rooms can accommodate single ski vacationers and larger groups.

SNOWPINE LODGE
P.O. Box 8062
Alta, UT 84092
801-742-2000
www.thesnowpine.com
Price: Inexpensive to Expensive
Credit Cards: MC, V
Handicapped Accessible: No
Pets: No
Special Packages: No

Another historic lodge, the Snowpine was built in 1938 when Alta was still a thriving mining town. It accommodates all needs, offering dormitory-style lodging as well as private rooms with private baths. The oldest lodge in Little Cottonwood Canyon, it has been retrofitted with a deluxe heated pool and Scandinavian spa. The breakfasts here can compete with those of the best bed & breakfasts, and guest dinners come in four courses. The lodge is located at the base of the Grizzly Tow Lift, which makes this a ski-in, ski-out lodge. This is arguably the best value at Alta. Dorm-style lodging available here as well, for much less money than at other hotels with this option.

On-site Dining

For on-the-go skiers' cuisine or a cup of hot chocolate, Alta has well-located coffee stands and grills. Hot beverages can be found at **Alta Java**, located in the Albion Day Lodge at the Albion Base Area. In the Wildcat Base Area, just next to the ticket office is the **Alta Ski Shop**, which sells espresso and tea right alongside its other merchandise. **Baldy Brews** is located in the all-new Watson Shelter at the mid-station of Collins Lift. Another spot for warming beverages is **Slopeside Joe's Café** in the Goldminer's Daughter Lodge in the Wildcat Base Area.

Hearty and quick lunch fare is served around the mountain. **Albion Grill** (Albion Base Area; 801-742-2500) is tucked at the base of the Albion and Sunnyside Lifts. Here you can satiate your high-altitude appetite with fresh pizza, hot chili, and other ski lodge fare. A salad bar and beer selection is available. Dining is cafeteria style. Similar in cuisine and atmosphere, **Alf's Restaurant** (Base of Cecret and Sugarloaf Lifts; 801-799-2295) is perfect for ravenous skiers not wanting to interrupt their skiing with a trip to the bottom of the mountain. While you refuel, be sure to sneak a peak at Devil's Castle, the massive limestone formation above you. A ski shop and demo center is also located on the premises. The **Watson Shelter** (Mid-Station at Collins Lift; 801-799-2296) has a couple of options, but the most efficient lunch option is the café and grill downstairs. Hamburgers, deli fare, salads, fruit, and beer make this as satiating as any ski lodge grill. This new building, with three of four walls mostly of glass, has excellent views. Also on-site is a coffee bar and the more deluxe **Collins Grill**.

For more serious dining, Alta has a few formal restaurants. **The Collins Grill** (Watson Shelter, Mid-Station at Collins Lift, upstairs; 801-799-2297) serves contemporary French cuisine, including seafood, lamb, duck, and rabbit with an emphasis on organic ingredients. A children's menu is also available. For the pleasure of your feet (and their carpet), slippers are available at the door to replace your wet, clunky boots. Serving lunch and very early dinner, the Grill suggests reservations for peak hours. **The Rustler Lodge Dining Room** (Alta's Rustler Lodge, between the Wildcat and Albion Base Areas; 801-742-2200) serves a small, but delicious selection of seafood, steak, and pastas with a wine list to match. **Shallow Shaft** (between the Wildcat and Albion Base Areas; 801-742-2177; www

Getting ready for the backcountry ski, Reynolds Pass Christine Balaz

.shallowshaft.com) serves a variety of gourmet entrées of varied origins, with slight Southwest and citrus inflections. The **Top of the Lodge Restaurant** (top floor of the Goldminer's Daughter Lodge, Wildcat Base Area; 801-742-2300) serves American and European cuisine, with a selection of traditional gourmet meat entrée selections as well as pasta.

On-site Après Ski and Nightlife

The **Alta Peruvian Bar** (Alta Peruvian Lodge, Wildcat Base Area; 801-742-3000) is a beloved hot spot for post-ski conversation, relaxation, and spirits. The Peruvian serves complimentary popcorn and appetizers. The low-key room is busy with wood paneling, heavy wooden bar furniture, taxidermy, and thick timber beams and rafters. A large window faces the ski slopes so you can reminisce about your day. The **Goldminer's Saloon** (Goldminer's Daughter Lodge, Wildcat Base Area; 801-742-2300) brings more food to the après ski experience, padding your stomach with tasty finger foods like pizza, nachos, and calzones, before you bombard it with any of the 13 fermented grain beverages on tap. For more après ski options, you may venture to Snowbird.

A word of warning to guests not staying at or near Alta: The après ski festivities here can have surprising results. Many people doubt the effect of 3.2 beer, but there are other important factors in the equation. At Alta, you will have been between 8,000 and 11,000 feet above sea level all day in the intense Utah sun and bone-dry western air. Though the skiing day is over, technical turns are not; a long, steep, and winding descent down the canyon awaits. It is often complicated by traffic and extremely hazardous black ice. Heed warning signs for curves and black ice, but expect unsigned hazards as well. No person under the age of 21 is allowed in a bar, even if the person is a child accompanied by a parent.

Lessons

Alta offers a variety of lessons at its **Alf Engen Ski School** (P.O. Box 8064, Alta, UT 84092; 801-359-1078; www.alta.com). Private lessons are offered at hourly, half-day, and full-day rates. After the first student, the cost of each additional person is significantly less. Private lessons are available for adults, children, and women-only, as well as for parent and child pairs. The ski school also offers first-come, first-served group lessons for children, meeting on the snow in front of the Albion Ticket Center. Meeting times vary, so call ahead or visit their Web site (www.alta.com/pages/children.php) for explicit instructions. Reservations for private lessons are required; no reservations are accepted for children's group lessons.

Child Care

The **Alta Children's Center** (801-742-3042) is Alta's on-site child care service. They take children as young as six months old and offer special winter sports programs for kids too young to ski, but old enough to want to play outside. Reservations are strongly suggested, as capacity is limited. **Guardian Angels** (801-598-1229; www.guardianangelbaby.com) is not affiliated with Alta, but it is a popular service around the Wasatch Region that sends sitters to your room.

On-site Rentals

Deep Powder House (above the Alta Lodge; 801-742-2400; www.deeppowderhouse.com), alpine ski demos, rentals, repairs, retail, and tuning

Mother Lode Ski Haus (in the Goldminer's Daughter Lodge; 801-742-9753; www.deep powderhouse.com), alpine ski demos, rentals, repairs, retail, and tuning

Rustler Powder House (in the Rustler Lodge; 801-742-2705; www.deeppowderhouse .com), alpine ski demos, rentals, repairs, retail, and tuning

Snowbird Ski and Summer Resort

Highway 210
Little Cottonwood Canyon
Snowbird, UT 84092
1-800-232-9542
www.snowbird.com
Average Annual Snowfall: 500 inches (13 m.)
Snow Phone: 801-933-2100
Area Elevation: 7,760–11,000 feet (2,365–3350 m.)
Vertical Drop (without hiking): 3,240 feet (990 m.)

Lifts: 1 tram, 4 high-speed quad chairs, 6 double
Trails: 89
Area: 2,500 acres
Difficulty: 27 percent beginner, 38 percent intermediate, 35 percent advanced
Lift Hours: 8:30–4:30
Full Day: $72 adult chair and tram, $62 adult chair only, $59 senior chair and tram (65 and over), $51 senior chair only, $15 6 and under (free chairs only), $39 children 7–12 ($29 chairs only), $85 Alta & Snowbird combination, multiple day pass discounts, beginner lift discounts
Half Day: $62 chair and tram, $55 chair only (9–1 and 12:30–3:30)
Special Features: Bottom-to-top tram access, access to backcountry skiing, combination pass with Alta

Snowbird, like Alta, is one of Utah's most famous prize mountains. The main side of Snowbird, visible from Little Cottonwood Canyon, has 3,240 continuous, vertical feet of lift-served terrain. One tram ride and you'll be more than half a mile above the base area. The tram is wildly popular among ski zealots. Behind the Little Cottonwood face of Snowbird is Mineral Basin. You can access this by the tram, Little Cloud Lift, or the new "magic carpet" tunnel at the top of the Peruvian Express. Mineral Basin features open-bowl, ungroomed steeps. Two lifts serve Mineral Basin, and both bring skiers back to the ridge from which they can access the main side of Snowbird.

Because of Snowbird's open-face topography, the wind often picks up toward the top of the mountain. When the wind whips on one side of the mountain, it is often still on another. So if it howls in Mineral Basin or by the tram, head to the western side of the mountain and the Gad Lifts.

Backcountry skiers often use Snowbird's Mid-Gad Lift to access the Whitepine Basin. The ski patrol requires that you check in at their hut at the top of the lift and show that you have a transceiver, shovel, and partner. For current avalanche conditions, visit the Web site **www.avalanche.org**. Both Alta and Snowbird share access to a crown gem of bragging rights: Baldy Mountain and its chutes. These chutes are exceptionally steep and narrow, yielding extremely high avalanche conditions. The patrol blasts these regularly, but is only able to open them a handful of days each ski year. If you have the ability, and are lucky enough to find them open when you visit, you must take the opportunity. The hike from Snowbird's tram is significantly shorter than from the Alta side.

Snowbird has a quite elongated base area with several exits off Little Cottonwood Canyon Road (UT 224). Regarding skiing, you will ideally arrive via the first, second, or third entries. Parking is found along these roads entering the area, and in designated lots alongside them. The first entry most directly accesses the Creekside Base Area. Here is a grill, ticket office, and the bottom of the Mid-Gad and Gad Zoom Lifts. The second entry also accesses the Creekside Area by making your first (very sharp) right-hand turn. If you park near this junction and already have a lift ticket, you can take the Wilbere Lift from right there. If you instead continue left at the junction, you will reach the Resort Plaza with ticket office, cafés, General Gritts (café, store, and state liquor store), and the base of the tram and Peruvian Lift. There is no central parking lot at Snowbird; rather, parking is scattered along the area roads that connect the various base areas and exits. If you must park in an odd spot, remember that ticket booths exist both at the Resort Plaza and the Creekside Area.

Regarding lodging, the third entry accesses the Iron Blosam, The Inn, and the Lodge at Snowbird. All of these establishments are within easy walking distance of the Wilbere Lift and the Resort Plaza. The fourth entry accesses the massive Cliff Lodge. The Cliff is a comfortable walking distance from the Resort Plaza.

Because Little Cottonwood Canyon is a protected watershed, no pets are allowed in the canyon.

On-site Accommodations

For **vacation rentals** other than these lodges, see the "Alta" section of this chapter.

THE CLIFF LODGE & SPA

Snowbird Lodging
P.O. Box 929000
Snowbird, UT 84092
1-800-232-9542
www.snowbird.com
Price: Expensive to Very Expensive
Credit Cards: AE, Disc, MC, V
Handicapped Accessible: Yes
Pets: No
Special Packages: Flight, spa, and ski packages

The Cliff Lodge functions as more of a community center than a hotel. With over 500 rooms and suites, a day spa, several restaurants, pools, hot tubs, and soaring lobbies, the Cliff is Snowbird's most famous lodge. In 1988 it hosted this country's first World Cup rock climbing competition on its western wall. Built in 1973, it underwent a nearly $6 million renovation. Completed in the summer of 2006, this increased its size and spiffed up the amenities. Suspended in the 11-story lobby, and covering much of the floor space, is North America's largest Oriental rug collection. For restaurants, the Cliff cannot be beat; many people drive up the canyon just for an evening of dining in **The Aerie**, overlooking Little Cottonwood Canyon below. Other restaurants include the **Aerie Lounge & Sushi Bar**, **The Atrium**, and **El Chanate**. Guest rooms vary from small hotel-style to expansive suites. Each room has a fantastic view, no matter which direction it faces. **Camp Snowbird**, Snowbird's child care service, is found in the Cliff Lodge.

THE INN AT SNOWBIRD

Snowbird Lodging
P.O. Box 929000
Snowbird, UT 84092
1-800-232-9542
www.snowbird.com
Price: Moderate to Very Expensive
Credit Cards: AE, Disc, MC, V
Handicapped Accessible: No
Pets: No
Special Packages: Flight, spa, and ski packages

Like the Cliff Lodge, the Inn was built in 1973, and has since undergone a series of renovations, rendering its facilities clean and modern. Accommodations vary from hotel-style to loft apartment, but all are privately owned. Owners have first priority for booking, so if you wish to stay in a specific style of room at a certain time, be sure to book well in advance. With an outdoor heated swimming pool, hot tub, and exercise room, it has all the amenities of a larger hotel, but in a mellow, small-scale fashion.

THE IRON BLOSAM LODGE

Snowbird Lodging
P.O. Box 929000
Snowbird, UT 84092
1-800-232-9542
www.snowbird.com
Price: Moderate to Very Expensive
Credit Cards: AE, Disc, MC, V
Handicapped Accessible: No
Pets: No
Special Packages: Flight, spa, and ski packages

The spelling for this lodge was taken from the phonetic spelling of an early Little Cottonwood Canyon mine. Opened in 1975, it was the first timeshare property in North America, and a fixed schedule of Saturday-to-Saturday rentals is still the policy here. Though options go to timeshare owners first, plenty of slots open up to unaffiliated guests. To enter the reservations pool, contact Snowbird Lodging. Guests here enjoy a spa and dry sauna, steam room, massage services, and walking-distance proximity to the Wilbere Lift. The **Wildflower Restaurant** (801-933-2230), serving gourmet Italian cuisine, is the Iron Blosam's on-site dining.

THE LODGE AT SNOWBIRD

Snowbird Lodging
P.O. Box 929000
Snowbird, UT 84092
1-800-232-9542

www.snowbird.com
Price: Moderate to Very Expensive
Credit Cards: AE, Disc, MC, V
Handicapped Accessible: No
Pets: No
Special Packages: Flight, spa, and ski packages

Located conveniently near the resort center's tram and Gad and Peruvian Lifts, the Lodge offers its guests ultimate convenience for skiing, dining, and nightlife. The on-site **Lodge Bistro** (801-933-2145) serves French and contemporary American dishes. All rooms in the Lodge are condominium units. Like Snowbird's other lodges, this early 1970s building underwent a comprehensive renovation that revamped the rooms and expanded and improved the pool and sauna areas.

On-site Dining

Baked and Brewed (Snowbird Center, second floor; 801-933-2466) serves teas, espresso, and also a variety of pastries. This is Snowbird's only Internet café. **The Birdfeeder** (Plaza Deck, adjacent to base of the tram) is a window café that serves coffee drinks and other hot beverages, as well as a variety of snacks and sandwiches. Inside the Mid-Gad Restaurant is the **Mid-Gad Espresso Bar** (top of the Mid-Gad Chair; 801-933-2245). Food items can also be purchased in the café-style restaurant.

For midday feasts, Snowbird has many skier-savvy eateries dishing up large quantities of hot, high-calorie foods. The **Creekside Café and Grill** (Creekside Base Area; 801-933-2477) is located in the lower level of the Creekside Building. They serve standard ski café fare as well as fabulous hot chocolate. For breakfast and lunch, **The Forklift** (across from the base of the tram; 801-933-2440) is a favorite for families for whom wait service is easier than cafeteria dining. Though not a restaurant, **General Gritts** (lower level, Resort Plaza; 801-933-2466) has all the fixings and cold sandwiches for a cold lunch. General Gritts also contains a selection of general store wares and a **Utah State Liquor Store**. Because it is a government-regulated establishment, liquor prices are (by law) the same as in non-resort Utah. (In the event of a "interlodge" closure, during which avalanche danger forces everyone at the mountain to remain in the base area, hurry to the liquor store before supplies run out; you may not be able to drive out of the canyon for a day or more!) The **Mid-Gad Restaurant** (mid-mountain along the Mid-Gad Lift; 801-933-2245) enables you to feast properly on pizza and chili fries—and perhaps a side of beer—without descending to the base of the mountain. **Pier 49 Sourdough Pizza** (second level, Resort Plaza; 801-933-2476) is a small pizza stand serving their dish by the slice or whole. Beer is also sold here. (By now you have probably noticed that Utahans like beer.) **The Rendezvous** (second level, Resort Plaza; 801-933-2466) is a place for mixed skier and non-skier groups to gather for a healthier, casual, lunch. Their specialties are an extensive salad bar, bread-bowl soups, wraps, and hot and cold sandwiches. **Superior Snacks** (level three, Cliff Lodge; 801-933-2466) services hungry cliff-dwellers near the pool. Foods are quick for kids, and beer is fun for the parents.

Perched high on the top level of the Cliff Lodge, **The Aerie** (Level 10, Cliff Lodge; 801-933-2160) is likely Snowbird's finest dining in one of the most attractive spaces. The floor-to-ceiling windows around the dining room give guests a priceless view of the surrounding mountains and canyon below. Cuisine is gourmet American and includes gourmet interpretations of dishes from overseas. The Aerie is a highly respected restaurant with an extensive wine list. **The Aerie Lounge** (Level 10; Cliff Lodge; 801-999-2160) is a chic watering hole and sushi bar. The atmosphere is casual, with couches as well as bar seating, and the establishment is privy to some of the same amazing views as The Aerie. Peer out at the darkening mountain and be grateful for the fireplace in front of you. **The Atrium** (Level B, Cliff Lodge; 801-933-2140) is located in the bottom of the 11-story, glass-enclosed lobby and is filled with sunlight and the greenery of potted trees. A high-end breakfast and lunch establishment, it dismantles the connotations of the word "buffet." Sunday comes with a superb brunch. **El Chanate** (Level A, Cliff Lodge; 801-933-2025) is Snowbird's Mexican eatery. It has a bright, artsy layout with earthen, red walls, wooden chairs reminiscent of beach furniture, and desert paintings. **The Lodge Bistro** (Lodge at Snowbird; 801-933-2145) is a French and American bistro with a large amount of windows and skylights. The menu is heavy with delicious beef preparations, but it does include limited vegetarian and fish items. Surf and turf with organic tendencies describes the fare of **The Steakpit** (Level 1, Snowbird Plaza; 901-993-2260). The unassuming, wood-paneled atmosphere and simple layout leave it to the cuisine to attract the crowds. Amazingly, this is one of the few Utah restaurants serving prime beef. Legendary desserts please the children. **The Wildflower** (Iron Blosam Lodge; 801-933-2230) brings a little of Italy's palate to Little Cottonwood Canyon. Here guests dine on delicately prepared traditional pasta dishes as well as heartier steak and fish entrées.

On-site Après Ski and Nightlife

Utah's canyons and their communities have always deviated from the norm of the Latter-day Saints (LDS) churches. Today Little Cottonwood and Snowbird are no exception, particularly since the advance of Utah's skiing fame. Though establishments here must abide by Utah's liquor laws, the social scene at ski areas tends to be much more concentrated and lively than elsewhere. Snowbird's capacity to host many guests fuels its own fire, as does its proximity to Alta's fun-loving crew. In addition to bars, Snowbird has Little Cottonwood Canyon's liquor store tucked right inside the Resort Plaza Building, at General Gritts (lower level, Resort Plaza; 801-933-2466). Because this is a state liquor store, prices are kept the same as the rest of the state all year. During your visit, be sure to monitor the events calendar on **www.snowbird.com**. Snowbird hosts many festivals, concerts, and competitions. No person under the age of 21 is allowed in a bar, even if the person is a child accompanied by a parent.

The Aerie Lounge (Level 10, Cliff Lodge; 801-999-2160), just outside The Aerie Restaurant, offers the same soaring views and chic atmosphere, but in a relaxed environment with room for lounging. A sushi bar here is open during the winter months. **El Chanate** (Level A, Cliff Lodge; 801-933-2145) makes you glad you're staying at the resort and even happier if you're staying right in the Cliff Lodge. This has Utah's most extensive tequila collection, and some of the finest available in the state. **The Lodge Bistro Lounge** (The Lodge at Snowbird; 801-933-2145) is a completely relaxing and informal bar for après ski beers and burgers. The lights dimmed slightly over the wooden bar and dining tables take the edge off the day's end. If your favorite team is playing, cut out a few runs early and head to the **Tram Club** (Level 1, Resort Plaza; 801-933-2222). With 13 television sets, you'll be able to catch almost any game being broadcast. The open layout and guest tables of **The Wildflower Lounge** (Iron Blosam Lodge; 801-933-2230) make it a relaxing space to have some appetizers and listen to live music.

Lessons

Snowbird's Mountain School (801-933-2170) is your resource for any kind of lessons, ski or snowboard. Snowbird offers more than a dozen varieties of lessons, varying in duration, age of participant (from children to seniors), and skill level. Special beginner packages are offered that include rentals, lift ticket, and lessons. Some advanced groups meet with the purpose of introducing you to Snowbird's bountiful terrain. Groups meet at the Resort Plaza. Times vary, so when you choose your lesson, make a note of meeting times; all group lessons fill on a first-come, first-served basis. Reservations are taken for private lessons only. Check **www.snowbird.com/mtnschool** for special camp listings, including women's, big mountain, and even yoga camps.

Child Care

Camp Snowbird (Cliff Lodge; 801-933-2256) keeps your kids happy and warm while you milk the tram. Reservations are only required for children under three. **Guardian Angels** (801-598-1229; www.guardianangelbaby.com) is not affiliated with Snowbird, but is a popular service around the Wasatch Region that sends qualified, certified sitters to your room.

On-site Rentals

Christy Sports (Level 3, Snowbird Resort Plaza; 801-742-2871; www.christysports.com), alpine ski and snowboard rentals, repair, retail

Cliff Sports Demo & Rental (Level 1, Cliff Lodge; 801-933-2265), telemark and alpine ski and snowboard demos, rentals, repair, retail, tuning

Creekside Rentals (Gad Valley Building, Creekside Base Area; 801-933-2414), alpine ski and snowboard rentals

Legend Demo Center (Resort Plaza Deck and inside Cliff Sports, Level 1, Cliff Lodge; 1-800-232-9542), demos, online reservations

Superior Ski and Board (Level 3, Resort Plaza; 801-742-2871; www.superiorski.com), alpine ski and snowboard rentals, repairs, tuning, boot fitting

SALT LAKE VALLEY LODGING

If you are in Salt Lake City primarily to ski, but cannot get resort-side lodging (or do not want to foot the elevated bill), there is a sufficient amount of lodging west of canyon bases in Sandy and Midvale. Vacation rentals are scattered throughout the area. Valley rental services include Utah Ski Lodging (8016 Sunnyoak Circle, Salt Lake City; 801-943-2426 or 1-800-943-2426; www.utahskilodging.com), and Wasatch Front Ski Accommodations (2020 East 3300 South, Salt Lake City; 1-800-762-7606; www.wfsa.com).

Major hotels are located a few miles west of the canyons, on the valley floor. Located along Fort Union Boulevard are many familiar national chain hotels, including **Courtyard by Marriott** (10701 South Holiday Park Drive, Sandy; 801-571-3600; www.marriott.com), **Days Inn** (7251 South 300 West, Midvale; 801-566-6677; www.daysinn.com), **Homewood Suites by Hilton** (844 East Fort Union Boulevard/7200 South Street, Midvale; 801-569-5999; www.homewoodsuites.com), **La Quinta Midvale** (7231 South Catalpa Street, Midvale; 801-566-3291; www.lq.com), and **Super 8 Motel** (7048 South 900 East, Midvale; 801-255-5559; www.super8.com).

Park City

Park City is literally surrounded by its three ski resorts. The northernmost resort, The Canyons, is a five-minute drive from downtown. Park City Mountain Resort's base area abuts the historic downtown, and its Town Lift actually services downtown. Deer Valley is the southernmost resort, and its resort villages make up many of Park City's neighborhoods. Because of the nearness of the base areas to the town center, slope-side and in-town lodging are virtually interchangeable. Additionally, skiers here can easily dabble in all of the resorts and participate in the cultural offerings of the town without a major commute. Park City area accommodations options are listed at the end of this section.

Transportation

People in Park City can easily get away without renting a vehicle. The services listed below offer private and group shuttles to and from Salt Lake City International Airport. Once in Park City, you can ride the Park City Transportation Division's Free Bus Service. A favorite of locals, this service connects downtown Park City to all of the ski resorts, eliminating the hassle of driving and parking. The only limitation to these prolific buses is the lack of late-night hours. For specific route information, see www.parkcity.org or call 435-615-5350.

Advanced Transportation (1-866-647-3999; www.advtransportation.com), private and group direct shuttle service between Salt Lake Airport and ski areas

All Resort Express (1-877-658-3999; www.allresort.com), private and group direct shuttle service between Salt Lake Airport and ski areas

Canyon Transportation (1-800-255-1841; www.canyontransport.com), private and group direct shuttle service between Salt Lake Airport and ski areas

Le Bus (1-800-366-0288; www.lebus.com), group shuttle service; charter buses and large charter vans available

Lewis Stages (1-800-862-5844; www.lewisstages.com), charter buses, as well as private and small group shuttle service (see All Resort Express above)

Park City Transportation (1-800-637-3803; www.parkcitytransportation.com), private and group shuttle service from Salt Lake Airport to Park City vicinity

Park City Transportation Division Bus Service (435-615-5350; www.parkcity.org), free public shuttle buses across town

Wasatch Crest Shuttles (801-330-5711; www.wcshuttle.com), all private shuttles to Park City

XPress Salt Lake City (1-800-397-0773; www.xpressshuttle.com), individual and group direct shuttle service between Salt Lake Airport and ski areas

The Canyons

4000 The Canyons Resort Drive
Park City, UT 84098
435-649-5400 or 1-888-226-9667
www.thecanyons.com
Average Annual Snowfall: 355 inches (9 m)
Snow Report: 435-615-3456
Area Elevation: 6,190–9,990 feet
(1,890–3,040 m)
Vertical Drop (without hiking): 3,190 feet
(970 m)
Lifts: 17 total, combination of gondolas, high-
speed and fixed chairs, towropes

Jonathan Echlin

Trails: 152
Area: 3,700 acres
Difficulty: 14 percent beginner, 44 percent intermediate, 42 percent advanced
Lift Hours: 8:30–4:00
Full Day: $81 adult, $48 children 7–12 and seniors 65 and over, free 6 and under
Half Day: $53 (9:15–1 and 1–4)
Special Features: 8 major peaks and 5 distinct bowls, 6 half-pipes, 2 terrain parks, skiing
only, access to backcountry skiing

When people describe The Canyons, one of the first words that you'll hear is "Huge!" There
really is something for everyone on this resort's eight distinct mountains, with corduroy
grooming, backcountry powder stashes, green runs, and black diamond faces. With 17 lifts
accessing the terrain, The Canyons can be a destination for several years running.

Conveniently, most of The Canyons Village is in one location, with the lifts fanning out
from this single point. For day guests, parking is available in a large central lot at The
Canyons Base Camp. This area comes up very quickly after you turn onto The Canyons
Drive, and it is on your left. From here, a gondola called Cabriolet takes you to the heart of
the resort base. Lift tickets can be purchased at the base of Cabriolet or at the top. If you are
staying on the mountain, proceed past the base camp to your vacation rental or hotel.

The driving immediately becomes the trademark convoluted spiderweb of ski resort
driving, but the massive hotels are landmarks impossible to miss, and some amount of signage guides you along the way. The Sundial Lodge and Grand Summit Resort Hotel offer in-
Village underground parking (and free skiing with your stay).

Some of The Canyons vacation rentals are outside this immediate area. This lodging
extends southward and up into the hillsides a bit. Ski runs cut right through the neighborhoods, with bridges to resolve junctions between ski trails and neighborhood lanes.

On-site Accommodations

For all accommodations questions, contact **The Canyons Central Reservations** at 1-866-
604-4171, or visit **www.thecanyons.com**. Hotel lodging at The Canyons is simple. Your
choice of hotels will be among the **Grand Summit Hotel** (4000 The Canyons Resort Drive,
Park City, UT 84098; 1-866-604-4171; www.thecanyons.com), the **Sundial Lodge** (4000
The Canyons Resort Drive, Park City, UT 84098;1-866-604-4171; www.thecanyons.com),

or the **Westgate Resort** (3000 The Canyons Resort Drive, Park City, UT 84098; 435-940-9444). Because of their general popularity, exceptional quality, guest services, and surroundings, these hotels are included in the "Accommodations" section of Chapter 2, Park City. Guests of these hotels ski free.

On-site Dining

First Tracks (lobby, Grand Summit Hotel; 435-615-8033) starts your day with coffee and warms your body with midday hot chocolate. **Powder Daze Coffee & Creperie** (Resort Village; 435-649-0085) is a fast, warming treat for breakfast or lunch. For mid-mountain hot chocolatiers, go to the **Dreamscape Grill** (base of Dreamscape Lift; 435-649-5400), **Lookout Cabin** (Lookout Peak; 435-615-2892), **Red Pine Lodge** (top of the Flight of The Canyons Gondola; 435-615-2888), or the **Sun Lodge** (top of Sun Peak Lift; 435-615-2890).

Doc's at the Gondola (Resort Village; 435-615-8068) serves satiating ski lunches, as well as après ski drinks and appetizers. Although Doc's serves food, it is primarily a bar and thus only open to those 21 and over with valid ID. **The Dreamscape Grill** (base of Dreamscape Lift; 435-649-5400) is the classic mountain lunch venue, with burgers, pizza, and more to choose from. **Lookout Cabin** (Lookout Peak; 435-615-2892) is also an excellent lunch spot. With wait service and finer fare, it provides more than basic caloric satisfaction. Kick your ski boots off and enjoy their fresh fish, salads, sushi, and full bar. Call ahead for reservations. **The Red Pine Lodge** (top of the Flight of The Canyons Gondola; 435-615-2888) is your mid-mountain cafeteria-style dining option for a simple, filling hot lunch. **The Sun Lodge** (top of Sun Peak Lift; 435-615-2890) offers similar fare, but is often less crowded than the Red Pine because of its location. **The Western Grill** (in Red Pine Lodge, top of the Flight of The Canyons Gondola; 866-604-4171) serves gourmet barbecue for lunch and dinner. With table service, it is perfect for tired parents, and kids love the cowboy theme. Reservations are required. **The Westgate Grill** (Westgate Hotel, Resort Village; 435-655-2260) is another lunch spot with table service for those wishing for a longer, more relaxing lunch. **The Westgate Marketplace & Deli** (Westgate Hotel) sells to-go sandwiches that you can eat on the lift, so as to have a completely uninterrupted ski day.

You'll want to shower and freshen up before a dinner at the **Alpine House** (Sundial Building, Resort Village; 435-615-4828). This was the first full-service restaurant at the resort, it continues to serve high-end, contemporary American cuisine. A "small bites" menu allows guests to sample a broader spectrum of the cuisine. Open to the public at 4:30 daily for après and dinner. Call ahead for reservations. **The Cabin** (Lobby Level, Grand Summit Hotel; 435-615-8060). As you might guess from the name, the cuisine is a collection of western fare, but with a gourmet interpretation. Sample from their wine list as you savor your elk loin entrée. The Cabin also serves breakfast and lunch. Reservations are strongly encouraged. **The Viking Yurt** (between Tombstone Express and Saddleback Express; 435-615-9878) is one of the most romantic dinner locations at The Canyons. Each evening begins with a sleigh ride (pulled by a snowcat, of course) to this tiny, cozy hut. The Yurt serves a set menu that changes nightly, so be sure to check ahead, especially if you have special dietary needs. The presentation and preparations are exceptional and cuisine varies, but it is usually American and European. Dinner lasts from 6–10 PM. **The Westgate Grill** (Westgate Hotel, Resort Village; 435-655-2260) serves breakfast, lunch, and dinner of American cuisine. The menu has carnivorous tendencies.

On-site Après Ski and Nightlife

Sit at the bar or high table for après ski conversation, drinks, and appetizers at **Doc's at the Gondola** (Resort Village; 435-615-8068). Doc's serves simple lunches and après ski snacks. **Smokey's Bar and Grill** (Resort Village; 435-615-2891) is The Canyons' classic sports bar with sun deck, pool tables, draught beer, and several TV screens. For a real evening on the town, venture to Park City's Main Street. A short, free shuttle ride away, this is where the nightlife really happens. In Utah no person under the age of 21 is allowed in a bar, even if the person is a child accompanied by a parent.

Lessons

Lessons at The Canyons are all orchestrated by their **Ski School** (435-615-3449; www.the canyons.com/ski_school.html). Group lessons are available for kids, adults, or women only. Other specialty workshops take place, as scheduled. Lessons are offered to skiers and snowboarders alike. Adult lessons are for those 15 and older. Regardless of age, all abilities are welcome. Meeting times and lesson duration vary. Book ahead.

Snowboarder rips into Utah's fluff (at Snowbird) Jonathan Echlin

Child Care
The Little Adventures Children's Center (435-615-8036; www.thecanyons.com/daycare
.html) is The Canyons' on-site daycare. They accept children as young as six weeks old. For
older children, a full-day combination of ski lesson and daycare is available. Reservations
are required. **Guardian Angels** (435-640-1229; www.guardianangelbaby.com) is not affiliated with The Canyons, but is a popular service around the Wasatch Region that sends
first-aid- and CPR-certified sitters to your room.

On-site Rentals
Aloha Ski and Snowboard Rentals (between Sundial and Grand Summit Lodges, Canyons
  Resort; 435-647-2990 or 1-877-222-7600; www.alohaskirentals.com), alpine ski and
  snowboard demos, rentals, repairs, tuning
Black Tie Ski Rentals (delivery to The Canyons, Deer Valley, and Park City Mountain
  Resort; 435-649-4070 or 1-888-333-4754; www.blacktieskis.com), alpine ski and
  snowboard rentals, retail, free children's rentals
Breeze Ski Rentals (Park City Mountain Resort Plaza; 435-655-7066 or 1-888-427-3393;
  www.breezeski.com), demos, rentals, retail, discounts with reservations, ski and snowboard storage
Canyon Mountain Sports (4000 The Canyons Resort Drive; 435-615-3440; www.the
  canyons.com), demos, rentals, repairs, retail, tuning, boot fitting
The Canyons Rental and Solid Edge Repair (Canyons Resort Village; 435-615-3441; www
  .thecanyons.com), alpine ski and snowboard rentals, repairs, retail, tuning, ski and
  snowboard storage
KinderSport Junior Ski & Snowboard Rentals (The Canyons Resort Sundial Lodge; 435-
  615-3385; www.kindersport.com), children's ski and snowboard rentals, retail
Ski Butlers (delivery to The Canyons, Deer Valley, and Park City Mountain Resort; 1-877-
  754-7754; www.skibutlers.com), ski and snowboard equipment delivery
Skis on the Run (delivery to The Canyons, Deer Valley, and Park City Mountain Resort;
  1-888-488-0744; www.skisontherun.com), alpine ski and snowboard rentals, tuning

Deer Valley Resort
P.O. Box 1525
Park City, UT 84060
www.deervalley.com
Average Annual Snowfall: 300 inches (7.5 m)
Area Elevation: 6,570–9,570 feet (2,000–2900 m)
Vertical Drop (without hiking): 3,000 feet (915 m)
Lifts: 21 total, combination of gondolas, high-speed and fixed chairs
Trails: 91
Area: 1,875 acres
Difficulty: 27 percent beginner, 38 percent intermediate, 35 percent advanced
Lift Hours: 9–4:15
Full Day: $86 adult, $62 senior (65 and over), $53 children 4–12, $21 age 3 and under
Half Day: $60 adult, $43 senior, $42 children, $14 toddlers (12:30–4:15)
Special Features: Excellent guest services and grooming

Though it seems nearly everything in Park City is upscale and glittery, Deer Valley seems to be the crème de la crème for extremely deluxe accommodations, dining, and guest services. Deer Valley has a pervasive reputation for outstanding service, from customer relations on-mountain to grooming, vacation planning, and ski lessons. For those willing to pay the price, the experience is fabulous.

Deer Valley gives guests a feeling of seclusion. Slightly offset from Park City, it seems to truly be a self-contained destination resort. Some of North America's finest restaurants are located within the resort's three villages, as are some of Park City's most fabulous rental and private homes.

For day skiers, the most convenient access point is Deer Valley's main base area, Snow Park. Everything, from parking to ticket purchase, is unambiguous here. There is but one expansive and highly visible parking lot, and the equally obvious Snow Park Lodge. Within the lodge is everything skiers need, from locker rooms to equipment shops and ticket sales. For guests lodging on the mountain, the options become quite a bit more diversified. Deer Valley's three main villages, Empire Pass, Silver Lake, and Snow Park, are described below.

On-site Accommodations

Deer Valley has extensive lodging options. The on-site lodging falls into three areas, the **Snow Park Village**, **Silver Lake Village**, and **Empire Pass**. **Snow Park Village** is located at the effective resort center and base area of Deer Valley. From here, the Silver Lake, Carpenter, Snowflake and Burns lifts take skiers to the mountain. Major lodges here are the **Black Diamond Lodge**, **Courschevel**, **The Lodges at Deer Valley**, **Powder Run**, and **Red Stag Lodge**. Smaller establishments and vacation rentals include condominium units in **Aspenwood**, **Boulder Creek**, **Bristlecone**, **Chaparral**, **Comstock**, **Daystar**, **Deer Lake Village**, **Fawngrove**, **Glenfiddich**, **In the Trees**, **Lake Side**, **Pine Inn**, **Pinnacle**, **La Maconnerie**, **Queen Esther**, **Stonebridge**, **Trail's End**, and **Wildflower**. Descriptions of the Lodges at Deer Valley and Red Stag Lodge can be found in the "Accommodations" section of Chapter 2, Park City.

Silver Lake Village is the second-highest village at Deer Valley, reached by traveling south out of Park City on UT 224. Turn north (left) on Guardsman Connection toward the Silver Lake Village before UT 224 swings uphill and becomes Guardsman Pass Road. (It can also be reached by the Snow Park Village at the base of Deer Valley Resort.) Silver Lake Village has many of the big hotels at Deer Valley, including **Blackbear Lodge**, **Goldener Hirsch Inn**, **The Inn at Silver Lake**, **Mont Cervin**, **Ontario Lodge**, **The Ridge**, **Silver Bird**, **Stein Eriksen Lodge**, **Sterling Lodge**, and **Twin Pines**. The more intimate lodging options at the Silver Lake Village are **Aspen Hollow**, **Belle Harbor Homes**, **Bellemont Homes**, **Chateau at Silver Lake**, **Enclave**, **Little Belle**, **Ridge Point**, **Sterlingwood**, **Trailside**, and **The Woods**. A write-up of the Goldener Hirsch Inn and Stein Eriksen can be found in the "Accommodations" section of Chapter 2, Park City.

Empire Pass, the highest of the three Deer Valley villages, is reached by taking **Marsac Avenue** as it winds south out of Park City and up the slopes of Deer Valley's mountainside villages. The Silver Strike Lift originates in the lower section of this neighborhood along Marsac Drive. Near this lift you will find the **Arrowleaf**, **Larkspur**, **Paintbrush**, and **Shooting Star** accommodations. Farther up Marsac, you will find the **Ironwood** and **Grand Lodges** near the Northside Lift. The most popular of the lodges and hotels are described in the "Accommodations" section of Chapter 2, Park City.

You can expect all of Deer Valley's accommodations to be comfortably modern and spacious. For specific quality, taste, and location, contact Deer Valley Central Reservations at 435-645-6528 or 1-800-558-3337. Deer Valley's reservations Web site, **www.deervalley centralreservations.com**, can help you narrow your selection and orient you. Additionally, any of the lodging services listed in the "Accommodations" section of Chapter 2, Park City, will be able to assist you with Deer Valley booking.

On-site Dining

Deer Valley's restaurants, like the rest of their service, will please you with high quality when you least expect it. Although many of these restaurants are among the best in the nation, Deer Valley also has casual eateries. **Bald Mountain Pizza** (Silver Lake Lodge) offers a slightly different take on a quick ski lunch. Serving gourmet pizzas with fresh, house-made sauces, Bald Mountain's pizzas are significantly tastier (and healthier) than the typical heat-lamp ski lodge pizza. Pastas and salads are also available. At the top of Flagstaff Mountain is **Cushing's Cabin**, serving hot and cold snacks and small meals. Seating space is limited. **The Empire Canyon Grill** (Empire Canyon Lodge) serves continental breakfasts and à la carte lunch. You have the choice of unique sandwiches, grill items, baked goods, and panini, as well as filling chili and soup. **Royal Street Café** (Silver Lake Lodge; 435-645-6632) is open daily for lunch, après ski, and dinner. The menu offers contemporary American cuisine of gourmet preparations alongside specialty burgers and simpler fare. A popular restaurant with table service, reservations are required. **Silver Lake Restaurant** (Silver Lake Lodge) serves cafeteria-style breakfast and lunch daily during ski season. This eatery has an offering of buffet and grill items taken up a notch with fresh ingredients, as well as more deluxe roast carvings. **The Snow Park Restaurant** (Snow Park Lodge), like the Silver Lake Restaurant, offers cafeteria-style breakfast and lunch. For lunch a selection of carved roasts also appears here, as well as an extensive salad bar, different soups and stews, and a daily entrée. **Snowshoe**

O'Shucks Bar & Grill, Park City |Jonathan Echlin

Tommy's (top of Bald Mountain) serves quick skier snacks and warming drinks to keep you going without a major detour from your recreation. For an exceptional group lunch, reserve **Sunset Cabin** (adjacent to Sunset Lift; 435-645-6650) for a private party with fondue. Seventy-two-hour advance notice is required to reserve this cabin.

If Deer Valley's lunch establishments tend to be one or two notches nicer than those of most ski areas, the dinner eateries tend to be two or three notches finer. In fact, many are nationally acclaimed restaurants. **Fireside Dining at Empire Canyon Lodge** (Empire Canyon Lodge; 435-645-6632) is a special affair, occurring only Wednesday, Thursday, and Friday evenings during the winter season. Three course meals are actually prepared using the grand fireplaces. Swiss and European cuisine is the flavor here. Each night has a unique set menu. An extensive wine list and full bar are available to dinner guests. To complete an utterly romantic evening, consider a post-dinner sleigh ride. Make your sleigh reservations during the same phone call as your dinner reservations. Available every Wednesday, Thursday, and Friday night from 6–9. **The Mariposa** (Silver Lake Lodge; 435-645-6632) is Deer Valley's premier restaurant and has even been ranked as the nation's number-one restaurant by *Zagat*. Mariposa offers time-tested European and American dishes and original creations, as well as sampler dishes and vegetarian fare. You can opt for an entrée of regional game or a lobster tail. Open for dinner Tues.–Sun.; call for reservations. **Royal Street Café** (Silver Lake Lodge; 435-645-6724) serves lunch and dinner, with casual cuisine listed alongside gourmet dishes on the menu. Most items center around some form of meat, but there is a salmon dish for those not interested in munching on land-dwelling animals. The name **Seafood Buffet** (Snow Park Lodge; 435-645-6632) describes the restaurant exactly, although the connotation of buffet does not fit into the picture. This restaurant has an extensive offering of hot and chilled seafood, shellfish, sushi, appetizers, and entrées. For non-seafood types, other grilled items are available, as well as pasta.

On-site Après Ski and Nightlife

Deer Valley, like its Park City sisters, hosts many major events, so be sure to check the Web site's calendar. World Cup aerials and bumps competitions attract people from around the region, filling the parking lots. These events are accompanied by free concerts given by national bands tough enough to play in the chilly mountain air.

When 2:30 rolls around, head to the **Snow Park Lounge** (Snow Park Lodge), pick at some appetizers, and sip the cocktail or wine of your choice. Entertainment ranges from live music to televised sporting events and games of pool. The deck becomes popular during warm spring afternoons. **The Royal Street Café** (Silver Lake Lodge) also sees its share of après ski drinks and appetizers. As with The Canyons and Park City Mountain Resort, people wishing to roll an après ski into a full evening out usually head to Park City's Main Street. No person under the age of 21 is allowed in a bar, even if the person is a child accompanied by a parent.

Lessons

Whether you are a beginner or an expert unfamiliar with the terrain, a lesson with **Deer Valley's Ski School** (435-645-6648 or 1-888-754-8477) can be informational. The ski school offers lessons to six different levels, from first-timers to expert. If you wish to purchase your lessons in person, go to the Stein Eriksen Lodge (Silver Lake Village), Lodges at Deer Valley (Snow Park Village), Children's Center (main level, Snow Park Lodge), or Snow Park Ski School.

Child Care

Deer Valley's **Children's Center** (main level, Snow Park Lodge; 435-645-6648) is a state-licensed facility that cares for kids aged two months to 12 years. Because the center comes under high demand, advanced booking is important if child care is a necessary part of your trip. Popular weekends fill up months in advance. **Guardian Angels** (435-640-1229; www.guardianangelbaby.com) is not affiliated with Deer Valley, but is a popular service around the Wasatch Region that sends first-aid- and CPR-certified sitters to your room.

On-site Rentals

Black Tie Ski Rentals (delivery to The Canyons, Deer Valley, and Park City Mountain
Resort; 435-649-4070 or 1-888-333-4754; www.blacktieskis.com), alpine ski and
snowboard rentals, retail, free children's rentals

Cole Sport (Silver Lake Village; 435-649-4601; www.colesport.com), demos, rentals,
repairs, retail, tuning

Deer Valley Rentals (Silver Lakes Village, Snow Park Lodge; 1-888-754-8477; www.deer
valley.com), demos, rentals, repairs, retail, tuning

KinderSport Junior Ski & Snowboard Rentals (Deer Valley Silver Lake Village; 435-649-
8338 and Deer Valley Snow Park Lodge; 435-649-6229; www.kindersport.com), children's ski and snowboard rentals, retail

Ski Butlers (delivery to The Canyons, Deer Valley, and Park City Mountain Resort; 1-877-
754-7754; www.skibutlers.com), ski and snowboard equipment delivery

Ski 'N See Ski and Snowboard (Silver Lake Village; 435-615-1106; www.skinsee.com),
demos, rentals, repairs, retail, tuning, discounts on reservations, select discounted lift
tickets

Skis on the Run (Delivery to The Canyons, Deer Valley, and Park City Mountain Resort; 1-
888-488-0744; www.skisontherun.com), alpine ski and snowboard rentals, tuning

Stein Eriksen Rental (The Chateaux at Silver Lake, Stag Lodge, Stein Eriksen Lodge; 435-
658-0680; www.steineriksen.com), alpine ski and snowboard rentals, repairs, tuning

Park City Mountain Resort

P.O. Box 39
1310 Lowell Avenue
Park City, UT 84060
1-800-331-3178
www.parkcitymountain.com
Average Annual Snowfall: 355 inches (9 m)
Snow Phone: 435-647-5449
Area Elevation: 6,900–10,000 feet (2,100–3,050 m)
Vertical Drop (without hiking): 3,100 feet (945 m)
Lifts: 15 total, combination high-speed and fixed chairs
Trails: 104
Area: 3,300 acres
Difficulty: 17 percent beginner, 50 percent intermediate, 33 percent advanced
Lift Hours: 9–7:30
Full Day: $86 adult, $58 senior (65 and over), $54 children 7–12, free 6 and under
Half Day: $68 (12:30–4)
Special Features: Terrain parks, World Cup facilities, snowcat skiing, night skiing

Park City is a vibrant mountain with skiers of all sorts. You'll quickly learn that the mountain is naturally partitioned by its guests, based on the diverse offerings of each region. On
the lower mountain, the Payday Lift (the high-speed six-pack departing from the resort
center) is usually dominated by snowboarders dressed in their baggy—yet expensive and
allegedly fashionable—suits. As you ride up, look to your left and you'll see the tail end of a
terrain park and bodies flying off jumps. The skiers' left side of the lower mountain is used

Cisero's Restaurant, Park City Jonathan Echlin

by the U.S. Ski Team, National Disabled Team, Park City Ski Team, and Rowmark Ski Academy for training and races. On the upper mountain, McConkey's and Jupiter Bowls, as well as some traverse-accessed skiing, attract the crusty experts. Because of its array of choices, Park City is great for mixed-skill groups, with groomed runs and off-piste trails adjacent to each other.

With regards to driving and parking, Park City is simple to navigate. Almost as soon as you turn into the area, you will be surrounded by parking lots for day skiers. An underground parking garage is located directly below the resort center. It has fairly low ceilings, not allowing for vehicles much taller than an SUV. The fee for parking in the garage is five dollars.

Park City's major hotels, the **Lodge at Mountain Village**, **Marriott Mountainside**, and **Resort Center Inn** are all located right in the resort center. Many vacation rentals are distributed just downhill of the parking lots, within short walking distance of the resort center. Specific lodging locations are described with each establishment.

On-site Accommodations

Because the resorts in Park City are an integral part of the town, many of the major hotels of the city are on resort property. As a result, the on-site hotel accommodations for **Park City Mountain Resort**, **The Lowell** (1335 Lowell Avenue; 1-888-727-5248; www.thelowellpark city.com), the **Loft at Mountain Village** (1386 Lowell Avenue; Park City Mountain Reservations: 435-647-5440 or 1-800-331-3178; www.parkcitymountain.com), **Marriott's Moun-**

tainSide (1305 Lowell Avenue; 435-940-2000; www.marriott.com), and **Resort Plaza at Park City Mountain Resort** (Park City Resort Center; Park City Mountain Reservations: 435-647-5440 or 1-800-331-3178; www.parkcitymountain.com) are described in the "Accommodations" section of Chapter 2, Park City.

On-site Dining

Most of Park City's lunches are served at the resort center, although a number of establishments are strategically scattered around the mountain. Housed in a yurt, the **Five-way Café** (beneath Bonanza and Silverlode Lifts, along Homerun) offers hot beverages and European-style goodies like crepes, sandwiches, and soups. The **Legacy Lodge** (resort center, near base of Payday Lift), with an outdoor patio and expansive dining area, is the go-to dining place on the mountain. The cafeteria includes an impressive salad bar boasting nutritious and gourmet components. A grill, pizza bar, and chili stand are also available. Weather permitting, the staff fires up the grill on the outdoor patio. **The Mid-Mountain Lodge** (near Pioneer and McConkey's Lifts) is the legendary old Silver King Mine's bunkhouse, which was relocated to prevent demolition. Still quite functional, it today serves simple fare like soups, pizza, pasta, and salads. **Payday Pizza** (second floor, Legacy Lodge) serves fresh pizza, cold beer, and more. The fireplace makes it hard to leave on a cold day. Sports fans appreciate score updates and games on the big-screen TVs. For lunch on a beautiful day, the **Snow Hut** (near the base of Silverlode Lift), with its expansive patio and limited inner seating, is perfect. Its cafeteria setup and mid-mountain location make it a quick way to eat without interrupting your day. **Summit House** (top of Bonanza Lift and near the top of Thanes Lift) has everything you could want in a large, modern ski lodge. It has panoramic views, a grill, bakery, deli, and coffee drinks, plus a heated deck for sunny day dining. With a beer you'll want to linger, but this lodge closes at 3 PM. For a full dinner, Park City Mountain Resort skiers must travel to downtown Park City or Kimball Junction.

On-site Après Ski and Nightlife

The newly renovated **Legends Bar and Grill** (adjacent to Payday Lift, First Level, Resort Center; 435-649-8111) is a perfect spot for adults to enjoy a peaceful après ski among friends in a modern establishment. Fine liquors and appetizers are available, as is dinner. For a relaxed, jovial evening, the **Pig Pen Saloon** (adjacent to the National Ability Center, Second Level, Resort Center; 435-655-0070) may be your choice. Equally close to the hill, this is the kind of bar where teams and groups of friends gather, pull tables together, and share pitchers of beer. Much of the serious nightlife moves on to Main Street after a few drinks. Free shuttle buses between town and the resorts operate until about 10 PM. No person under the age of 21 is allowed in a bar, even if the person is a child accompanied by a parent.

Lessons

Park City has a very visible and thriving **Mountain School** (children's and group lessons: 1-800-227-2754). Private and group lessons are available for telemark and alpine skiing, as well as snowboarding. An entire sector of the school is dedicated to children's lessons. Park City's most unique opportunity for instruction is the world-class **National Ability Center** (435-649-3991; www.nac1985.org). This organization brings winter sports to disabled people of all skill levels. During the summer, they offer another full array of sports.

Flat Rabbet Vintage Poster Gallery, Park City Jonathan Echlin

Child Care

Though **Guardian Angels** (435-640-1229; www.guardianangelbaby.com) is not affiliated with Park City Mountain Resort, they are a popular choice for locals and guests. First-aid and CPR-certified sitters come to your room to stay with the kids for a very reasonable rate.

On-site Rentals

Aloha Ski and Snowboard Rentals (Park City Mountain Resort Center; 1-877-222-7600; www.alohaskirentals.com), alpine ski and snowboard demos, rentals, repairs, tuning

Bahnhof Sport (base of Town Lift, Park City Mountain Resort/Park City downtown; 435-

645-9700 or 1-866-451-9425; www.bahnhof.com), alpine ski and snowboard rentals, repairs, retail, tuning

Bazooka's Freeride Shop (Park City Mountain Resort Center; 435-649-0520; www.cole sport.com), demos, rentals, repairs, retail, tuning

Black Tie Ski Rentals (delivery to The Canyons, Deer Valley, and Park City Mountain Resort; 435-649-4070 or 1-888-333-4754; www.blacktieskis.com), alpine ski and snowboard rentals, retail, free children's rentals

Breeze Ski Rentals (Park City Mountain Resort Center; 435-649-1902; www.breezeski .com), demos, rentals, retail, discounts on reservations

Cole Sport (Park City Mountain Resort Center; 435-649-4600; www.colesport.com), demos, rentals, repairs, retail, tuning

Jake's Slope Side Sports (Park City Mountain Resort Center; 435-649-0355; www.rent skis.com), ski and snowboard rentals, repairs, tuning, ski and snowboard storage

KinderSport Junior Ski & Snowboard Rentals (Park City Mountain Resort Center; 435-649-5463 or 1-877-350-5463; www.kindersport.com), children's ski and snowboard rentals, retail

Max Snowboard (Park City Mountain Resort Center; 435-647-9699; www.breezeski.com), demos, rentals, retail, discounts on reservations

Park City Park and Ride (Park City Mountain Resort Town Lift/Park City downtown; 435-940-0140; www.pcparkandride.com), snowboard rentals, clothing rentals, retail

Park City Sport (Park City Mountain Resort Center; 435-645-7777; www.rentskis.com), ski and snowboard rentals, repairs, tuning, ski and snowboard storage

Ski Butlers (delivery to The Canyons, Deer Valley, and Park City Mountain Resort; 1-877-754-7754; www.skibutlers.com), ski and snowboard equipment delivery

Ski 'N See Ski and Snowboard (Park City Mountain Resort Center; 1-800-722-3685; www.skinsee.com), demos, rentals, repairs, retail, tuning, discounts on reservations, select discounted

Skis on the Run (delivery to The Canyons, Deer Valley, and Park City Mountain Resort; 1-888-488-0744; www.skisontherun.com), alpine ski and snowboard rentals, tuning

Summit Demo Center (top of Bonanza and Silverlode Lifts, Park City Mountain Resort; 435-649-8111 or 1-800-226-0047; www.parkcitymountain.com), alpine ski rentals, repairs, tuning

Surefoot (Park City Mountain Resort Center; 435-649-6016; www.surefoot.com), boot-fitting and footwear specialists

Utah Ski & Golf (Shadow Ridge Condos at Resort Center; 435-655-8367; www.utahski golf.com), demos, rentals, repairs, retail, tuning, discounts on reservations, select discounted lift tickets

PARK CITY AREA LODGING

Vacation rental services available in the Park City area include Affordable Luxury Lodging (1-866-786-3755; www.affordableluxurylodging.com), Park City Mountain Reservations (435-649-8111 or 1-800-331-3178; www.parkcitymountain.com), Snow Valley Connection (435-645-7700 or 1-800-458-8612; www.snowvalleyconnection.com), Utah Travel Connection (801-453-1128; www.utahtravelconnection.com), and Western Leisure (435-649-2223; www.westernleisure.com). These agents are described more fully in the "Accommodations" section of Chapter 2, Park City.

Ogden Valley

In the peaks surrounding Ogden Valley and the towns of Eden and Hunstville are the resorts Powder Mountain, Snowbasin, and Wolf Creek Utah. During the winter, these mountains offer every activity you could want, including Nordic skiing, tubing, snowshoeing, and world-class alpine skiing. During the summer, the best of Utah's recreational opportunities, like waterskiing on the Pineview Reservoir, mountain biking, and fishing, are all available here. With activities comparable to more popular Utah destinations, the Ogden Valley's major advantage is its utter lack of crowding by people and buildings alike. This comes with lower costs for skiing, lodging, dining, and recreation.

Of the three ski resorts in the area, Powder Mountain and Snowbasin are the full-sized resorts. They attract skiers from Salt Lake City who deem the trip a worthwhile trade for the solitude of these areas. The terrain and annual snowfall here can easily be compared to that of the Cottonwood Canyons, but the crowds and prices are much less.

A third ski area in the Ogden Valley, Wolf Creek Utah, is a very small hill, perfect for beginner skiers. With only one major face, it does not claim to be a full ski resort, but rather a great area for families and novices wanting to try their new skills. It will not be fully described in this book, although its contact information and rates are listed. Guests of Wolf Creek Utah will have the same accommodations pool from which to select.

Transportation

The lowered population in Ogden Valley is a gift to skiing but a bane for public transportation. Choices are much more limited, forcing visitors to rent cars. However, the money saved in lodging, lift tickets, and dining in the Ogden Valley probably eclipses the added cost of car rental.

Advanced Transportation (1-866-647-3999; www.advancetransportation.com), individual and group direct shuttle service between Salt Lake Airport and ski areas

All Resort Express (1-877-658-3999; www.allresort.com), individual and group direct shuttle service between Salt Lake Airport and ski areas

Lewis Stages (1-800-862-5844; www.lewisstages.com), charter buses, as well as individual and small group shuttle service (see All Resort Express above)

Powder Mountain Shuttle Service (801-745-3772; www.powdermountain.com), morning shuttles operating from Ogden Valley's Moose Hollow, Red Moose Lodge, and Wolf Lodge to Powder Mountain; call to set up special pickup times

XPress Salt Lake City (1-800-397-0773; www.xpressshuttle.com), individual and group direct shuttle service between Salt Lake Airport and ski areas

Powder Mountain

P.O. Box 450
Northern Terminus of UT 158
Eden, UT 84310
801-745-3772
www.powdermountain.com
Average Annual Snowfall: 500 inches (13 m)
Snow Phone: 801-745-3771

Roofer working in Park City winter Jonathan Echlin

Area Elevation: 6,895–8,900 feet (2,100–2,700 m)
Vertical Drop (without hiking): 2,005 feet (610 m)
Lifts: 7 total, combination high-speed and fixed chairs, towropes
Trails: 113
Area: 5,500 acres
Difficulty: 10 percent beginner, 50 percent intermediate, 40 percent advanced
Lift Hours: 9–4:30
Full Day: $58 adult, $46 senior (62–69), $25 senior (70 and over), $31 children 12 and under, free 5 and under on Sundance Lift

Half Day: $48 (9–1); $49 (12–9)
Special Features: Night skiing, terrain parks, most skiable acres of any resort in the United States, snowcat skiing, helicopter skiing, backcountry tours

Powder Mountain's real claim to fame is its 5,000 acres of terrain—the most of any North American resort. Its snowfall matches that of Snowbird and Alta, yet the lack of crowds and expansive terrain keep fresh powder stashes for several days after the snow has stopped falling. Powder Mountain sells remarkably inexpensive snowcat passes to ticket holders. This opens up even more terrain beneath Lightning Ridge.

For as huge a mountain as this, it has a very simple arrangement: Only five major lifts are required to access all of this terrain, which is characterized by open bowls, chutes, and light tree patches. All resort parking and base services are centrally located in the Timberline Area. Powder Mountain is located within a protected watershed and no pets are allowed there.

On-site Accommodations

COLUMBINE INN
Powder Mountain Resort Center
801-745-1414
www.powdermountain.com
Price: Moderate to Very Expensive
Credit Cards: AE, MC, V
Handicapped Accessible: No
Pets: No
Special Packages: Limited air and car rental packages

Adjacent to the Powder Mountain Lodge, this is the ultimate Powder Mountain location. Guest rooms range from hotel style to three-bedroom condominiums. Hotel rooms are equipped with basic amenities like a small refrigerator, coffeemaker, and microwave. Condominium units have all the necessary accommodations for a ski vacation, including in-room fireplace and full kitchen. This is a slightly older establishment with an endearing hodgepodge decor.

POW MOW SKI-INN CONDOS
Office: P.O. Box 1015
Eden, UT 84310
801-458-9112
www.powmowcondos.com
Price: Very Expensive
Credit Cards: Personal checks only
Handicapped Accessible: No
Pets: No
Special Packages: No

Spacious and simply decorated, each unit leaves you plenty of room to unwind without feeling crowded by wet ski gear. The condominiums have three separate bathrooms and a sun porch for enjoyment of good weather. The modern loft-style structure is adorned with raw pine furniture, simple stonework, and regional art. A two-car garage is available at each unit. Extra perks include the gas grill and ski-tuning bench in each condominium. A minimum stay of three nights is required.

POWDER RIDGE CONDOS AND LODGE
6172 Powder Ridge Road
Eden, UT 84310
801-745-3722
www.powderridgevillage.com
Price: Expensive to Very Expensive
Credit Cards: MC, V
Handicapped Accessible: No
Pets: No
Special Packages: No

The condominiums at Powder Ridge Village share common horseshoe pits, a pool, tennis courts, and proximity to Powder Mountain. Remodeled in 2000, units have one, two, or three bedrooms, and have a modest, yet clean, feel. These moderate condominiums are simple, yet comfortable. As these are some of the only ski-in, ski-out accommodations at Powder Mountain, it would be wise to book ahead. The condominiums are located near the top of the Hidden Lake Lift.

SUNDOWN CONDOMINIUMS
Across from Sundown Lift
Powder Mountain Resort
801-745-1414
www.powdermountain.com
Price: Expensive to Very Expensive
Credit Cards: AE, Disc, MC, V
Handicapped Accessible: No
Pets: No
Special Packages: Limited air and car rental packages

Each unit is built to satisfy families or small groups, with sleeping capacities from six to ten. To ensure comfort during your stay, each condominium has been equipped with a fireplace, kitchen, laundry facilities, and single-car garage. The condominiums are simple, but you will hardly notice—and you may appreciate it—when you toss your wet ski clothes off.

VALLEY LODGING AT WOLF CREEK
See "Ogden Valley Lodging," below

Valley Lodging has a two-bedroom town house available for rent near the Sundowner Lift. This home has laundry facilities and a one-car garage.

On-site Dining
Because of its slope-side location, **Hidden Lake Lodge** (top of Hidden Lake Lift) is a popular lunch spot with two levels of seating to accommodate its guests. The views from the second level of the lodge are unbeatable; at 8,000 feet above sea level, you can see four different states on a clear day. Another favorite lunch spot because of its grill, the **Powder Keg** (lower level, Powder Mountain Lodge) slides easily into après ski mode with appetizers and draught beer. **The Powder Mountain Restaurant** (resort center) is a great place to grab a quick, cafeteria-style breakfast, lunch, or post-skiing snack. **The Sundown Lodge** (adjacent to Sundown Lift, resort center) is Powder Mountain's all-day establishment. Breakfast begins here at 9 AM and drinks end at 10 PM. Throughout the day, you can indulge in grilled sandwiches and sides of fries.

On-site Après Ski and Nightlife
Powder Mountain's best two après ski spots are the **Sundown Lodge** (adjacent to Sundown Lift, resort center), open until 10 PM, and the **Powder Keg** (lower level, Powder Mountain Lodge), open until 6 PM on weekends and 5 PM on weekdays. **The Powder Mountain Restaurant** (resort center) also serves beer, but closes at 4:30 PM.

Lessons
Powder Mountain's **Snow Sports School** (801-745-3772; call between 10am and 4pm) offers both ski and snowboard lessons to a variety of targeted groups. For adult groups, first-time ski and snowboard lessons are available, and there are lessons for adults of various skill levels and women-only groups. Two different children's groups are available according to age, as well as a teenager-specific group. Private lessons are also available. Regardless of which lesson you opt to take, call ahead to ensure availability of an instructor.

Child care
Though no on-site child care is available at Powder Mountain, the **Old Firehouse Learning**

Shops on Park City's historic Main Street   Jonathan Echlin

Academy (2612 North Highway 162, Eden Utah 84310; 801-745-5600) is just a few minutes away.

On-site Rentals

Resort Center Rentals (Resort Center; 801-745-3772; www.powdermountain.com), alpine
   ski and snowboard rentals, retail
Sundown Rentals (Sundown Lodge; 801-745-3772; www.powdermountain.com), alpine
   ski and snowboard rentals, retail

Snowbasin Resort

3925 East Snowbasin Road
Huntsville, UT 84317
801-620-1000; 1-888-437-5488
www.snowbasin.com
Average Annual Snowfall: 400 inches (10 m)
Snow Phone: 801-620-1100
Area Elevation: 6,400–9,469 feet (1,950–2,890 m)
Vertical Drop (without hiking): 2,959 feet (900 m)
Lifts: 12 total, combination gondolas, high-speed and fixed chairs, and towropes

Trails: 104
Area: 2,483 acres
Difficulty: 7 percent beginner, 29 percent intermediate, 64 percent advanced
Lift Hours: 9–4
Full Day: $65 adult, $53 senior (65–79), free senior (80 and over), $40 children 7–12, free 6 and under
Half Day: $54 (12:30–4)
Special Features: Terrain parks, tubing hill, Nordic skiing

Another beautifully craggy northern Wasatch Mountain, Snowbasin has all of the snow and terrain of Snowbird, with the ultradeluxe atmosphere of its parent resort, Sun Valley. Five hundred inches of snow fall annually onto its rolling knolls, jagged cliffs, long ridges, and open bowls. Snowbasin has everything from steep steeps to flat flats. Massive antler chandeliers, cathedral ceilings, thick timbers, and floor-to-ceiling windows are the signature style of these posh lodges. The amount of snow and quality of terrain is comparable or superior to many destination resorts, yet the price and crowds are dramatically less for lift tickets and lodging.

For alpine skiers, the base area is extremely simple. Two large, adjacent parking lots are immediately below the ticket offices and base of the lifts. Nordic skiers can park in the same location, ideally in Lot 2. All trails start and end here. Snowbasin has no on-site lodging.

On-site Dining

Earl's Lodge (Main Plaza; resort line: 801-620-1020) takes ski lodge fare several echelons higher than the norm. Roasts and poultry carvings, fresh sushi and Asian cuisine, and gourmet salads are served right alongside deli sandwiches, grill fare, and brick-oven pizza. Dinnertime brings out meat-based western entrées, as well as contemporary American and more exotic dishes. **Earl's Lodge Lounge** waits with a full bar and two beers specially crafted for Snowbasin. (Only persons over the age of 21 are admitted.) **Needles Lodge** (top of Needle Express Gondola; resort line: 801-620-1021) is yet another grand facility that you will not want to leave. Another roughly cafeteria-style eatery, you can home in on the general cuisine of your fancy, and then order directly from the chef, watching as your food is prepared. Dine on the Needle's Austrian cuisine fireside under elaborate chandeliers while sitting on high-backed leather chairs. You'll be surprised both by the extremely high quality of the food and the reasonable pricing. Excellent views of surrounding peaks can be seen through the gaping window of the **John Paul Lodge** (top of John Paul Lift; resort line: 801-620-1021), which sits at the base of Mount Ogden. In classic Snowbasin fashion, the lodge has grand stone fireplaces, massive timber beams, and premium carpeting. On a nice day, you can enjoy your pizza, soup, or tasty grilled lunch on the deck.

On-site Après Ski and Nightlife

Earl's Lodge Lounge (Earl's Lodge, Main Plaza; 801-620-1021) is a highly relaxing place to sit and sip cocktails or either of the two beers brewed specially for Snowbasin. Guests are welcome to bring their meal in from the main dining room or order from their appetizer menu. Because the lounge is defined by the State of Utah as a bar, no one under the age of 21 is allowed here, even if the person is a young child with a parent.

Lessons

Snowbasin's **Snowsports Learning Center** (801-620-1016) has a fleet of more than 100 instructors to cater to your specific instructional needs. Children's and adults' lessons range from first-time beginner to advanced levels. Specialty lessons are available for freeriding, racing, and Nordic skiing. Lesson meeting times and durations vary, so call ahead. Reservations are strongly suggested for private lessons.

Child Care

In case you need a day—or even just a few runs—to yourself, Snowbasin's **Grizzly Cub's Den** (Grizzly Center; 801-620-1111) will entertain your child. During busy times, call ahead to ensure there will be room for your child.

On-site Rentals

Snowbasin Resort Grizzly Center (3925 East Snowbasin Road, Huntsville; 801-620-1120; www.snowbasin.com) rentals, repairs, retail, tuning

Wolf Creek Utah

3567 Nordic Valley Way
P.O. Box 1089
Eden, UT 84310
801-745-3511
www.wolfmountaineden.com
Average Annual Snowfall: 400 inches (10 m)
Area Elevation: 5,500–6,500 feet (1,675–1,980 m)
Vertical Drop (without hiking): 1,000 feet (305 m)
Lifts: 3 total, 2 fixed chairs and 1 ski carpet
Trails: 19
Area: 3,300 acres
Lift Hours: 9–9
Full Day: $26 adult ($32 adult weekend), $23 senior (65 and over) or military ($28 weekend), $15 children 12 and under ($20 weekend)
Half Day: $23 (1–9); $28 weekend
Special Features: Terrain parks

If you would like to check out an evening of night skiing on perfectly groomed trails, or feel a bit shaky on skis, Wolf Creek Utah (formerly **Wolf Mountain**) is a low-cost and low-intimidation mountain. With one "magic carpet" for true beginner skiers, a mid-mountain chair, and a single major chairlift accessing more difficult terrain, this ski area is an excellent location for learning. Certified by the Professional Ski Instructors of America, the **Wolf Creek Utah Learning Center** (801-745-3511) offers a variety of lessons to match your duration of stay and age. Freestyle lessons are available for youngsters, and a women-only lesson group meets as well.

Though no on-site child care is available at Wolf Creek Utah, the **Old Firehouse Learning Academy** (2612 North Highway 162, Eden Utah 84310; 801-745-5600) is just a few minutes away.

OGDEN VALLEY LODGING

Because the Ogden Valley resorts are in close proximity to each other and very near the towns of Huntsville and Eden, hotels and vacation rentals in these towns make excellent lodging options for skiers at any of these areas. Many of these properties are condominium vacation rentals in the style that you would expect slope-side at any resort. The short morning drive to the ski area will seem minor, and you will leave your options open as to which area you want to visit each day. Keep in mind that Eden is closer to the base of Powder and Wolf Creek Utahs, and Huntsville and the Pineview Reservoir are nearer Snowbasin.

ATOMIC CHALET

6917 East 100 South
Huntsville, UT 84317
801-745-0538; 1-866 209-9503
www.atomicchalet.com
Price: Inexpensive to Moderate
Credit Cards: MC, V
Handicapped Accessible: No
Pets: No
Special Packages: No

This bed & breakfast was built with European ski tradition in mind. Each morning guests awake to copious, healthy breakfasts of fruits, granolas, oatmeal, and other whole foods that help you make the most of your ski day. Rooms are quaint, yet thoroughly comfortable with pillow-top king beds, private baths, and down comforters that you will greatly appreciate at the end of a long day outside. Guests have common access to a recreation room and ski locker with crucial boot dryers. The guests and innkeepers take skiing seriously, and a quiet atmosphere is enforced. A home for some of the U.S. Ski Team during the 2002 Olympics, the Atomic Chalet still flies the team's flag. Young children are not allowed.

LAKESIDE VILLAGE

6486 East Highway 39
Huntsville, UT 84317
801-745-3194; 1-866-745-3194
www.lakesideresortproperties.com
Price: Moderate to Very Expensive
Credit Cards: AE, Disc, MC, V
Handicapped Accessible: Limited (inquire; require assistance)
Pets: No
Special Packages: Discounts on extended stays

Located on lakefront property along Pineview Reservoir, the Lakeside Village offers its guests uninterrupted views across the lake and a glimpse of all of the nearby peaks. The Village's refreshing natural settings are a perfect place from which to embark on adventures. These modern, mountain lodge—style units give you privacy as well as the benefit of shared resources like the resort's tennis courts and pool. All of the Ogden Valley ski areas are within a few minutes' drive from the private balcony hot tub.

MOOSE HOLLOW LUXURY CONDOMINIUMS

3605 North Huntsman Path
Eden, UT 84310
1-877-745-0333
www.moosehollowcondos.com
Price: Moderate to Expensive
Credit Cards: AE, Disc, MC, V
Handicapped Accessible: No
Pets: No
Special Packages: Ski packages with Powder Mountain and Snowbasin

Moose Hollow is your source for some of the valley's finest and newest accommodations. For the excellent quality, you will incur only a slightly elevated cost. All units are on an expansive campus of guest condominiums and town houses. A neighborhood atmosphere is given by winding residential lanes with carefully landscaped lawns reminiscent of a golf course. A volleyball court, sauna, hot tub, tennis courts, and pool are on the premises. **The Powder Mountain Shuttle** stops by the complex upon request (1-877-745-0333).

THE RED MOOSE LODGE & HOTEL

2547 North Valley Junction drive
Eden, UT 84310
801-781-4155; 1-800-771-7037
www.theredmooselodge.com
Price: Inexpensive to Expensive
Credit Cards: AE, Disc, MC, V
Handicapped Accessible: Yes
Pets: No
Special Packages: Ski packages with Powder Mountain and Snowbasin

The fully modern Red Moose Lodge was built to resemble the thick-timbered, log cabin ski lodges of the 1930s. A low-profile, yet grand lodge, Moose Hollow is surrounded by lush lawns, a pool, gazebos, and picnic areas. Inside, timber rafters and peaked ceilings in the billiards room create a rustic feel that integrates with the modern stonework, luxury furniture, and immaculate cabinetry. In your room, the oversized mountain-style woodwork, overstuffed chairs, and stone fireplaces will make you feel pampered before you even sleep here.

SKINNER'S OGDEN VALLEY CONDOMINIUMS

3615 North Wolf Creek Drive
Eden, UT 84310
801-745-2621; 1-800-345-8824
Price: Moderate to Expensive
Credit Cards: AE, Disc, MC, V
Handicapped Accessible: No
Pets: No
Special Packages: Discounted rates, as available

These condominiums are fully furnished homes, each with a kitchen and fireplace. Located in Eden, they are each just a short drive from Powder Mountain, Snowbasin, or the smaller Wolf Creek Utah. The 144 modern condominiums have the benefit of many shared amenities. Business travelers have access to a meeting room, and all guests can enjoy the indoor and outdoor hot tubs. For summer visitors, a tennis court, an outdoor pool, or even the nearby Pineview Reservoir can be a way to enjoy an afternoon in this mountain valley setting.

SNOWBERRY INN

1315 North Highway 158
Eden, UT 84310
801-745-2634; 1-888-746-2634
www.snowberryinn.com
Price: Moderate to Expensive
Credit Cards: MC, V
Handicapped Accessible: No
Pets: No
Special Packages: Romantic, extended stay, and summer recreation packages

The guest rooms at the Snowberry Inn are decorated individually with subdued themes and simple charm. Raw pine furniture, quilts, and ski memorabilia give this a cozy ski lodge ambience. Fragrant breakfasts greet you each morning. Famous for good cooking, the inn posts a handful of their recipes online each month. Many guests enjoy the fact that the rooms do not have television sets (with the exception of "the apartment"), and enjoy playing pool, darts, games, or even the piano in the game room.

VALLEY HOUSE INN

7319 East 200 South
Huntsville, UT 84317
801-475-8259; 1-888-791-8259
www.valleyhouseinn.com
Price: Moderate to Expensive
Credit Cards: V, MC
Handicapped Accessible: No
Pets: No
Special Packages: Romantic packages

Housed in a refurbished 1872 colonial brick home, the Valley House Inn has cozy, simple rooms with the fun, quirky angles required to fit them into the building. A wraparound porch and on-site restaurant give guests the option to lounge on the premises without rushing off for meals. The restaurant serves contemporary American cuisine ranging from prime rib to seafood, and brunch is served on Sundays. Guests have access to a complimentary breakfast every day.

VALLEY LODGING AT WOLF CREEK

3718 North Wolf Creek Drive
Eden, UT 84310
801-745-3787; 1-800-301-0817
www.valleylodging.com
Price: Moderate to Very Expensive

Credit Cards: AE, MC, V
Handicapped Accessible: Limited (inquire)
Pets: No
Special Packages: Ski and recreation packages

Valley Lodging at Wolf Creek has lodging options in Eden and Huntsville in various resort village locations, as well as at Powder Mountain. All units are fully furnished vacation rentals that range from condominiums to town houses and single-family homes. These units range from moderate to very deluxe. The ownership and staff are very outdoors- and ski-savvy and will assist you in your selection with regards to summer and winter recreation. Ski bus vouchers are available.

Provo Area

Sundance Resort

RR3 Box A-1
Sundance, UT 84604
801-225-4107; 1-800-892-1600
www.sundanceresort.com
Average Annual Snowfall: 320 inches (8 m)
Area Elevation: 6,100–8,250 feet (1,875–2,500 m)
Vertical Drop (without hiking): 2,150 feet (650 m)
Lifts: 1 quad, 1 triple, 1 surface tow
Trails: 41
Area: 450 acres
Difficulty: 17 percent beginner, 50 percent intermediate, 33 percent advanced
Lift Hours: 9–4:30
Full Day: $47 adult, $15 senior (65 and over), $25 children 6–12, free 5 and under
Half Day: $38 (12:30–4:30)
Special Features: Low crowding, Nordic skiing, night skiing

Much more than "just" a ski area, the Sundance Resort is a holistic soul retreat. The accommodations are subtly elegant and in tune with the mountain surroundings. Dining features delicately prepared local foods, from herbs to wild game. Artists in residence fill the studios with life and creativity.

Everything about Sundance was designed to afford guests the greatest luxuries in the simplest and most down-to-earth fashion. Skiing at Sundance is no exception. Groomed trails slice softly through the woods, and powder is piled on the steeps. Though Sundance

Resort is modest in size, it offers a full spectrum of alpine terrain. A full Nordic ski and snowshoe facility are also available on-site. All lodging, dining, and ticketing needs are found centrally in the resort village.

On-site Accommodations

SUNDANCE LODGING
Sundance Resort Reservations
1-800-892-1600
www.sundanceresort.com
Price: Very Expensive
Credit Cards: AE, Disc, MC, V
Handicapped Accessible: No
Pets: No
Special Packages: Limited seasonal offers

The Sundance's private rentals are located around the resort village. Decorated with tasteful western flair, each **Sundance Studio** has 405 square feet of living space, as well as basic kitchen appliances to keep you relatively self-sufficient, although you will not have a full kitchen. But more important than the refrigerator and microwave are the down comforter, queen-sized bed, and fireplace. Selected units also have a private balcony. **The Sundance Suites** are decorated with subtly beautiful woodwork, stone, and southwestern Native American craftwork. The Suites have just been expanded to include 700 square feet and a kitchenette. Vaulted ceilings with pine timber beams make each unit feel more spacious. The next step up in size and accommodations are the **Mountain Suites** and **Lofts**, which measure 900 square feet and have a full kitchen and master bedroom. Some units also include extra sleep space in the form of loft or sleeper sofa, as well as steam showers.

On-site Dining

The Foundry Grill (Village Center; 1-866-932-2295) epitomizes the Sundance Resort with its casual atmosphere, yet richly prepared foods. A small menu is available especially for kids. Breakfast, lunch, and dinner are available daily, with a special brunch on Sunday. Dinner at the **Tree Room** (Village Building, Village Center; 1-866-627-8313) is no casual affair. With national acclaim and a serious wine list, the cuisine here is regional, and fresh according to season. The Tree Room is closed on Sun. and Mon., and for a short time in the late fall.

On-site Après Ski and Nightlife

The Owl Bar (Village Center; 801-223-4222) is one of Sundance's—and Utah County's—favorite evening spots. The bar itself is actually a relocated, restored rosewood piece from Thermopolis, Wyoming. Butch Cassidy and his gang frequented this bar in its original location. Live music is often heard here, and the schedule is listed on www.sundanceresort.com. No person under the age of 21 is allowed in a bar, even if the person is a child accompanied by a parent.

Lessons

Sundance's **Ski & Snowboard School** (801-223-4140) offers lessons for individuals, small groups, and larger groups. Adult and children's lessons are available. For less than the cost

Top of Big Cottonwood Canyon in Winter Christine Balaz

of a day pass at most other ski areas, beginners can get a package deal including a half-day lesson and full-day ticket.

Child Care

Though **Guardian Angels** (801-310-2761; www.guardianangelbaby.com) is not affiliated with Sundance Resort, they are a popular choice for locals and guests. First-aid- and CPR-certified sitters come to your room to stay with the kids for a very reasonable rate.

On-site Rentals

Sundance Mountain Outfitters (Resort Village; 801-223-4120; www.sundanceresort .com), alpine ski and snowboard rentals, repair, retail

NORDIC FACILITIES AND TRAILS

Facilities

The Wasatch region has as many fantastic opportunities for Nordic skiing as it does for its famous alpine skiing. These facilities are perfect if you prefer lessons or a fast-paced work-out to a wooded nature stroll. All of these facilities offer groomed trails and most have rental services.

MOUNTAIN DELL

I-80, Exit 134
Salt Lake City, UT 84109
801-582-3812
Cost: $5 donation
Rentals and Lessons: None

Mountain Dell is a canyon golf course by summer and a looping Nordic ski track in winter. After exiting I-80, follow signs to the nearby clubhouse. Park as you would for golfing and follow the trampled snow to the groomed trails. Loops depart from either side. Built into a canyon, this course naturally has some pitch, although much less than other facilities in the area. A five-dollar donation is required for access to the trails.

SOLDIER HOLLOW

2002 Olympic Drive
Midway, UT 84049
435-654-2002
www.soldierhollow.com
Cost: $18 adult, $15 senior (65 and over), $9 children (7–17), free 6 and under
Rentals and Lessons: Classic and skate ski rentals, demo center, lessons

Soldier Hollow, the Salt Lake Winter Olympics Nordic racing grounds in 2002, is a state-of-the-art facility perfect for recreational skiers and competitive skiers alike. Miles of trails groomed for skate and classic skiing trace loops around flat and hilly terrain. With a full demo center, expansive lodge, and available lessons, Soldier Hollow is truly a complete facility. The on-site tubing hill makes Soldier Hollow an attractive destination for families.

SOLITUDE MOUNTAIN RESORT

12000 Big Cottonwood Canyon Road
Solitude, UT 84121
801-536-5774
www.skisolitude.com
Cost: $16 adult ($11 after 12:30), free senior (70 and over), free 10 and under
Rentals and Lessons: Classic and skate-ski rentals, lessons, special clinics

Solitude's Nordic skiing facilities are among the locals' favorites. High in Big Cottonwood Canyon, this hilly course is a treat for people seeking fresh mountain air. Because of its Solitude Mountain location and proximity to Brighton Resort, the Nordic facility is a great place for families whose interests are split between downhill and cross-country skiing. Open 8:30-4:30.

SNOWBASIN RESORT

3925 East Snowbasin Road
Huntsville, UT 84317
801-620-1000; 1-888-437-5488
www.snowbasin.com
Cost: Free
Lessons and Rentals: Skate and classic rentals, group and private lessons at the Grizzly Center

Snowbasin grooms 16 miles (26km) of trails for skate and classic skiing. Skiers have a choice among easy, moderate, and challenging terrain. Additionally, the U.S. Forest Service (801-236-3400) maintains miles of trails that connect to Snowbasin's trails, but are outside the resort. All trails originate from the Olympic Parking Lot at the base area. Easier loops stay near the resort base, while longer trails depart from the area.

SUNDANCE RESORT CROSS COUNTRY SKI CENTER
RR3 Box A-1
Sundance, UT 84604
801-223-4170; 1-877-831-6224
www.sundanceresort.com
Cost: $16 adult ($12 half day), $9 children 11–17 ($6 half day), free 65 and over and 10 and under
Lessons and Rentals: Skate and classic rentals, group and private lessons

Just 1.5 miles on the Alpine Loop Road south of the Resort Village is the Sundance Resort's full-service Nordic center. A few dozen trails of various difficulty meander through the woods, totally 26 kilmoeters of grooming. With a compact, interconnected format, these loops are easy to link, and your route can be lengthened or shortened as you wish. Open 9-5. Half day rates start at 2 PM. Check out the other "Sundance-eque" options, such as couples' moonlight skis and owling tours.

WHITE PINE TOURING CENTER
1790 Bonanza Drive
Park City, UT 84060
435-649-6249; 1-888-649-8710
www.whitepinetouring.com
Cost: $18 adult ($10 after 3 PM), $8 children 6–12, free 65 and over and 6 and under
Lessons and Rentals: Skate and classic rentals, lessons (435-649-6249)

Literally in the center of Park City, the White Pine Touring Center could not be more convenient for visitors looking for an afternoon of aerobic activity. The 12.5 miles (20km) of trails include 3, 5, and 10k loops. Some of the loops stay on the valley floor, while a few advanced trails gain some elevation in the nearby wooded hills.

Trails
For Nordic skiing away from developed centers, the possibilities are virtually endless. Nearly anywhere you can hike, you can ski—with the exception of very steep hiking trails. For Salt Lake City skiers, Millcreek Canyon is the go-to convenient and free destination. The upper section of the canyon road is closed to automobile traffic between November and March. During these months it becomes a cross-country ski track that follows the road for another 5 miles up into the canyon. A popular destination, it sees some crowding that disperses soon after you leave the parking area. If the people are too much for you, you can simply park and ski from any of the hiking trailheads along the canyon road. During warm winter weeks, the trails on the north-facing slopes retain their snow much longer. There is a $2.25 day-use fee for the canyon, to be paid upon leaving.

Near Park City is the favorite **Wasatch Mountain State Park**, a valley park surrounded by small peaks. Though this is not a full-blown facility, rentals are available here (435-654-

Putting skins on the backcountry skis Christine Balaz

1791), and groomed skiing can be enjoyed in relative solitude. The park is just south of Park City, on the northeast side of Midway.

The Nordic Skiers of Provo enjoy the close proximity of **Rock Canyon**. The gate at the mouth of the canyon keeps all motor vehicles out of the area, lending it serenity. Aptly named, Rock Canyon is a deep, craggy canyon of limestone and quartzite.

BACKCOUNTRY SKIING

Although Utah's Wasatch Range has many world-class resorts, they cover only a fraction of the available terrain. This is where snowcats, helicopters, and your legs come in. The backcountry skiing in Utah is as vast and good as it gets anywhere in the Rocky Mountains. With excellent terrain and some of the planet's best snow, Utah gives its backcountry skiers great rewards.

What a lot of people do not realize is that the tops of Millcreek Canyon, Little Cottonwood Canyon, Big Cottonwood Canyon, and the back of The Canyons Resort are actually fairly near each other. Tens of thousands of acres of skiing are available with a set of skins and free-heel bindings. If considering a backcountry trip on your visit, be 100 percent confident in your avalanche safety knowledge and skills. Then go to the **Utah Avalanche Center**'s Web site, **www.avalanche.org**, or call the advisory at 801-364-1591. This has extremely current information. Because Utah's backcountry is so vast, you might consider consulting a guidebook or local for explicit instructions and recommendations based on snowpack.

Guide Services

Utah Mountain Adventures (formerly Exum Mountain Guides) (www.utahmountain adventures.com) is the consummate guide service, leading beginners through expert trips in backcountry skiing, ice climbing, mountaineering, and more. They also give introductory safety courses, and custom tours are available.

Ski Utah Interconnect Tour (801-534-1907; www.skiutah.com/interconnect) is a favorite guide service of Park City and Salt Lake skiers. They operate two tours: one out of Deer Valley Resort and the other out of Snowbird. On these tours, you cross many ridges and link canyons you probably didn't know were adjacent.

Helicopter and Snowcat Skiing

Many ski resorts offer snowcat skiing in addition to their lift fare. Utah resorts that have this service are Alta, Deer Valley, Park City Mountain Resort, and Powder Mountain.

Diamond Peaks Heli-Ski Adventures (801-745-4631; www.diamondpeaks.com), located in Ogden Valley, has a staff composed entirely of U.S. Ski Patrol members. Diamond Peaks has over 15,000 acres of private ski terrain and welcomes intermediate skiers as much as it does experts. Pass options include pure heli-skiing days and combination passes with Powder Mountain. Special packages are available to groups and couples.

Park City Powder Cats (435-649-6596; www.pccats.com) operates heli- and snowcat skiing out of Park City. They have a very flexible scheduling service that accommodates your needs and group size. They even offer combination deals with massage service. Their helicopter fleet serves more than 42,000 acres.

Wasatch Powderbird Guides (801-742-2800 or 1-800-974-4354; www.powderbird.com) is the Salt Lake vicinity's most famous heli-ski service. In addition to transporting skiers around the Wasatch Range, they also give scenic tours.

RENTALS

Although all ski areas have on-site rental shops as listed in this chapter, you may prefer to rent in town. Renting in town is often less hectic than renting at the ski hill, and it takes a stressful step out of arriving at the resort. Additionally, Nordic and backcountry skiers may need to rent in town if their destination is a simple trail or an undeveloped facility, such as Mountain Dell.

Salt Lake City: Base of Big and Little Cottonwood Canyons

Breeze Ski Rentals (2354 Foothill Drive; 435-649-1902; www.breezeski.com), alpine ski

Sugarhouse Park and Wasatch backdrop, Salt Lake City Jonathan Echlin

and snowboard demos, rentals, retail, discounts on reservations, ski and snowboard
storage, free children's rentals

Canyon Sports Ski and Snowboard (517 South 200 West, Downtown; 1-800-482-4754 or
1844 East Fort Union Boulevard, Cottonwoods; 1-800-736-8754; www.canyonsports
.com), Nordic and alpine ski and snowboard rentals, repairs, retail, tuning, discounts
on reservations, select discounted lift tickets

Lifthouse Ski & Snowboard Shop (3698 East Fort Union Boulevard; 801-943-1104),
alpine rentals, repairs, retail, tuning, discounts on reservations, select discounted lift
tickets

REI (3285 East 3300 South, South Salt Lake; 801-486-2100; www.rei.com/stores/19),
touring, Nordic and alpine ski and snowboard rentals; mountaineering and snowshoeing equipment as well

Sidsports (3900 South 265 East; 801-261-0300; www.sidsports.com), alpine, and Nordic
ski rentals, repairs, tuning

Ski 'N See Ski and Board (102 West 500 South, Downtown; 801-333-7767; or 772 East
9400 South, Sandy; 801-571-2031; or 2125 East 9400 South, Cottonwoods; 801-942-
1780; all 1-800-722-3685; www.skinsee.com), Nordic and alpine ski and snowboard
demos, rentals, repairs, retail, tuning, discounts on reservations, select discounted lift
tickets

Utah Ski & Golf (134 West 600 South, Downtown; 801-355-9088; or 2432 East Fort Union
Boulevard, Cottonwoods; 801-942-1522; www.utahskigolf.com), alpine ski and snowboard rentals, repairs, retail, tuning, discounts on reservations, select discounted lift
tickets

Wasatch Touring (702 East 100 South; 801-359-9361; www.wasatchtouring.com), alpine,
telemark, randonee, and Nordic ski rentals, repairs, retail, tuning, discounts on reservations, select discounted lift tickets

Wild Rose Sports (702 3rd Avenue, Avenues District, Salt Lake City; 801-533-8671; www
.wildrosesports.com), Nordic ski racing and recreational, telemark rentals, repairs,
retail, tuning

Park City: Base of The Canyons, Deer Valley, and Park City Mountain Resort

Aloha Ski and Snowboard Rentals (580 Main Street; 1-877-222-7600; www.alohaski rentals.com), alpine ski and snowboard demos, rentals, repairs, tuning

Colesport (1615 Park Avenue; 435-649-4806; www.colesport.com), demos, rentals, repairs, retail, tuning

Destination Sports (738 Main Street; 1-800-247-6197; www.destinationsports.com), alpine ski and snowboard rentals, repairs, retail, tuning

Jans Mountain Outfitters (1600 Park Avenue; 435-649-4949; www.jans.com), demos, rentals, repairs, retail, tuning

Peak Experience (875 Ironhorse Drive; 1-800-361-8824; www.pcpeakexperience.com), alpine ski and snowboard rentals, repairs, discounts on reservations

Ski Butlers (delivery to The Canyons, Deer Valley, and Park City Mountain Resort; 1-877-754-7754; www.skibutlers.com), ski and snowboard equipment delivery

Skis on the Run (delivery to The Canyons, Deer Valley, and Park City Mountain Resort; 1-888-488-0744; www.skisontherun.com), alpine ski and snowboard rentals, tuning

Sports Authority (1780 Park Avenue; 435-649-6922; www.sportsauthority.com), alpine ski and snowboard rentals, repairs, retail, tuning

Turner Ski (Hotel Park City; 435-940-5000, Marriott Park City; 435-655-7941, Sweetwater Lift Lodge; 435-615-8829, The Yarrow; 435-655-4489; www.turnerski.com), alpine ski and snowboard rentals, repairs

Utah Ski & Golf (698 Park Avenue; 435-649-3020; www.utahskigolf.com), alpine ski and snowboard demos, rentals, repairs, retail, tuning, discounts on reservations, select discounted lift tickets

White Pine Touring (1790 Bonanza Drive; 435-649-8710; www.whitepinetouring.com), Nordic ski rentals, city center 12.5 mile (20km) ski track

Provo and Orem: Base of Sundance

Park's Sportsman (644 North State Street, Orem; 801-225-0227 or 1-800-789-4447; www.parkssportsman.com), Nordic and alpine ski and snowboard rentals, retail

Kiosk, downtown Provo Christine Balaz

Pedersen Ski & Sports (1300 South State Street, University Mall, Orem; 801-225-3000), Nordic and alpine ski and snowboard rentals, repairs, retail

Ogden: Base of Snowbasin, Powder Mountain, and Wolf Creek Utah

All American Playground, Inc. (6658 South UT 89; 801-476-8080), alpine ski and snowboard rentals, repairs, and retail

Alpine Sports (1165 Patterson Street; 801-393-0066; www.alpinesportsutah.com), alpine ski and snowboard rentals, repairs, select discounted lift tickets

Canyon Sports (705 West Riverdale Road; 801-621-4662; www.canyonsports.com), telemark, Nordic, and alpine ski and snowboard rentals, retail, repair, select discounted lift tickets

Diamond Peak Ski & Sport (2429 North Highway 162, Eden; 801-745-0101; www.peak stuff.com), Nordic and alpine ski and snowboard rentals, repairs, retail

Miller's Ski & Cycle Haus (834 Washington Boulevard; 801-392-3911), Nordic and alpine ski and snowboard rentals, repairs

Ski Mania (4035 Riverdale Road; 801-621-7669), Nordic and alpine ski and snowboard rentals, retail, tuning

5

CALENDAR OF EVENTS

JANUARY

Utah Winter Games (435-658-4208; www.utahwintergames.org) is a monthlong community festival of competitions in alpine and Nordic skiing, ski jumping, snowboarding, biathlon, speed skating, luge, curling, and freestyle skiing. Events take place across Utah; call or peruse the Web site for specific information.

The **Huntsman Cup** (Park City Mountain Resort; 435-649-3991; www.nac1985.org) takes place around the first weekend of January. This is one of the nation's premier disabled ski races.

The **Sundance Film Festival** (Park City and Salt Lake City; 1-877-733-7829; www.sundance.org) descends on Park City every third week of January, bringing with it many of the year's best new independent films, as well as Hollywood stars, concerts, parties, and intensity.

The **FIS** (Fédération Internationale de Ski) **Freestyle World Cup at Deer Valley** (Deer Valley Resort; 1-800-424-3337; www.deervalley.com) brings much more than a ski competition each year. Deer Valley's night skiing lights illuminate the hill for all to see, free concerts are given by major national bands, beer is served, and of course the best freestyle athletes in the world are seen doing bumps and aerials competitions.

Slamdance Film Festival (Park City and Salt Lake City; www.slamdance.com) is an edgier alternative to the Sundance festival. It takes place in Salt Lake City and New York City, usually in the third week of the month.

FEBRUARY

Winter Choirfest (various locations; 1-800-978-8457; www.byuarts.com), takes place in Utah Valley in early February. This features the area's best collegiate choirs.

Utah Winterfest (Salt Lake City, Ogden, Provo; 1-800-453-1360) is an entirely appropriate, weeklong party celebrating winter sports and ... partying. The kickoff to the event is the International Pedigree Stage Stop **Sled Dog Races**, followed by concerts, fireworks, and the whole shebang. Part of Salt Lake City's celebration is 10 Gay Days/Winter Pride (www.slcwinterfest.com). The festival takes place across Utah, but it is most concentrated in Park City where the ski and snowboard races, moonlight snowshoeing, and sculpture competitions take place.

Rock climbing competition in downtown Salt Lake City atop Shiloh Inn Christine Balaz

MARCH

Nordic Combined Junior Olympics (435-658-4200; www.olyparks.com or www.ski
jumpingcentral.com) comes to Park City early in March. This competition includes
Nordic aerial jumps, which are quite a sight.

The **U.S. Freeskiing Championships** (1-800-232-9542; www.snowbird.com) are hosted
by Snowbird during the second week of March. This is a big mountain skiing competition during which competitors try to ski the most difficult lines down the most technical
faces—with the most style.

The **World Superpipe Championships** (Park City Mountain Resort; 435-649-8111; www
.worldsuperpipe.com or www.parkcitymountain.com) brings some of the most talented
pipe skiers and snowboarders to Park City Mountain Resort's half-pipe during the second week of March. It is truly an impressive display of skill and daring.

In the middle of March, The Canyons (435-649-5400; www.thecanyons.com) hosts two
events. **The Canyons Slopestyle Competition** brings out some of the nation's best
freeskiers. **The Canyons Pond Skimming Contest** brings out local bravery, beer, music,
and more beer. This month also marks the beginning of **The Canyons Spring Concert
Series**.

The **Red, White, and Snow Wine, Culinary, and Ski Festival** (435-200-0985; www.red
whiteandsnow.org), a benefit for the National Ability Center, takes place in Park City
during one weekend in March. It combines some of the best parts of life to raise funds
for one of the area's best foundations.

The **Annual Brigham Young University Jazz Festival** (www.byu.edu) also occurs in March.

APRIL

The **Easter Sunrise Service and Easter Egg Hunt** (1-800-232-9542; www.snowbird.com) is a local favorite. Hunters catch a 5:30 AM tram to Hidden Peak for an Easter egg hunt and nondenominational sunrise service.

The **Semiannual LDS World Conference** (Salt Lake City) is one of Salt Lake City's major conferences, attracting tens of thousands of visitors. During this time, the Temple Square area comes alive.

The **Salt Lake Bees AAA Baseball** (801-325-2273; www.slbees.com) season begins in April. A game in the immaculate Franklin Covey Stadium, with its spectacular Wasatch Range backdrop, is one of the best ways to spend a summer afternoon in the city.

MAY

The **Great Salt Lake Bird Festival** (801-451-3278; www.greatsaltlakebirdfest.com) takes place on Antelope Island, one of the most unique inland bird habitats in the country. The festival attracts bird lovers from around the country and involves lectures, sea-kayaking, and bird-watching.

Days of '47 (801-250-3890; www.daysof47.com), a truly authentic Utah tradition, is Salt Lake City's oldest parade commemorating early Utah Mormon pioneers. All sorts of family-friendly fun ensues.

The **Utah Asian Festival** (South Town Exposition Center; 801-467-6060; www.utahasian festival.com) takes place in Salt Lake City and celebrates the Asian and Pacific Island cultures.

Farmers Market at The Canyons (435-649-5400; www.thecanyons.com) begins in May. This takes place Wednesdays from 2–7 PM.

JUNE

The **Downtown Farmers Market** (Pioneer Park, 300 South 300 West; 801-359-5118; www.downtownslc.org) of Salt Lake City begins early in June and lasts through October. It takes place Saturday mornings starting at 8 AM.

The Scottish Festival and Highland Games (www.utahscots.org) is a Thanksgiving Point in Lehi carnival of Scottish culture and athletics, that takes place during one of the first weekends of June.

The **Utah Arts Festival** (230 South 500 West; 801-322-2428; www.uaf.org) is a community-wide festival in Salt Lake City that takes place at the beautiful Library Square. The festival usually occurs during the third week of June. Check the Web site for other events listings throughout the year.

Around this time, watch for the **Salt Lake City Classic 5 & 10K Races** and **Salt Lake City Marathon and 5K** (801-412-6060; www.saltlakecitymarathon.com), **Park City Marathon** (www.pcmarathon.com), and **Wahsatch Steeplechase** trail run (www.wahsatchsteeplechase.com).

Pedalfest (1-800-424-3337; www.deervalley.org) is a part of the Intermountain Mountain Biking Cup that takes place in the second weekend of June at Deer Valley.

Gallivan Center Concerts (801-535-6110; www.gallivanevents.com or www.slcgov.com

/Arts/twilight), one of Salt Lake City's best traditions, begins in June. These Thursday evening concerts begin at 7 PM and turn this downtown outdoor pavilion into a family-friendly dance floor and beer garden. Park City Performing Arts Foundation (435-655-3114; www.ecclescenter.org) sponsors **free concerts at Deer Valley** throughout the summer.

The **Saturday Freestyle Big Air Show** (Utah Olympic Park, Park City; 435-658-4206; www.olyparks.com) showcases some the nation's best aerialist skiers performing their tricks over a pool of water.

The **Park City International Music Festival** (801-943-0169; www.pcmusicfestival.com) also begins and takes place in several different venues around Park City and Salt Lake City.

Lehi Round-up Rodeo (801-766-3951; www.lehicity.com/roundup) is part of a town-wide celebration of history and western culture that takes place in the last full week in June.

Children's Celebration of the Arts (Pioneer Park, 500 West Center Street; www.provo.org) is a festival especially for children and families that includes a parade, musicians, and crafts.

JULY

Deer Valley Music Festival (www.deervalleymusicfestival.org) summer concerts begin in the last weeks of July, weather permitting. These varied concerts take place in Deer Valley Resort's outdoor amphitheater.

Snowbird's Folk and Bluegrass and **Rock and Blues Festival** (1-800-232-9542; www.snowbird.com), attract prominent musicians and large crowds. This usually takes place in the second weekend of July and at the end of the month.

The **Sundance Institute Outdoor Film Festival** (801-328-3456; www.sundance.org) takes place at Park City Municipal Park during the first week of July. Every Friday you can enjoy a free outdoor screening of an independent film.

Springville World Folkfest (801-489-4811; www.worldfolkfest.com) brings folk dance from around the world to Springville during the first two weeks of July. Locations vary.

The Sundance Resort's **Summer Theater** (801-225-4107; www.sundance.org) is a thriving performing drama program that attracts people from around Utah Valley.

America's Freedom Festival (www.freedomfestival.org) is a gigantic celebration of Utah and the Mormons' arrival here. This takes place all month across Provo. Traditional **Fourth of July** celebrations take place in Park City and Salt Lake City.

AUGUST

The **Kimball Arts Festival** (435-649-8882; www.kimballartcenter.org) takes place during the first week of August. It completely takes over Main Street and attracts thousands of spectators and roughly 200 of the nation's premier artists.

Oktoberfest (1-800-232-9542; www.snowbird.com) at Snowbird actually begins during the last week of August and lasts through the first week of September. This brings Bavaria right to the base area, with beer gardens and folk bands. This is mostly a daytime festival.

Park City International Jazz Festival (435-649-1000; www.parkcityjazz.org) takes place in

Deer Valley's Snow Park Village outdoor amphitheater and is a series of free concerts that features artists and groups from around the world. Concerts take place Friday, Saturday, and Sunday throughout the summer.

The **Timpanogos Storytelling Festival** (801-229-7050; www.timpfest.org) is a huge, family-oriented festival that takes place over Labor Day each year. The three days are filled with storytelling, most of which takes place at Mount Timpanogos Park.

Many eclectic festivals around greater Utah take place in August. **The Utah Belly Dance Festival** (1-800-232-9542; www.snowbird.com) at Snowbird, **Festival of the American West with World Championship Dutch Oven Cookoff** (in Wellsville), **Annual Railroaders Festival** (Golden Spike National Historic Site, Promontory Point), and **Swiss Days** (Midway; www.midwayswissdays.com) may be worth a short drive (though the Swiss Days *may* take place in early September).

Many athletic competitions also unfold during the weeks of August. Watch for the **E100 Century** mountain bike race and **Jupiter Steeplechase** trail run in Park City.

September

The **Miner's Day Parade and Celebration** (435-649-6100; www.parkcityinfo.com) takes place in early September in Park City. This is a classic, old-town festival that pays homage to the mining roots of the area.

Soldier Hollow (435-649-6619; www.soldierhollow.com) hosts the **Sheepdog Championships and Highland Games**. This is a festive introduction to the culture and skills of the world's sheepherders.

Snowbird's celebration of Oktoberfest continues. Look at the Web site (www.snowbird .com) for an extensive race calendar. Somewhat related, the **Utah Brewers Festival** takes place downtown at the Gallivan Center (www.gallivanevents.com).

The **Utah State Fair** (155 North 1000 West, Salt Lake City; 801-538-8400; www.utah-state -fair.com) occupies about a week and a half in the beginning of September.

World of Speed at the Bonneville Salt Flats (801-485-2662; www.saltflats.com) is an event you don't want to miss if you are around. It is unlike anything you have ever seen before.

Dine O' Round (www.downtownslc.com) is an unmatched opportunity to try some of the best restaurants in town for an exceedingly good price. Not a festival, this is a period of time during which participants create a Dine O' Round menu for a set price (either $15 or $25, depending on the establishment). This is often more than a 50 percent savings.

The legendary **Wasatch Front 100 Mile Endurance Run** (www.wasatch100.com) also takes place in September. Crazy people from around the country come to participate in this grueling trail run with 25,000 feet of elevation gain—and loss.

October

October brings with it a slight lull between summer and winter festivities, but it also brings a revival session of the **Semiannual LDS World Conference**, during which the streets and businesses of Salt Lake City bustle with these guests.

November

The **Antelope Island Buffalo Roundup** (1-800-322-3770; www.utah.com/stateparks) at Antelope Island State Park is enhanced by the surreal environment of the island and Great Salt Lake.

The **Utah Jazz** (www.nba.com/jazz) begin their season when November rolls around. Their home stadium is the EnergySolutions Center in Salt Lake City.

The annual **Lighting of Temple Square Holiday Lights** (www.lds.org), after Thanksgiving, kicks off the Christmas season beautifully. Tens of thousands come to see the lighting. Temple Square takes on a magical aura during this time.

The **Luge World Cup** comes to the Utah Olympic Park (435-658-4200; www.olyparks.com) the last weekend of November and lasts four days. (This is followed immediately by the Bobsled and Skeleton World Cup in early December.)

December

The **Bobsled and Skeleton World Cup** (435-658-4200; www.olyparks.com) continues Utah Olympic Park's competition.

Deer Valley (1-800-424-3337; www.deervalley.com) hosts one of the strangest festivals of all, the **Celebrity Ski Fest**, during the first few days of the month.

The **Mormon Tabernacle Choir Christmas Concert** (Mormon Tabernacle, Temple Square, Salt Lake City; www.mormontabernaclechoir.org) occurs during the middle of the month. For Christmas celebrations, it doesn't get much finer.

Ballet West (801-323-6900; www.balletwest.org) also puts on a traditional Christmas show: **The Nutcracker**. This takes place in the Capitol Theater in Salt Lake City.

Deer Valley's **Torchlight Parade** and The Canyons' **New Year's Eve Celebration** end the month with a bang (www.deervalley.com).

Like many other cities, Salt Lake City hosts a **First Night** (www.downtownslc.org). This is more subdued than in many cities, but it gives people a chance to stroll the streets and enjoy street vendors and musicians. Provo also hosts a First Night (www.provo.org).

Index